EBERHARD JÜNGEL

An Introduction to his Theology

J. B. WEBSTER

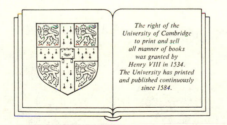

The right of the
University of Cambridge
to print and sell
all manner of books
was granted by
Henry VIII in 1534.
The University has printed
and published continuously
since 1584.

CAMBRIDGE UNIVERSITY PRESS

Cambridge

London   New York   New Rochelle

Melbourne   Sydney

Published by the Press Syndicate of the University of Cambridge
The Pitt Building, Trumpington Street, Cambridge CB2 IRP
32 East 57th Street, New York, NY 10022, USA
10 Stamford Road, Oakleigh, Melbourne 3166, Australia

First published 1986

Printed in Great Britain by
the University Press, Cambridge

British Library cataloguing in publication data
Webster, J. B.
Eberhard Jüngel: an introduction to his theology.
1. Jüngel, Eberhard
I. Title
209′.2′4   BX4827.J8

Library of Congress cataloguing in publication data
Webster, J. B. (John Bainbridge), 1955–
Eberhard Jüngel; an introduction to his theology.
Bibliography: p.
Includes index.
1. *Jüngel, Eberhard. I. Title*
BX4827.J86W43   1986   230′.092′4   85-12730

ISBN 0 521 30708 2

Eberhard Jüngel

Contents

v

'Unterscheiden heisst: in Beziehung setzen'

Preface

It is a pleasure to record a large debt of gratitude to many friends and teachers. George Newlands of the University of Cambridge first started me reading Jüngel, supervised my doctoral studies and has always been generous in his encouragement, as were Nicholas Lash and Rowan Williams, along with Brian Hebblethwaite and John Macquarrie who examined my thesis.

The present, very different work has been written in three places. In Sheffield I enjoyed the encouragement of John Rogerson and the financial support of the Trustees of the Sir Henry Stephenson Fellowship. In Durham I, like many others interested in systematic theology, have profited from the advice of Stephen Sykes. And a visit to Philadelphia afforded me not only the time to complete the book but also the opportunity of working with Darrell Guder. My thanks to them all, as also to Robert Williams of Cambridge University Press for his patience and editorial skills, and to Jean Field, for sorting out a messy typescript.

But my greatest debt is to my wife Jane and our little son Tommy, from whom I have been apart too much too often. Dedicating this book to them is the very least I can do to express my thanks.

JOHN WEBSTER

St John's College, Durham
Advent 1984

A note on references

I have generally made my own translations of Jüngel's works after consulting available translations.

Abbreviations employed in the notes can be found before the bibliography on pp. 169–70. The essays republished in the collections *Unterwegs zur Sache, Was ist ein Sakrament?, Von Zeit zu Zeit, Anfechtung und Gewissheit des Glaubens, Entsprechungen,* and *Barth-Studien* are quoted after their pagination in those volumes, not in their original place of publication. Sets of theses are referred to by abbreviation and thesis number, without page references.

Acknowledgement

Some parts of chapters 4, 7 and 8 have appeared in a different form under the title 'Eberhard Jüngel on the Language of Faith' in *Modern Theology* I (1985) 253–76. I am grateful to the publishers, Messrs Basil Blackwell, for their readiness to allow republication.

Introduction

The aim of this book is simple: to provide a reliable guide to Jüngel's work for English readers, and to offer some initial evaluation of its main features.

There can be little doubt that Jüngel's achievement to date has been remarkable. His professional advancement has been rapid even by German standards: after teaching in Berlin and Zürich, he succeeded to one of the most prestigious chairs of systematic theology in Germany, at the University of Tübingen, at the age of 36. Within a publishing career of just over two decades, he has produced major contributions on New Testament studies, classical philosophy, the work of Luther, the philosophy of religion and the theory of language, as well as a good number of more popular works. He is widely regarded as one of the most able living interpreters of Barth. And his prowess as preacher and lecturer has won him acclaim from audiences wider than those of specialist theologians.

Yet the impediments to the fruitful reception of such a startling achievement are considerable, and go some way towards explaining why his prominence in German theology has not been matched by thorough discussion of his work in English-speaking countries. Problems of cultural distance are immediately apparent to anyone beginning serious study of his work. Jüngel shows almost no awareness of English-language discussions of, for example, the nature of theological language or the philosophy of history, which might sharpen his own writing in these areas as well as provide helpful points of contact. And conversely, the disciplines, debates and specialist literatures with which he often assumes familiarity have not always been adequately attended to beyond Germany. The reasons for this mutual isolation of English- and German-language theology are historically complex and cannot be typified by a few generalised slogans about supposed national mental habits

I

or religious tempers.[1] It would be more accurate to say that over
the course of their recent histories both German and English
theology have evolved a variety of styles which sometimes overlap
but which are often quite sharply divergent. Jüngel's work suffers
fairly acutely from the results of this divergence.

Moreover, his work is also to a degree out of joint with some of
the main trends of Protestant dogmatics in Germany. His concern
to eschew modernity for its own sake has meant that his engagement
with contemporary theological debates has often been tangential
and critical. This can be seen, for example, in his constant
reference to certain problems in religious and theological language,
problems which no longer catch the imaginations of most of his
peers. And it is especially present in his stout adherence to the
primacy of theory over practice, and in the sharply critical
comments on 'political theology' to which this has led him. Jüngel
has carved out his own very distinctive idiom, one shared by few
of his fellows, and he has consequently sometimes declared himself
to be misunderstood and misinterpreted by native German
audiences.[2] The introduction of his work to an unfamiliar intellectual milieu can hardly be said to lessen the problems.

Nevertheless, it is just these difficulties which make an overview
of his theological programme imperative. With one or two notable
exceptions, such appraisal as has appeared in English has been
largely ill-informed and lacking in astuteness. Critics have often
fastened upon a theme in his writing which connects with
fashionable theological trends (the death of God,[3] a trinitarian
theology of the cross,[4] a 'processive' account of the divine being[5]),
wresting his discussions out of context, and making him appear
to be, for instance, merely one more example of modern theo-
paschite theology. Both the general reader and the close student
are inhibited by the lack of a comprehensive survey which traces
the main lines of his work, showing their interrelations and the
stages of their evolution, and highlighting the issues to which
Jüngel is addressing himself: this I have sought to provide. It is,
doubtless, a hazardous undertaking to map the work of a thinker
whose development is by no means at an end. Yet even the partial
and inevitably open-ended account which can be offered here is
preferable to the present vacuum.

The exposition of Jüngel's work is roughly chronological: in this
way I have tried to demonstrate the evolution and the inner

consistency of his theology, and to make his main preoccupations as plain as possible. Jüngel is by no means an easy thinker. Although he has written works aimed at a more general audience, his more strictly theological works are often abstract and technical, demanding an effort of unremitting concentration from the reader who wishes to master long passages of complex, nuanced argument. But the sophistication is not born of self-conscious professionalism. Rather, it comes from his refusal to be cast in the role of *simplificateur*, sacrificing the claims of truth to those of popular appeal. 'Truth,' he writes, 'does not yield immediate satisfaction. The way to truth can be frustrating.'[6] Consequently, Jüngel's work does not readily lend itself to popularisation, unlike the work of Moltmann, with which it is sometimes and mistakenly compared. I have tried to make the main lines of Jüngel's theology clear: but in order to do justice to the subtlety of his thought, I have avoided cutting corners.

Perhaps the most engaging feature of Jüngel's work, and the one from which English readers may learn most, is his preoccupation with some of the major questions of classical Christian theology. Where many English contemporaries have lacked desire or confidence to produce positive dogmatics, Jüngel suffers from no such absence of desire or crisis of confidence. And it is the positive rather than interrogative tone of his work which is both its strength and its weakness.

This intellectual temper expresses itself in such stylistic features as a fondness for the generalised proposition, a preference for the abstract and an absence of exemplification. Combined with the rhetorical energy of much of his writing, such features suggest a mind at once confident of its chosen direction, schematic in its organization of its matter, and not susceptible to distraction by detail. It is a style which betrays an overall preoccupation with the *grandes lignes*. If this intellectual manner does at times prove to be a rather burdensome asset, its weakness is bound up with the massive strength of his work, which is what he himself has noted in Bultmann: 'the clarity of an...Either-Or'.[7] It has a coherence and firmness of line which originate in the tenacity with which he has grasped and held onto his principles. That tenacity may no doubt sometimes cramp him, making him appear to lack subtlety or self-criticism. But it also means that we may expect from future work what we have already been shown: the intensity, rigour and penetration of a powerful mind working within the structures of a passionate commitment. It is not easy to think of many contemporaries who offer this much.

In terms of substantive content, it is not easy to make a simple characterisation of Jüngel's work, for it has so far been broad-ranging, not content to be confined to one set of issues. If a larger trend is to be discerned throughout his theological engagement, however, it is a concern to develop a theology in the tradition of Barth in which God and man are *complementary*. God and his creation form two mutually imprescriptible and not mutually exclusive realities.

This theme, for which Jüngel's rubric is that of 'distinguishing between God and man', could be said to form the pivotal concern of the whole of his theological programme. For above all he is anxious to avoid a reduction of the two-foldness of God and man to a single, self-consistent stratum. Thus in his doctrine of God he urges the rejection of any theological scheme in which God is the only significant reality and which accordingly reduces man to a mere function of the divine, not possessed of freedom and authenticity. Man's contingency upon the creative Word of God is not the abolition but the affirmation of his humanness. Again, in the doctrine of man Jüngel has resisted any anthropocentrism in which the divine is a mere function of the human, and in particular one in which man's work arrogates to itself what is properly God's. And as we pass in review Jüngel's major works, the ramifications of this concern properly to distinguish between God and man will be traced in other areas where decisions about the relation of the divine to the human and worldly function beneath the surface of the debate. Such discussions include the nature of language and thought about God, theological ethics, the doctrine of baptism, questions concerning natural theology – in all these areas, Jüngel has urged that theology must find ways to state how 'the essence of Christian faith is joy in God and so concern for a more human world'.[8]

One of the most difficult factors in a book of this kind is the formulation of a critical response to the subject. The temptation is either to be so totally lacking in sympathy that one presents not so much a critical exposition as the trial and refutation of an absent offender, or to offer a mere reverent paraphrase in which critical acumen simply goes by the board. Steering a middle course between distaste and infatuation is a tricky business, but a necessary one, since Jüngel's work badly needs sensitive, informed but critical appraisal.

My most fundamental anxiety about Jüngel's work, an anxiety which underlies many of my detailed comments upon his work, is not concerned so much with any particular positions which he has espoused as with what might be called his intellectual manner. This manner could very loosely be termed 'monist'. That is to say, he tends to adhere very closely to one intellectual strategy to the exclusion of others, and tends to emphasise the coherent, unitary nature of his material. This is especially true in his work on the doctrine of man, where he is strong in defence of a view of human history as a consistent whole, a view which is reached by rigorous deployment of one method in theological anthropology. But throughout his work I often sense the need for greater awareness of the sheer complexity of what is the case and consequently of our response – intellectual, moral and religious – to what is the case. This is not, of course, to deny that Jüngel is a subtle and profound thinker. But his subtlety and profundity do not go hand in hand with an awareness of the unschematic and untidy character of the theological enterprise.

Among the letters which have come down from the last period of Karl Barth's life is one to a younger theologian who had written a book on Barth's earlier views on eschatology and history.[9] In the letter, Barth offers advice on how to write a study of another's theology:

For me it would be a canon of all research in theological history, and perhaps in all history, that one should try to present what has engaged another person, whether in a good way or a less good, as something *living*, as something that *moved* him in some way and that can and indeed does move *oneself* too; to *unfold* it in such a way that even if one finally takes some other route, the path of this other has an enticing, or, if you like, tempting attraction for oneself. Disregard of this canon, I think, can only avenge itself by rendering the attempted historical research unprofitable and tedious.[10]

I have tried to keep this canon in mind as I have written. For whilst in the end I would have to part company with Jüngel on many issues, I do find his chosen path enticing. And perhaps this book may entice others to the kind of sustained, serious and yet delighted study which his work both invites and richly rewards.

1. Paul and Jesus

Introductory

On any reading, Jüngel's doctoral dissertation *Paulus und Jesus*, published in 1962, is a remarkable work. Explicitly intended as an exploration of the relationship between the synoptic presentation of Jesus' parabolic teaching and Paul's doctrine of justification, its close scrutiny of larger philosophical, theological and rhetorical issues arising from the interpretation of the New Testament makes clear that he is offering much more than simply another monograph surveying the well-worn territory of the 'Paul and Jesus' theme.[1] And it is the way in which it addresses itself to these larger issues which makes the work of substantial interest for an appraisal of his dogmatic work. We shall examine one of these issues – his discussion of the relationship between historico-critical study and dogmatics – in a later chapter.[2] For the present, we focus on four areas where Jüngel urges significant shifts in our understanding of the New Testament. We look first in broad outline at how he conceives the nature of the texts with which he is dealing and the appropriate response to them. We then move on to discuss in turn his analysis of the parables, his account of the coherence between the theologies of the synoptic gospels and Paul, and his understanding of eschatology.

Initially it is important to note that *Paulus und Jesus* is written with considerable enthusiasm for the work of Jüngel's *Doktorvater*, the New Testament theologian Ernst Fuchs. Fuchs has received little attention from mainstream biblical scholarship in English, apart from the brief interest in his work which grew out of the period in the 1960s when the German debates associated with the so-called 'New Hermeneutic' flourished for a while in the United States and, to a lesser extent, in Britain.[3] He has also, it is true, had a more lasting influence on New Testament theologians who,

6

dissatisfied with the dominance of tradition-history in parable exegesis, have sought interpretative models which are apparently more alert to the ways in which the parables function as stories.[4] But beyond these fairly narrow confines, Fuchs' work remains largely unread and untranslated. The fortunes of his work with English readers have been such that if it is known at all – usually second-hand – it is chiefly for his theories of parable-interpretation and for the view of language (worked out through the use of categories closely similar to those found in Heidegger's later writings) with which they are bound up.[5]

It is everywhere apparent to the reader of *Paulus und Jesus* how deeply Fuchs has influenced Jüngel's presentation: 'their two voices become one,' judges Soulen, 'Jüngel expands and explicates the same thesis'.[6] But it should be noted that Jüngel is too shrewd and perceptive a reader of Fuchs simply to adopt wholesale a theory of language and a hermeneutic of the parables. Indeed, the lessons learnt from long and intense engagement with Fuchs' writings surface not only in his interpretation of the parables but elsewhere: in his reading of Barth, for example,[7] and most especially in his exploration of the relationship between language and temporality. This theme – arguably the core of Fuchs' own theology[8] – not only emerges in Jüngel's presentation of the eschatology of the parables but also forms a major preoccupation in his later theological anthropology. Fuchs, in other words, has not merely furnished Jüngel with a set of hermeneutical principles woodenly copied; he has provided a fertile stimulus to his own theological creativity, a stimulus still fresh beyond the enthusiasm of a young man.

The real force and direction of *Paulus und Jesus* is easily overlooked unless it is first made clear that Jüngel approaches the study with a particular understanding of the material which deviates quite widely from the styles of New Testament scholarship most commonly espoused. Jüngel envisages the New Testament as a collection of 'speech-events'. The meaning of this term, derived from Fuchs, will emerge as we look at his work in more detail. But as a preliminary it can be noted that Jüngel uses it to propose that the language of the New Testament is not simply an information-bearing sign, but is itself the presence of the realities which it articulates or 'brings to speech'. And so the 'content' of the New Testament cannot be discovered apart from the 'form' in which it is present: the realities of which the New Testament speaks are present as (and not without) their textual form.

In more detail, this means, first, that Jüngel does not read the New Testament texts as a means of access to matters which lie *behind* the texts (such as the mind of the primitive church, or the self-understanding of Jesus): the content of the texts resides in the texts themselves and not in states of affairs which can be reconstructed with their aid. It is this which forms the basis of his presentation of the relationship between Paul and Jesus. His approach is quite different from those which explore that relationship by analysis of the history of the Christological titles,[9] as well as from those which see Paul and Jesus linked along a continuum of 'salvation-history' or 'tradition'.[10] Both these kinds of approaches fail in Jüngel's eyes because of their inability to reckon with the fact that the 'speech-events' of the New Testament are ultimately primary and not to be resolved into anything beyond themselves.

This last point leads to a second feature of Jüngel's approach which is of significance for his entire theological programme. Since the 'speech-events' are ultimate and primary, Jüngel believes that they must determine the method by which the critical scholar approaches them. And hence he disallows any notion that the critic is free to treat the materials in a manner of his own choice. An autonomous and self-justifying critical method has to be replaced by a way of approaching the texts in which 'thinking is measured by the object of thinking':[11] in which, that is, the critical work of the scholar reverts to its proper secondary and subsequent position *vis-à-vis* its object:

I understand the method followed here as a method which looks to the history of the phenomena[12] on the presupposition that the 'intentional act' of the mind which presses towards the objects is preceded by an 'extentional act' from the objects themselves which conditions the mind's inquiry and understanding. For thinking may only ascend back to the objects themselves from the conceptual horizon of the human consciousness insofar as the objects themselves *have already* appeared as phenomena for the human consciousness – and in theology that means insofar as the objects themselves *have already* come to speech.[13]

What is being propounded in that very dense statement is ultimately a conviction that the language of the New Testament 'brings to speech' *revelation*, that it is the place where God's Word is encountered and so is both authoritative and determinative of the mind's response to it. The 'extentionality' of the texts forestalls any autonomous 'intentionality'. This conviction is very deeply embedded in Jüngel's work, and in *Paulus und Jesus* it testifies to the depth of his debt not only to Fuchs but also to Barth.[14] Examination of Jüngel's treatment of the parables shows how fruitfully the suggestion has been used.

Parables

What is most interesting in Jüngel's account of the parables is not his contentious assertion that 'the parables not only lead us to the centre of Jesus' proclamation but also point to the person of the proclaimer, to the secret of Jesus himself'.[15] Rather, it is his proposals about how the parables are to be interpreted. His thought here is quite complex, but can be elucidated over against the programme of interpretation whose weaknesses he discusses at some length, namely that of Jülicher.[16]

His analysis of Jülicher's work focusses on its dominance by Aristotelian literary categories.[17] Working from such a basis, Jülicher comes to propose 'that parable is constituted by the similarity of two propositions understood as logical judgements'.[18] Jüngel, in other words, criticises Jülicher for envisaging the parables as resolvable to propositions and proposing that all that is lost by that kind of resolution is the rhetorical weight which is added to the proposition by its being set in parabolic form. Parables thus function as what Jülicher calls a 'Beglaubigungsmittel',[19] a rhetorical ornament to add persuasiveness to Jesus' proclamation of the Kingdom of God.

It is precisely this conception of the separability of Jesus' proclamation of the Kingdom from its parabolic form that Jüngel wishes to avoid by deploying the notion of 'speech-events'. Jülicher's failure is not simply that of foisting inappropriate literary categories onto the parables; it is rather that of neglecting the way in which the parables are the actuality of the Kingdom and not merely an engaging literary illustration of its presence. Because he envisages the parables as resolvable to a comparison of propositions, Jülicher understands the relationship between the Kingdom and the parables as one between 'content' and 'form': 'content and form seem to have nothing to do with each other', objects Jüngel, 'they are apparently separable from each other like shell and kernel'.[20]

Over against this Jüngel proposes that 'Jesus' preaching is to be understood as a speech-event which from the start prohibits any

separation between Jesus' language as the "form" of what came
to speech and his proclamation as the "content" of that "form"".[21]
Jesus' parabolic language *is* the event of the Kingdom of God, so
that 'the form of the saying and that which is said are fundamentally
bound up together'.[22] Thus the Kingdom of God is not to be
misunderstood as 'a *thesis* proclaimed by Jesus':[23] the Kingdom
is inseparable from the language in which it presents itself. Hence
Jüngel summarises his discussion by formulating the axiom: 'The
eschatological Kingdom of God comes to speech in the forms of
speech of Jesus' preaching *as* these forms of speech.'[24] To shift out
of Jüngel's idiom, we might say that the relationship between the
parables and the Kingdom of God is quasi-sacramental: Jesus'
parables are the real presence of the Kingdom, the Kingdom is
'really present' as parable. This is perhaps the best way of understanding his cryptic thesis: 'The Kingdom comes to speech *in*
parable *as* parable. The parables of Jesus bring the Kingdom of
God to speech *as* parable.'[25]

Jüngel's refusal to see the parables as a 'medium of information'[26]
is quite clearly indebted to Fuchs, and, through him, to
Heidegger,[27] for both object to any divorce between language and
being, sign and referent: 'Language,' writes Fuchs, 'makes being
into an event.'[28] But it should also be noted that Jüngel is as much
influenced by Barth as by his masters in the hermeneutical
tradition, although the influence rarely becomes explicit. Jüngel
has very acutely perceived that both Barth and Fuchs conceive of
the object of theology as a Word which both prescribes the manner
of its own reception and which cannot be resolved into anything
more primitive. Fuchs approaches this from the direction of his
understanding of language as what might be called the 'sacrament
of reality'. Barth comes from a different direction, namely that of
the theology of revelation. But the insights of both coalesce in
Jüngel's deployment of the concepts of 'speech-event' and
'coming-to-speech', concepts which articulate theological as well
as hermeneutical convictions. If for Fuchs the parables cannot be
'translated' into propositions without irreparable damage, for
Barth revelation is similarly untranslatable, in that it bears its
authority within itself and so is irreducible and ultimately
primary.[29] Jüngel's work here derives much of its force from both
proposals.

The New Testament as a 'Sprachgeschichte'

Paul's doctrine of justification receives much less attention in *Paulus und Jesus* than the synoptic parables, basically because Jüngel's presentation of Paul is methodologically and substantively a good deal less contentious. After arguing briefly that 'the doctrine of justification is the controlling centre of Pauline theology',[30] he goes on to stress the Christological grounds of justification,[31] and to discuss the place of the law in Paul's thought. In the course of the discussion, Jüngel makes many interesting remarks, notably in the area of Paul's anthropology. But his most provocative proposal concerns the relationship between the theologies of the synoptic parables and the Pauline doctrine of justification. He is concerned to demonstrate the continuity between the two by 'seeking to understand two speech-events which follow each other as events in one linguistic history'.[32] Once again, the formulation is cryptic. But, however opaque the idiom in which it is couched, it is clear that Jüngel's concern is to affirm the unitary nature of the New Testament. Three areas are identified as providing significant clues to this unity: eschatology, the role of the law, and the nature of faith.

First, there is continuity at the level of eschatology in that both Jesus and Paul bring the eschaton to speech as that new act of God which brings the past to an end and opens up a new future for man in Christ:

For Paul the revelation of the eschatological righteousness of God means that the time of the law, which enslaves man to his past, is at an end. With the end of the law God appears as the end of the history of the sinner. And along with the eschatological Kingdom of God Jesus preached God's nearness to history and thus set a new word over against the old word of the law.[33]

Thus, in both Jesus and Paul, God's eschatological Word (the word of the Kingdom, the word of justification) erupts into human history in such a way that man is renewed as his past is dislodged from its place of domination.

This point is expanded somewhat in the second area of substantial continuity: the place accorded by Jesus and Paul to the law. 'In Jesus' preaching a new word is set against the old word of the law.'[34] Similarly, Paul opposes the *nomos tou Christou* (law of Christ) to the *nomos tēs hamartias kai tou thanatou* (law of sin and death). Consequently, Jüngel suggests 'that in both Paul and Jesus a fundamental eschatological theme comes to speech in the temporal difference of eschatological future and eschatological past'.[35] In this temporal difference, brought about by the event of the word of the Kingdom or of justification, the enslaving power of the law is brought to an end and man is liberated for a new history under God.

A third area of continuity is offered by the role of faith in Jesus' preaching and Paul's theology. Whilst faith plays little explicit role in Jesus' proclamation, his behaviour provokes faith, which after his death becomes explicit faith in his person: 'Jesus' behaviour silently provoked faith, in that it gave men a share in God's power and so in God's being.'[36] In that Paul continues this understanding of faith as participation in God's omnipotence, it is again possible to discern some measure of continuity.

On the basis of his discussion of these three areas, Jüngel suggests that it is possible 'to speak of a history of God's coming-to-speech or simply of an eschatological linguistic history within which the preaching of Jesus and the Pauline doctrine of justification are speech-events'.[37] Jüngel, that is, invites us to consider the different theologies of the New Testament as possessing a coherence guaranteed by their belonging to a single tradition of human speech about God's eschatological work of salvation.

Eschatology

The final shift in approach to the New Testament texts which Jüngel commends concerns eschatology. We have already seen that *Paulus und Jesus* is pervaded by the conviction that the realities of which the New Testament speaks should themselves be determinative of the manner in which they are approached. It was this conviction which lay behind Jüngel's desire to allow the parables to define themselves rather than to force them into unsuitable literary categories. And the same conviction informs his treatment of eschatology.

His presentation takes its rise from dissatisfaction with accounts of eschatology which work with unacknowledged and inappropriate presuppositions about the nature of time. Jüngel contends that much exegetical work has been marred by an understanding of time oriented fundamentally towards the experiencing subject. On such a reading 'the Kingdom is allocated a place in a space of time, which is measured by an "I" which exists in time, so that the *nearness* of the Kingdom is conceived in terms of its *distance* from a temporally existing *subject*'.[38] Ultimately such exegesis can make little sense of the eschatology of the New Testament, whose understanding of time is not oriented towards the temporal subject but towards God the 'giver' or 'mover' of time: 'the measure of time...is not oriented towards the present of the human subject... God is the measure of time...Time is moved time. Time is set in motion by the end of time.'[39]

Jüngel's suggestion lacks the analytic sharpness of a technical philosophical discussion: but it is for all that provocative. For he is recommending that the eschatology of the New Testament does envisage the present as an absolute moment in the history of a subject from which past and future can be measured. Rather, the present is that interstice between past and future which God himself creates by addressing man in his Word. Time is not an independent continuum whose coherence is guaranteed by the subject of temporal experience. On the contrary: God's action – which for Jüngel means God's speech-act – is itself the constitution of time. His interpretation of the antitheses of the Sermon on the Mount makes the point well. The antitheses accomplish what he calls a 'Zeitunterschied',[40] a distinction in time. 'A new time is set against the old time. This happens in a new *Word*, which *declares* a new time over against the old time of the mosaic law.'[41]

Jüngel understands the fundamental reality of time to rest in the content with which it is informed by the speech-event of God's 'coming-to-speech'. Thus his interpretation of the parable of the seed growing secretly (Mk 4.26–9)[42] turns on a contrast between the 'time of sowing' and the 'time of harvest'. Jesus' proclamation of the Kingdom is that Word which constitutes the distinction between the two 'times' and opens up the future as time for God: 'Jesus' announcement of the Kingdom of God vouchsafes to man the present as free from the past (the time of sowing) and as the time of hearing which is free for the future (the time of harvest).'[43]

Once again, the roots of Jüngel's presentation lie in the work of Fuchs and Barth. From Fuchs he has learnt an account of time as linguistically contoured, structured around the speech-events in which man is addressed by God.[44] From Barth he has taken an insistence that temporality is not the condition of revelation, but rather that, because revelation has occurred, time and history have been given to man.[45] 'It is in virtue of the presence and gift of God that temporality...belongs to human nature.'[46] And so: '*The concept of eschatology is no anthropological concept, but is eminently theological.'*[47]

Reflections

What is the significance of *Paulus und Jesus* for Jüngel's future dogmatic work? His dissertation raises many themes which will become preoccupations later. Throughout his work his conviction of the centrality of language will be evident: the category of 'word', with its many ramifications, is never very far from the surface in his writing. Again, his analysis of some of the anthropological corollaries of the doctrine of justification will become a major theme in later work on the doctrine of man. But given this, what is of primary interest in *Paulus und Jesus* for his subsequent development is not so much its explicit content as its manner of approach. Indeed, the dissertation is at its most interesting when read as an essay on theological method, and its most significant decisions and recommendations are made at this level.

Of these recommendations, perhaps that most easily identified from within the perspectives of current New Testament scholarship is that concerning the unity of the New Testament. *Paulus und Jesus* tends to work with a belief that the New Testament forms a unity: the whole drift of his attempt to demonstrate the coherence of Jesus and Paul as elements in one 'Sprachgeschichte' shows that he is persuaded that at its heart the New Testament is simple rather than plural in its theological direction.

Such an approach is certainly not without its weaknesses. It involves Jüngel in a degree of selectivity in his reading of the New Testament (such as finding the centre of Paul's teaching in the doctrine of justification, or the centre of Jesus' teaching in his parables), selectivity which needs more rigorous vindication than Jüngel offers. It also involves him in a certain inattentiveness to the occasional, contextual character of the New Testament writings, a neglect which much recent work on the plurality of theologies in the New Testament makes all the more regrettable.[48] But we shall see that Jüngel's conception of the Christian faith as an essentially simple *kerygma* rather than as a complex and in some ways unschematic assembly of *kerygmata* informs his dogmatic work at a deep level.

Furthermore, his account of the language of the New Testament threatens to become similarly simplified. If the effects of understanding the theology of the New Testament as a 'Sprachgeschichte' is a flattening-out of its diversity, the effect of the concept of 'Sprachereignis' is to reduce the plurality of types of language found in the New Testament. Jüngel rejects any notion of language as an information-bearing sign, in favour of a 'performative' or 'sacramental' conception of language. But the effect of this rejection of the dianoetic is in fact a narrowing of the scope of the language of the New Testament. Language functions in a variety of ways in the New Testament: it is not only imperatival but also informative or argumentative, for example. The category of 'speech-event', however helpful in retaining the transcendent reference of Christian speech, is in effect too generalised to offer a sufficiently nuanced account of the linguistic properties of the New Testament.[49] Here, as elsewhere in his work, Jüngel's prescriptions are weakened by a reluctance carefully and patiently to exemplify and describe.

Nevertheless, perhaps the most striking feature of the methodology of *Paulus und Jesus* is its rigorous objectivism. It is difficult to come away from the book without being impressed by the energy with which Jüngel wrestles to shape a language and conceptuality appropriate to the realities of which he believes the New Testament to speak. The ground of his reluctance to project the subject into the place properly occupied by the object is a certain confidence in the accessibility of that same object. Jüngel's next book, *Gottes Sein ist im Werden*, will explore some of the dogmatic grounds for such confidence.

2. God's being is in becoming

Gottes Sein ist im Werden[1] was Jüngel's first – and arguably his best – book in the area of dogmatic theology. Explicitly the book offers an analysis of the structure and function of Barth's doctrine of the Trinity, and as such it is a masterly treatment. It is, however, more than a *tour de force* of Barth interpretation, for it contains many shrewd observations on the doctrine of God which Jüngel will unpack in later studies. Stylistically, too, it is one of his best pieces: conceptually tight and clean, its disciplined argument contains considerable intellectual passion.

The occasion for the work was a debate which erupted in the early 1960s between the New Testament scholar Herbert Braun[2] and the 'Barthian' dogmatician Helmut Gollwitzer.[3] Braun had urged the need for a 'non-objectifying' account of God, abandoning as naively mythological all attempts to talk of God as an independent entity, and replacing them by speech about God as a subjective, anthropological reality. On such an account, 'God would not be understood as the one existing for himself' since 'I can speak of God only where I can speak of man, and hence anthropologically.' Thus 'God would...be a definite type of relation to one's fellow-man.'[4] Gollwitzer's study *The Existence of God as Confessed by Faith* was written to counter such moves, emphasising the need to retain an idea of divine independence in order to avoid what he regarded as Braun's collapse into subjectivism, in which God's 'being' is identical with the event in which man feels himself encountered and addressed.

Jüngel's contribution both clarifies the issues and moves out of the perimeters of the debate by attempting to uncover hidden assumptions on both sides. In particular, he tries to shift the discussion out of an unwarranted polarity between God's being in and for himself (*pro se*) and his being for us (*pro nobis*). This polarity is encouraged by both Braun and Gollwitzer, but it is one to which the work of Barth represents a massive counter-example, though one strangely unnoticed by both protagonists in the debate. Jüngel very acutely perceives that the whole thrust of Barth's theology is to make God's being *pro se* identical with his being *pro nobis*: God is himself in the event of his free self-bestowal to man in the history of Jesus Christ. Moreover, Jüngel goes on to spell out how the refusal of any polarity between the inner divine life and the being of God in the world is one of the chief purposes of the *trinitarian* structure of Barth's theology.

Some major themes

Divine triunity

Jüngel suggests that it is neglect of the trinitarian nature of the Christian doctrine of God which leads both Gollwitzer and Braun to drive a wedge between God's being for us and his being for himself – Braun by dismissing talk of God's being for himself as 'objectification', Gollwitzer by asserting that God's being for us is secondary, subsequent upon his prior being for himself. And he moves on to show that Barth's exposition of trinitarian doctrine in the context of the doctrine of revelation offers a significantly different way of conceiving the relationship between the inner divine life and the divine presence to man.

The crux of his argument is an observation that, for Barth, to speak of God as triune is to assert that 'God corresponds with himself' in the event of revelation: 'God's being *ad extra* corresponds essentially to his being *ad intra* in which it has its basis and prototype',[5] so that 'the ultimate and final statement which can be made about the being of God is: God corresponds to himself [*Gott entspricht sich*]'.[6] Thus Barth understands revelation 'as the self-interpretation of God in which God is his own "double"'.[7] Jüngel's paraphrase of Barth is condensed, and its purport not entirely transparent at first. But at its heart is an attempt to avoid setting God's being for himself in opposition to his being for us, by compacting together the works of God and his very essence. The essence of God is nothing other than the essence of the one who works and reveals.

What is the purpose of Jüngel's appeal to these categories? To the superficial reader, the discussion may appear a solemn and ultimately rather arid kind of conceptual game. But its surface abstraction conceals a very different purpose – namely, to show how the history of the man Jesus constitutes nothing less than the inner life of God, the very place where God's trinitarian relatedness is played out before the world. If this is true – if God's revelation of himself in Christ is not foreign to but identical with his own inner life – then Braun's objections to language about God's being for himself are considerably less forceful. For to talk of God's being in and for himself is not to talk of some abstract order, some entity in the skies essentially unrelated to the contingencies of the natural order. Rather it is to say that God's way of being himself is by being God for us. It is this which lies behind the concept of 'correspondence' (*Entsprechung*) which Jüngel uses to describe the inseparability of God's immanent life from his economic operations. For if God 'corresponds with himself' in the event of revelation, then his revealed being *pro nobis* is nothing other than his immanent being *pro se*. And so talk of God's immanent being does not remove God to an infinite distance from man or posit a remote divinity: it simply describes as it were the impetus of God's proximity. Precisely because there is no gap between God's being and God's being-revealed, then we may assert the intimate reality of God in the world without reducing 'God' to a cipher for a human state of affairs.

Jüngel's use of some central motifs in Barth's doctrine of God poses severe problems for Braun's critique. But it is no less critical of Gollwitzer, who trades upon the same polarity of 'immanent' and 'economic'. To counter Braun's 'subjectivism', Gollwitzer proposes a distinction between the will and the essence of God. Jüngel suggests that this distinction endangers the coherence of God by positing an essentially unrelated God (his essence) behind God's revealed relations to men (his will). In his desire to safeguard the independence of God, Gollwitzer imports an understanding of independence which threatens the identity between the *pro se* and the *pro nobis*. Jüngel's reply is to emphasise the absolute necessity of eschewing such distinctions: 'Whoever...wishes to maintain and think of God's independence cannot avoid the task of thinking of God's independence [*Selbständigkeit*] *out of* God's subsistence [*Selbstand*].'[8] Once again, the bare definition appears rather barren until we realise how it condenses and abbreviates something of the utmost fleshliness and historical density, namely a conviction that God's 'subsistence' is the man Jesus, in whose life and death the ways of God are to be traced.

Divine objectivity

Having scrutinised one false polarity, Jüngel moves on to deal with another, this time that between God as object and God as a subjective reality within the human scene.

Braun's critique of the notion of God as 'a quantity existing in and for himself'[9] is pervaded by a deep-seated suspicion of talk of God as object, on the grounds that such talk inevitably 'objectifies' God. Such objectification inevitably pushes God beyond the concern or reach of human subjectivity; it also hypostasises into an 'entity' the primordial anthropological content of talk of God. The core of Jüngel's protest is that talk of God as object is not necessarily an objectifying human projection, reifying human states of affairs into an objective order of divine being. Proper talk of God's 'being-as-object' (*Gegenständlich-Sein*)[10] is not the result of a movement originating in the human mind in which 'the knowing human subject...make(s) God available as an object'.[11] Rather, it results from a quite contrary motion, namely that of God's bestowal of himself upon the subject. God may thus legitimately be spoken of as an object because he gives himself to be known as such.

Clearly Jüngel counters Braun by a strong appeal to a concept of revelation in which God in his objectivity makes himself available for subjective apprehension:

God's being-as-object is his being-revealed. God is thus the object of knowledge insofar as he has interpreted himself. And insofar as God has interpreted himself in his revelation and so made himself the object of knowledge of God, he has also made man into the subject of the knowledge of God...That means...that God's being-as-object is not the result of human objectification of God....He *is* only objective as the one who has *made* himself objective.[12]

It is, however, very important to grasp the precise implications of Jüngel's move here. His deployment of the concept of revelation in no way reintroduces the notion which he is at pains to remove, namely that of God as a remote and unrelated 'entity'. On the contrary, God's being-as-object is in the fullest sense what he calls an 'anthropological existential'. God's objectivity, in other words, is to be understood from within its character as a determination of human existence. 'The anthropological significance of God's being-as-object consists in the fact that through his being-as-object God brings our existence into a definite relationship with his existence.'[13] Because of this, talk of God's objectivity in no way works for the exclusion or the suppression of the subjective reality of man. Rather, such talk already contains a subjective component in that through bestowing himself as object God draws human lives into a bond with his own life.

It is again worth pausing to note what Jüngel has sought to achieve. He has attempted to show that the polarisation of God's objectivity from the reality of God for human subjectivity is illegitimate. And he has tried – once again through very close attention to Barth – to discover a way of stating how God can be a determination of human existence without reducing the word 'God' to a cipher for a purely human state of affairs or equating God's existence with human existence. He has, moreover, tried so to characterise God's objectivity that God's being-as-object is not the antithesis but rather the inner possibility of the reality of God for man.

Divine becoming

Out of what he has observed so far about God's trinitarian being and his being-as-object, Jüngel comes to define a sense in which it is appropriate and necessary to speak of God's 'being-in-becoming'.

He is particularly concerned to make clear that to speak of God's being-in-becoming is not at all to make the being of God into a mere instance of a more general ontology of flux.[14] Rather, it is to speak of 'becoming' in a very particular sense, as the manner in which God chooses to be himself. In order to make the fullest sense of Jüngel's point here, it is important to grasp that his discussion is pervaded by two fundamental theological principles.

The first is that of what might be called the 'particularity' of the being of God and the attributes by which it is characterised. The attributes of God are not simply examples of more generally available qualities which could be predicated of other beings; they are peculiar to God himself. And so to talk of God's being-in-becoming, precisely because it is talk of *God's* being-in-becoming, uses the word 'becoming' in a sense unique to God: 'becoming' is a function of God, and not vice-versa. 'The becoming in which God's being is can evidently...signify neither an increase nor a decrease of God's being..."Becoming" indicates the manner *in* which God's being is, and thus can be understood as the ontological place of God's being.'[15] And so God's being-in-becoming is 'the becoming which is proper to God's being'.[16] The impetus, in other words, for Jüngel's formulation of the idea of God's being-in-becoming is not at all metaphysical, and its result is not the tying of God to inappropriate ontological categories. Rather, the impetus is Christological, in that Jüngel is concerned (after Barth) to specify the divine nature in accordance with the way in which that nature has been manifested in Jesus Christ: 'the God whose being is in becoming can *die* as a human being'.[17]

The second principle underlying the discussion is that of the freedom of God. 'Becoming' is not a general ontological category exemplified by the being of God. Rather, it is the place of God's eternal election of himself, a path chosen for himself which is actual in the history of Jesus. 'The ontological place of God's being...is the place of his choice.'[18] To speak of God's being-in-becoming is in no way to compromise his freedom or aseity; it is to attempt to describe the way in which that freedom and aseity are actual. God's being is in becoming because he has chosen to be himself in identity with the history of Jesus, which is no mere shadow of the divine life but its very substance. Once 'becoming' is understood in this fashion – as embraced by God's free election of himself – it can be seen as a category of considerable theological resonance. For it enables the theologian to incorporate into his doctrine of God the extreme peril to God's being at the event of Calvary. And yet it does so in such a way that God's being does not as it were collapse into the void. For whilst the path of God's becoming in the history of Jesus includes the moment of suffering and death, that moment does not constitute the negation of God. Rather, it is a moment which at once imperils God's life and is the occasion of his self-affirmation, since suffering and death are willed by God for himself. The act of *kenosis* at the cross is at one and the same time the act of divine *plerosis* such that, in the moment of self-denial, God becomes himself.

Accordingly, the force of the concept of God's 'being-in-becoming' is to try to specify the voluntary nature of God's self-sacrifice in identifying himself with the crucified Jesus. God's entry into history in the incarnation and the cross, his historicality and thus his possibility, is his own chosen goal. And so 'the definition of God's being as "being-in-act" is not contradicted when suffering is predicated of God. God's being-in-act is expressed in his suffering. But God's suffering is his being-in-*act*.'[19] God's freedom is thus his obedience to suffering in which he 'exposes himself to death'.[20] But 'suffering and death are not a metaphysical misfortune which happened to the Son of God who became man: God *chose* this "fate"'.[21] As in *Gott als Geheimnis* later, 'becoming' states how in transience we can discern both God's action and the durability of his will and purpose.

Gottes Sein ist im Werden in the context of Jüngel's development

As a piece of Barth-exegesis, the book is quite superb. This is not only because of its acute presentation of some of the central features of Barth's doctrine of the Trinity and their extraordinarily rich consequences in many fields, but because of its refusal of any easy or monochrome characterisations of Barth's work. In his recent collection of essays on Barth, *Barth-Studien*, Jüngel speaks of the danger of 'reducing the impressive language of Barth's texts to the one-dimensional prose of scholarship':[22] it is a danger which his intense and excited study of Barth has excluded from his own writing.

He has, however, never been interested in Barth interpretation simply for its own sake, but with the resources which Barth's *opus* contains for current dogmatic work (and this, indeed, goes a long way to explaining why he is so discerning a commentator). His engagement with Barth has sought 'to ponder...the possible enticements which in a good and a bad sense lie within the theology of this great man and which constitute not the least part of its greatness'.[23] 'A thinker is honoured through thinking.'[24] And from this perspective, Jüngel's first full-length study of Barth is of very great significance for tracing the path of his future work, and in two areas in particular.

The first is that of the doctrine of God. Jüngel has very firmly grasped the motives and effects of the kind of identity between God's being for himself and his being for us which Barth's doctrine of God proposes. And it is this which provides the platform for a good deal of his later work in many different theological areas. In the area of the doctrine of God, it is the lessons learnt from Barth which enable him to construct an account of the divine passion and death as the manner in which God's triune life is manifested. Again, his critique of what he regards as the traditions of metaphysical theism and its atheistic shadow centres on the separability of God's immanent essence from his economic existence which both traditions presuppose. And in the anthropological area, Jüngel's sense that God's being-for-us is his very being-for-himself furnishes the ultimate ground for his assertion that God is the human God whose humanity is the way in which he both becomes himself and affirms the humanity of his creatures.

Second, *Gottes Sein ist im Werden* is very instructive for the conception of the theologian's task with which it works and which it occasionally articulates, a conception which has remained stable through the development of Jüngel's theology. The conception is perhaps most pregnantly described when Jüngel observes that for Barth the ultimately primitive question is not (as for Bultmann) 'what does it *mean* to speak of God?', but rather 'in what sense *must* we speak of God, so that our speech is about *God*?'.[25] To set up the question in that way is to propose a radical epistemological shift, in which attention is focussed not so much on the subjective conditions of our experience of God as on the objective 'thereness' of that which is received in intelligent apprehension. Accordingly, 'the question of God' is not at all a question concerning some general anthropological possibility: it is a question which is itself as it were set in motion by the prevenient reality of God's self-gift to the world. 'The theological question concerning the being of God *reflects on* [*nachdenkt*] – the being of God. This means, however, that the being of God which is the subject of theological questioning *precedes* the inquiry...This being so *precedes* all theological questioning that in its course it paves the way for questions and...brings the questioning onto the path of thinking.'[26] What is primary is not the inquiring subject but God's self-bestowal which places the inquirer in a position of subsequence and humble dependence upon the divine act of grace. The convictions suggested here will receive full treatment in Jüngel's account of the 'Denkbarkeit Gottes' in *Gott als Geheimnis der Welt*.

Critics of *Gottes Sein ist im Werden* looked upon it as a kind of high scholasticism, an elaborate conceptual play using abstract counters taken over from the dogmatic tradition. Heinrich Ott wrote, for example, that Jüngel

does not succeed in an existential rendering of the Trinity...And hence Jüngel's expositions remain in a conceptual Heaven, that of the concepts of the dogmatic tradition in which he knows how to move about with agility, but they scarcely reach the earth, there to become illuminating and to show for preaching and all responsible speech about God what it means that the reality of God dwells among men.[27]

Such criticism, however, is difficult to sustain. This is partly because Jüngel's more recent work shows a lively concern for the anthropological dimensions of Christian belief (albeit on grounds very different from those proposed by Ott). But it is also because Ott has failed to catch the real tone of Jüngel's book. It is an abstract discussion: but its abstraction is not a flight from the contingencies of historical existence. Rather it is an attempt conceptually to clarify how one historical episode of the utmost contingency – the life and especially the death of Jesus of Nazareth – can be determinative of our understanding of the ways and works of God. Perhaps not the least of the features which make *Gottes Sein ist im Werden* such a remarkable book is its peculiar tautness as a piece of writing, a tautness which comes from the kerygmatic concern lying behind a densely conceptual exterior.

3. Christology: exegesis and dogmatics

It is almost a commonplace that, since critical study of the canonical gospels reached wider currency in the mid-nineteenth century, English Christology has very often been closely concerned with the effects of such study on the formulation of the doctrine of the Incarnation.[1] A book such as *The Myth of God Incarnate*,[2] together with its conservative rejoinders,[3] forms simply one more (undistinguished) episode in a tradition dominated by a particular understanding of the relationship between the historical and the dogmatic in Christology. This tradition is especially concerned with the question of whether the wedge driven by gospel criticism between the 'Jesus of history' and the 'Christ of faith' (as the latter is found in the gospels) leads to a position where incarnational formulae lack historical grounds and so cease to command assent. It was concern along these lines which led many orthodox English Christologians to concentrate their energies in the defence of the doctrine of the Incarnation as a doctrine resting on secure historical foundations. Lightfoot, remarks Morgan, 'inaugurated the century-long Anglican tradition of defending the doctrine of the Incarnation by maintaining the essential historicity of the gospels'.[4]

Anglican Christology in particular has often responded to historical criticism by urging that the doctrine of the Incarnation stands or falls by its historical grounds. Theologians might differ as to whether it does in fact stand or fall. But it is important to note how often certain types of English Christology construe the relationship between the doctrine and the history as primarily *evidential*: the history proves, or fails to prove, the dogma. When we look at some recent German Christological writing, however, it is striking that, whilst much critical work on the gospels has been German in provenance, or received its stimulus from German models, systematic theology in the same language has been much

more ready to absorb such critical work and to allow it to enlarge
the systematic theologian's understanding of his own task. Jüngel's
work on some fundamental problems of method in Christology is
a particularly good illustration of the point.[5]

Exegesis and dogmatics in Christology

Jüngel's early work is especially notable for the way in which it
straddles historico-critical study and dogmatics, frequently returning to the theme of the relationship between the critical biblical
scholar and the dogmatician. As we have seen from the first two
chapters, he shows himself to be particularly keen to observe his
own prescription that 'the exegete may no more release the
dogmatician from the obligation to engage in historico-critical
reflection than he himself may hold himself aloof from the hard
work of the dogmatician'.[6] Such convictions about the interrelation
of the exegetical and dogmatic tasks are partly the fruit of his
training in both critical New Testament scholarship and systematic
theology under figures like Fuchs, Ebeling and Vogel. But his early
writings also take up concerns which exercised many German
Protestant theologians in the later 1950s and early 1960s. It is
important to bear in mind that this period, in which Jüngel
received his theological training and wrote his doctorate, saw the
growth of widespread interest in *Hermeneutik* as a theological
discipline concerned with the interpretation of texts from the past
and with their proclamation in the present. Ebeling's work, for
example, and notably his 'discussion with Rudolf Bultmann' in
Theology and Proclamation[7] canvassed an understanding of hermeneutics as a theological task which embraces both historical study
and contemporary duties of proclamation and dogmatic affirmation.
It is in this connection also important to remember the continuing
influence of Barth's dogmatic programme and its understanding
of the relationship between the tasks of the biblical preacher and
the dogmatician.[8] Trained by thinkers preoccupied with such
questions, Jüngel became quite naturally very sensitive to the
issues involved.

These issues coalesced at an early stage in Jüngel's theological
development in the area of Christology. For it is in the area of
Christology that the coherence of the historico-critical method and
the dogmatic concerns of the systematician is under considerable
strain. The rigorous use of the historico-critical method seems to

militate against the indispensable historical component of dogmatic Christology. Ebeling observed that 'Modern historical thought has made the previously self-evident unity of historical and dogmatic speech so problematic that one might be tempted to despair of the unity of theology: indeed, to doubt its very possibility.'[9] It is precisely this question of the threat posed to the *unity* of theology which Jüngel seizes upon. His sense of the potential disruption of theology as a coherent intellectual exercise has led him into careful examination of the structure and logic of Christology, in the attempt to maintain the legitimacy and necessity of both historical criticism and dogmatics.

The unity of theology

Jüngel's earliest explorations of this theme are informed by his conviction that the different theological disciplines all stand in relation to the Word of God: 'Theology is a science which is related in all its parts to the event of the Word of God and constituted as a science through that relation.'[10] The idiom of his proposal is such that English readers may find it hard to appreciate its precise force. The category of 'the Word' often perplexes English readers of German theological works in which it occurs, most usually because the precise functions of that category are not always clearly grasped by such readers or made sufficiently clear by those who use it.[11] In Jüngel's case, the category is best understood in the present context as furnishing a bridge-concept to show that historico-critical work and dogmatics form 'a unity, whose origin lies in their common relation to the same Word'.[12] Theology is a coherent discipline in that it is a multi-faceted response to the one Word of God. Failure to appreciate this has disturbed the relationship between exegesis and dogmatics and brought about the situation in which they seem mutually incompatible. In his attempt to work through this situation, Jüngel suggests that a proper use of the historico-critical method will be alert to the relationship between the biblical texts and the Word of God which is discovered through them. In an – admittedly opaque – statement he claims that theology is 'interpretation [*Auslegung*] of the Word of God *secundum dicentem deum* on the basis of the interpretedness [*Ausgelegtheit*] of the Word of God *secundum recipientem hominem*'.[13] In other words, neither the historical nor the dogmatic tasks of theology can be dispensed with. Because it concerns itself with the 'interpretedness' of the Word of God, that is, with those texts which articulate that Word as it is received in traditions of human language, the task of historico-critical study is incumbent upon theology as the proper method of understanding human texts. But because theology is also 'interpretation' of the Word of God *secundum dicentem deum*, it is also a kerygmatic and dogmatic exercise, though one which may not leave behind the textual form which the Word of God takes. Put more briefly: as exegesis, theology inquires after the 'Word of God as text';[14] as dogmatics, theology inquires after the same Word 'as truth to be reiterated'.[15]

The kinds of moves that Jüngel is making here can perhaps be elucidated by comparison with Ebeling's study to which reference was made earlier. Ebeling there conceives of the continuity between exegesis and dogmatics in terms of the continuity between *traditum* and *actus tradendi*. Exegesis concerns itself with the tradition of Christian language as *tradition*, that is, with textual and chronological complexes of historical data. Dogmatics, like the proclamation which it is intended to serve, is concerned with the *actus tradendi*, and in this way participates in the handing-on of tradition. Both are united in their engagement with the Word of God as it is found in a tradition of human language.[16] Using different language and conceptuality, Jüngel makes much the same point: historico-critical study and hermeneutics (by which he means kerygmatic and dogmatic 'interpretation') are united in their concern with human language as the 'capture' or 'conquest' (*Eroberung*) of revelation:

> The historico-critical method...orientates itself (exclusively!) to the *captures* which revelation *has* made...The hermeneutical task of theology consists in bringing revelation as revelation to speech by using the historico-critical method. Hermeneutics is interested in the *capture* of language by revelation as it is perceived in the captures (texts!)...Thus the hermeneutical task of theology is the consistent *essence* of the historico-critical method in theology.[17]

To summarise what has been necessarily a rather laboured discussion: one of the larger issues towards which Jüngel's early work is directed is that of the coherence of exegesis and dogmatics, a coherence formulated through the use of the category of 'the Word'. His use of this category is not to be misconstrued as an attempt to circumvent the legitimate claims of the historico-critical method by claiming a privileged status for the biblical text; rather it is the attempt to acknowledge those claims whilst retaining the dogmatic and kerygmatic functions of theology.[18] Because of its relation to the Word of God, 'theology is in all its divisions an indivisible whole'.[19] The 'differentiation of theology...into several disciplines'[20] does not lead to its fragmentation; it is rather 'the expression of a necessary and meaningful division of labour'.[21]

History and dogma in Christology

In later Christological essays,[22] Jüngel moves on from here to look in greater detail at one area in which the maintenance of the unity of theology is an especially pressing necessity: the relationship between history and dogma in Christology. At significant points this later work builds upon earlier proposals about the unity of theology. In the same way that theology as a whole, grounded in the Word of God, faces both the historico-critical and the dogmatic tasks, so Christology in particular, because of the nature of its material, has both an historical and a dogmatic component. Like all theology, in other words, Christology is a coherent discipline because of its object.

There is, however, a significant shift in direction in the later work. For here Jüngel does not appeal to the category of 'the Word of God' in his search for theological unity. Rather, he examines the language of the gospel texts themselves. In simple form, his argument could be laid out as follows: an account of the relation between the historical and the dogmatic components of Christology is to take its bearings from the literary *Gattung* of the canonical gospels. These texts furnish normative language about Jesus Christ and so constitute the measure of all contemporary language about him. Close analysis of the mode of speech found in the gospels shows that it is both historical and interpretative. It tells us who Jesus Christ is by narrating who he was, presenting the past in the light of his present significance. This means that a theological response to those texts must embrace both historico-critical investigation and dogmatic reflection. Because it is reflexive upon the gospel texts, Christological language is both historical and dogmatic.

This shift towards analysis of the textual form of the gospels is significant in two respects. First, it represents a greater concreteness in Jüngel's approach, in that he takes his bearings not from the rather abstract category of 'the Word of God' but from a particular tradition of language. Second, it highlights a more general feature

of his work, namely his concern to identify the particular mode of
speech which is appropriate to theology. 'Theology has the
responsibility to ensure that its subject-matter is expressed in
appropriate language. One of the most fundamental tasks of
theology as a science is thus to come to an understanding of the
different modes of speech which a state of affairs demands if it is
to be articulated.'[23] In the case of Christology, attention to the
specific nature of religious language reveals a fundamental distinction between 'theological affirmation and historical [*historisch*]
observation'.[24] This distinction concerns 'the relationship of
dogmatic and historical [*historisch*] perception in theology'.[25]
Jüngel insists on the need to be clear about this relationship,
because of his sense that mistakes at this level can put the whole
Christological enterprise out of joint, either by denying any
historical reference in Christological language or by supposing that
historical 'facts' can be neatly separated from their significance for
the interpreter. The point can be clarified a little by looking at how
Jüngel puts the distinction to work in talking about the death of
Jesus.[26]

Historical perception approaches the death of Jesus '*from the
direction of the life he lived*',[27] and it is accordingly limited to
showing how Jesus' death was the factual consequence of that life.[28]
However much it may investigate questions of Jesus' own
understanding of his death or of the legal and political details of
his trial, the language of historical perception cannot give a full
account of the connection between the life and the death of Jesus:
that connection remains 'ambivalent in meaning'.[29] Jüngel is not,
of course, rejecting such historical investigation *tout court*, but
rather seeking to identify its limits, and to preserve the demarcation
between historical perception and 'dogmatic responsibility'.[30]
This is necessary because when historical perception annexes to
itself the dogmatic tasks, it absolutises its own findings into a
normative interpretation, and the result is an objectification in
which 'the place of Jesus himself is taken by a picture of Jesus
which sacrifices the livingness of the historical [*geschichtlich*]
phenomenon'.[31] This kind of objectification can, moreover,
threaten to become an 'historicizing metaphysic of salvific facts'.[32]
Such a metaphysic is an abuse of historical perception, which
maintains continuity between event and interpretation only by
objectifying historical factuality. The effect of this objectification
is to freeze the past, by isolating it from the present in which it

is significant. In order to counteract this, Jüngel makes a suggestion about the nature of history.

His denial of absolute status to the results of historical perception means the rejection of 'a theology of the facts, which asserts that the so-called brute facts constitute the primary factor and their historical [*geschichtlich*] i.e. theological meaning a secondary factor to be distinguished from the primary'.[33] As an alternative to this, he sketches an understanding of the nature of historical truth which denies any hiatus between fact and meaning and so makes both the historical and theological tasks legitimate and necessary. At the heart of his sketch is a suggestion that 'historical being'[34] is 'more than "bare actuality", more than "naked factuality"'.[35] This 'more' is what he labels the 'truth' of historical being, which is identified as the possibilities which a past event opens up in the present: 'the possibilities which a reality brings with itself and leaves behind make a fact which happens in history into something like an event of historical [*geschichtlich*] truth'.[36] Jüngel is suggesting, that is, that part of the true nature of an event is the effect which it has upon subsequent history. The meaning of a past event cannot be discovered by lifting that event out of the stream of history: both the event and its effects need to be understood together. And so the significance of the history of Jesus cannot 'be exclusively limited to what we know of him historically [*historisch*]'.[37] Rather, that history is to be interpreted within the larger context of 'the effectiveness of Jesus',[38] that is, from faith in his history as 'salvation-event'.[39]

This complex of event and 'effective history' is the concern of dogmatic perception. As a 'judgement about the death of Jesus expressed in the language of faith',[40] dogmatic perception approaches that death from the standpoint of God's relation to it as revealed in the resurrection and expressed in the language of faith. It would be a mistake to envisage this approach as an unwarranted imposition of interpretation upon fact: it is rather an acknowledgement of the inseparability of fact and meaning. Equally, it would be a mistake to interpret Jüngel as offering a docetic Christology in which interpretation is cut loose from event. He is certainly proposing that it is only from faith in Jesus as the mediator of salvation that the facts of his life have theological significance. There is, however, a *necessary* connection between contemporary experience of salvation and the historical ministry of Jesus. For as he noted in *Paulus und Jesus*, 'The question of the preaching of Jesus (gen. obj.) includes the question of the preaching of Jesus (gen. subj.).'[41] This connection Jüngel identifies through analysis of the literary form of the gospels.

In that literary form Jüngel notes what he calls a 'kerygmatically necessary return to the tradition about Jesus'.[42] The very literary form of the gospels shows the inseparability of kerygma and historical actuality. This can be seen, for example, in the way in which the gospels accomplish a '*communicatio idiomatum* between the earthly Jesus and the risen One',[43] so that 'in the post-Easter light of the risen and exalted Lord the earthly Jesus becomes a hermeneutical aid to the kerygma'.[44] Again, the application of post-Easter titles to the earthly Jesus in the gospel narratives,[45] or the device of synecdoche in which the presentation of a particular incident in the life of Jesus becomes 'the presentation of a way of behaviour which characterised the whole of Jesus' existence',[46] demonstrates that past event and present meaning are bound up together. The language of the presentation of Jesus in the gospel narratives is thus 'the paradigm case for a hermeneutic of theological logic'.[47] Those texts are normative for Christology, not simply because they furnish historical 'data', but because they 'introduce...the distinction of historical [*historisch*] and dogmatic perception insofar as they identify Easter faith as an event which qualifies the *past* anew, an event whose consequences can be perceived historically [*historisch*], for example, in the alteration of the logia of Jesus'.[48]

In drawing attention in this way to the blend of historical and theological reference in the language of the gospels, Jüngel is attempting to make theological capital out of a feature which has become axiomatic for study of those texts. That is to say, he is using this characteristic of the gospel *Gattung* as the basis for a Christological programme in which historical and dogmatic work will be able to co-exist, and in which historico-critical exegesis will not stifle but encourage contemporary reflection. 'Dogmatic perception is interpretation of historically [*historisch*] perceived speech as speech of faith in the past, with the aim of laying bare the speech which is possible and necessary for faith in the present.'[49]

Like the gospels, then, Christological language is language about the past which refuses to isolate event from interpretation. In the canonical gospels, there is no separation between formative events and presentation of and commentary upon those events from the standpoint of the experience of salvation. They do not ask who Jesus Christ *is* without narrating who he *was*, nor do they narrate his past without advertising his contemporary significance.[50] Consequently, theological reflection upon the past of Jesus is inseparable from historical work on that past, and vice versa. Because he is engaged with the gospel texts, the theologian must do 'historical [*historisch*] work *as* theological work',[51] for the narrated past is effective in that it lays bare possibilities in the present.

To narrate history means: to examine its unique and irrevocable actuality, going back to the *past* possibility out of which it came, looking forward to its *future* possibilities, and in this way vouchsafing a future to that past actuality. Over against the arbitrariness of fable, and over against the necessary character of concepts, narrative is potent discourse in which it comes about that past history sets newly at liberty its real possibilities.[52]

The person of Christ

So far Jüngel has not published a systematic Christological treatise, but has concentrated for the most part on the hermeneutical questions outlined above and on questions concerning the relationship between Christology and other areas of theology. However, remarks on dogmatic issues in Christology are scattered throughout the corpus of his writings. Drawing some of these together will help outline some of the main features of his substantive Christology.

The concept to which Jüngel's writing in this area returns more than any other is that of *identification*. His Christology could be summarised over-schematically in two propositions: God is the one who has identified himself with the crucified Jesus; Jesus Christ is the man with whom God has identified himself. What is the meaning and the function of the concept of identification?

First, language about the identification of God with Jesus expresses a judgement made about the death of Jesus in the light of faith in his resurrection. Indeed, faith in the risen Jesus is for Jüngel primarily faith in the fact that, at the cross, God identified himself with the crucified. The resurrection is not to be conceived as temporally successive to the death of Jesus, a second stage after Calvary. Rather, the resurrection discloses 'God's relation to the death of Jesus of Nazareth',[53] a relation for whose description the language of identification is appropriate. 'The meaning of the death of Jesus, which is revealed in the resurrection of Jesus Christ, comes to speech as faith in the identity of God with the crucified man Jesus.'[54]

This strong emphasis on the death of Jesus will be examined later when we come to look at Jüngel's doctrine of God. However, it needs to be stressed that the field of reference of talk about the identification of God with Jesus disclosed at the resurrection stretches back into the life Jesus lived. This is a point of some considerable significance for it illustrates well the continuity between the earthly Jesus and the exalted Lord which Jüngel is at pains to stress.

The basic conceptuality through which Jüngel articulates the point is very ancient, namely that of 'anhypostasia' and 'enhypostasia'. Whilst the history of these terms in the Fathers shows a complex and flexible usage, a central core of meaning can be discerned.[55] 'Anhypostasia' describes the conviction that the human nature of the incarnate Christ did not have a personal centre of subsistence, but was rather incorporated into the person of the eternal Word with which it was united at the incarnation. 'Enhypostasia' stresses that the personal humanity of Jesus became hypostatic in the person of the Logos, who thus includes within himself all the attributes of perfect humanity. As Pannenberg puts it, the doctrine of enhypostasia means that 'Jesus' human existence in the whole of its historical course has the ground of its unity and meaning (and thus also of its facticity) in the fact that Jesus is the eternal Son of God'.[56]

Both 'anhypostasia' and 'enhypostasia' have been subjected to criticism for a failure fully to reckon with the humanity of Christ: 'anhypostasia', because of its implicit monophysitism (especially when deployed by Cyril of Alexandria), 'enhypostasia', because of its abstraction from 'the actual event of the unification of God and man in the temporal execution of the course of Jesus' existence'.[57] However, Jüngel seeks to use both concepts in a way which takes full account of the fact that the unity of God and man is historically mediated: both concepts are a way of talking of a human life and not of timeless realities which that human life merely illustrates. Thus 'anhypostasia' is a way of articulating the fact that Jesus is, as it were, so totally taken up with his proclamation of the Kingdom of God that his whole being could be defined by reference to that Kingdom. His 'life and his death was an ex-istence out of the coming Kingdom of God and an insistence on God's fatherly will'.[58] Jesus was not 'one who pleased himself',[59] but rather 'was himself in his selflessness'.[60] He was what he was because of the Kingdom that he proclaimed, so that his being was 'a being in the act of the Word of the *Kingdom of God*'.[61]

The grounds of this 'anhypostatic humanity',[62] however, remain hidden or ambivalent in meaning during the actual course of Jesus' life: it is only in faith in Jesus' resurrection that Jesus' selflessness is perceived to be grounded in his ontological relationship to God. The resurrection reveals that Jesus' existence in the Kingdom of God is ultimately to be traced to 'the relation of the Logos to Jesus as that which made Jesus' relationship to the Father possible'.[63] The resurrection, that is, discloses the enhypostatic grounds of Jesus' anhypostatic existence, the concept of 'enhypostasia' formulating how Jesus' existence is '*ontologically* grounded in the fact that his humanity is enhypostatic in the mode of being of the Logos'.[64]

This language of an- and enhypostasia, by which Jüngel elucidates the concept of identification, serves not only to advertise the ecstatic or relational structure of Jesus' existence. It also provides an explanatory framework by which to demonstrate the relation of the post-Easter kerygma to Jesus himself. As such, it functions as a dogmatic counterpart to the theory of 'effective history' outlined in the previous section. For such language offers a means of interpreting the death of Jesus as the *integral* of his existence: 'On the basis of faith in the resurrection of Jesus Christ the death of Jesus comes to have formal meaning as an integral of his earthly existence.'[65] Out of resurrection faith in God's identification with Jesus we are enabled to see Jesus' history 'as a unity'[66] with shape and firm contours, informed with inexhaustible significance and no longer 'ambivalent in meaning'.[67]

Finally, on a somewhat different note, Jüngel insists that the identification of God with Jesus is an *event*. His concern here is to avoid a position in which the historical relationship of God and Jesus would be simply the highest instantiation of a more general, structurally-fixed relationship of God and man. Such a position would not only abstract from the actual occurrence of God's act of identifying himself with this particular human history. It would also run the risk of undermining the distinction between God and the world: 'If his identity with the man Jesus were not understood as the event of his identifying, of his coming to the world, God would be thought of as part – and only part – of the world.'[68] The identity of God with Jesus has to be thought of 'as a continuing event',[69] to retain the concreteness of the history of Jesus as a set of events whose significance would be irreparably damaged if thought simply to exemplify a more general truth. Jüngel notes in Hegel – a thinker with whom he has very great sympathy – precisely this dissolution of the unique event of identification:

> Hegel's definition, in which through the incarnation and death of God there occurred the raising of an absolute spirit uniting divine and human nature in general, must be challenged by theology...as a threat to the concrete being of Jesus Christ as well as to the proper distinction between God and man. The *theological* criterion of a correct definition of the Christological unity of divine and human nature is respect for the uniqueness of Jesus Christ.[70]

The hypostatic union is a *history*, 'insofar as it is to be thought out of the event of the *unitio*'.[71]

The event of identification, then, offers an explanatory key to the being of Jesus: Jesus' anhypostatic existence in the Word of the Kingdom is rendered univocal when the resurrection discloses that this existence is to be understood from the perspective that 'it is the *self-renunciation* and *self-abasement* of the eternal Word of God which makes it possible for the man Jesus to exist...in the act of God's Word of the Kingdom of God'.[72] With the corollary notions of an- and enhypostasia, the concept of identification is used to explore aspects of the way in which the history of the man Jesus can be the actuality of God in the world. Jüngel only rarely makes reference to the conceptuality and terminology of 'incarnation'. But many of the functions of such language are performed by the cluster of notions: 'identification', 'anhypostasia' and 'enhypostasia'. In his lectures on Christology, Bonhoeffer quarrelled with the language of enhypostasia as docetic;[73] but the way in which Jüngel uses the term shows that it may equally be language which fulfils Bonhoeffer's desire that 'Of this man, we say: He is God for us.'[74]

Christology and theological method

The Christological concept of 'identification' performs not only a dogmatic function in Jüngel's theology: it is also a methodological principle of very great import. For the identification of God with Jesus is significant not only for our understanding of the person of Christ but equally for the definition of God and man, indeed, for any area of theological reflection. The event of the hypostatic union functions heuristically in the discovery of truth about human and divine nature: 'Out of this Christological event theological thinking has to let it be said what may properly be called God and man.'[75] Such a statement should not be taken as a rather crude extension of the 'two natures' Christology (a dogma about which Jüngel's strong Lutheran emphasis on the *communicatio idiomatum* between the humanity and the divinity of Christ makes him markedly reticent).[76] It is better understood as a remark about theological procedure: Christological assertions lie at the heart of authentically Christian doctrines of God and man.

This resolute Christocentrism pervades the whole structure of Jüngel's theology, providing its most fundamental commitments and most characteristic styles of argument. Jüngel does not envisage Christology as merely one doctrine in a series with other doctrines. Rather, it provides the platform for work in all other areas, and is normative and regulative for the whole corpus of Christian teaching. And it has this function precisely because in Jüngel's theology – as, of course, in that of his *doctor veritatis*, Barth – the doctrine of the person of Christ has come to occupy the place of the doctrine of revelation. God's self-declaration is identical with the history of Jesus Christ, which thus becomes the standard by which all dogmatic affirmations are to be judged.

Dogmatic inquiry discovers that there is a structural and essentially Christological pattern running throughout the whole body of our theological knowledge, which can be studied and used as a norm or criterion for helping to shape the true form of each doctrine, for testing and proving the different doctrines to see whether they really fit into the essential structure of the whole.[77]

Jüngel's Christocentrism will be amply illustrated as we look in detail at different aspects of his work, and its methodological and dogmatic viability will be assessed in the conclusion. For the present, it is important to note that Jüngel is primarily interested in procedural issues in Christology – with questions of the structure and logic of Christological assertions, with questions of the foundational role of Christology for the whole dogmatic edifice. His concern, in other words, has been with the area of fundamental theology.

Jüngel's preoccupation with issues concerning the structure, logic and method of Christology makes his work seem somewhat tangential to many contemporary Anglo-Saxon discussions of the field. Yet his very obliqueness to those debates may have a great deal to teach us. Large tracts of recent Anglo-Saxon writing on Christological themes, notably in the area of the doctrine of the incarnation, are deficient not so much at the substantive level but because they do not address themselves with sufficient clarity to the logical and procedural issues involved. As a result, the task which patristic incarnational Christologies sought to undertake is misconstrued (as 'hellenisation' or 'metaphysical speculation'), and objections are urged against such theologies which are not uncommonly inappropriate. In the course of a very perceptive review of *The Myth of God Incarnate*, E.F. Osborn noted in that book 'a remarkable failure to comprehend what the early Christian thinkers were doing'[78] – a remark which has much wider application than the particular volume to which it refers.

Osborn's counter-proposal is that elucidation of the precise problems to which the Fathers addressed themselves would prevent the kind of misconstructions and misunderstandings which have marred much recent debate.[79] It is at this level that Jüngel's contribution might be especially valuable. Concern carefully to specify the mode of Christological discourse prevents him from what Ian Ramsey called 'mistaken logical allocations',[80] and so alerts him to the real nature of some of the tasks facing the theologian of the person of Christ. Jüngel's attentiveness to logic and argumentative form – strangely lacking in some other areas of his work – is indeed a rare virtue.[81]

4. God the mystery of the world (1): speaking about God

Jüngel's *magnum opus* to date is the lengthy study *Gott als Geheimnis der Welt*, and themes from this book will be explored in the next three chapters. *Gott als Geheimnis* is a diffuse work whose main thrust is not easily identified from a cursory reading: it is indeed a 'Studienbuch'[1] which makes considerable demands on the student. Jüngel has three main areas of concern in the course of the book: language about God, thought about God, and the nature of God himself. He is led to range over such a breadth of issues in prolegomena and substantive dogma because of the book's underlying conviction that issues of method and content cannot be separated. Indeed, in some ways the book is an object lesson in the many-sidedness of serious theological work. Stylistically, too, it is a curious piece, blending together historical analysis with highly abstract writing on metaphysical and dogmatic themes. Once again, the juxtaposition conveys a conviction about 'the bond between systematic thinking and historical analysis'.[2] There are certainly times when the reader is left wondering whether the book operates on so many different fronts that its energy is dissipated. Nevertheless, it is a book of very considerable strength, with passages of real brilliance. We turn to the first of its main themes, that of Christian speech about God.

The 'linguistic displacement' of God

Mention has already been made of the centrality of the category of 'the Word' for Jüngel's theology, and of the difficulty which many Anglo-Saxon theologians may experience in identifying with his concern. It is, however, important to grasp Jüngel's sense that the speech of faith is rendered acutely difficult by its present linguistic context. For whilst 'the content of the Christian faith demands to be spoken',[3] nevertheless 'the language of our world has become

more worldly'.[4] Jüngel thus envisages himself addressing a
situation in which 'God...has no place in our language. He is not
met with, he has no *topos* [place]...We live in the age of the
linguistic displacement of God.'[5]

From this assessment emerges Jüngel's pressing concern with the
linguistic situation of faith as it is adversely affected by the
narrowing of the scope of language.[6] At many points *Gott als
Geheimnis* returns to this theme: the need more satisfactorily to
relate the necessity to speak of God and the worldliness of the
language in which God must be articulated. Two issues in particular
can be identified.

First, Jüngel insists that language about God must be authentically human language. Of course, he is firm in the conviction that
language about God is only possible on the basis of God's revelatory
utterance, and that such language does not take its rise from within
human language since it is demanded of man from beyond the
horizons of worldly discourse.[7] But he affirms with equal conviction
that language about God is not the suspension of human language
or its devaluation. Language about God is certainly not immanent
within the structures of ordinary human speech. Yet it does not
so transcend those structures as to lose its human character.
Language about God is a demand which goes against the grain of
man's natural linguistic resources; yet it is not thereby *less* but *more*
human than 'ordinary' discourse.

Second, Jüngel is at pains to identify the heavy demands which
speech of God makes upon human language, and to analyse the
semantic consequences of such demands. Language which properly
'brings God to speech' is *catachrestic*: it uses human language in
unfamiliar ways by applying words to new referents. These
catachrestic elements of religious language are to be taken with full
seriousness: instead of premature dismissal of religious language
as intolerable abuse of words, what is needed is an expansion of
our understanding of the referential relationship between language
and what is the case. For the meaning of religious language will
remain suppressed without a more flexible semantics and a more
catholic spectrum of modes of reference.

These issues naturally coalesce in questions about the place of
parable, analogy and metaphor in our speech of God. It is in the
exploration of such tropes that a solution to the problem of the
linguistic displacement of God is to be sought. For tropic language
is both fully human and catachrestic: it demonstrates both the

human context from which religious discourse is drawn and also the demands which are made upon language by a divine referent. Such language thus meets both Jüngel's conditions for proper speech about God, namely, that such speech both be authentically human and also 'bring God to speech'. It is only in more recent work that Jüngel has fully explored the curious interplay of familiar word and unfamiliar referent in metaphor and analogy as a possibility for Christian religious language. The background to these later studies is a series of earlier pieces which are less successful in their correlation of the human and the divine.

The Word of God and the word of man

In these earlier studies, the catachrestic elements of Christian speech tend so to be emphasised that the humanity of such speech is neglected. In *Paulus und Jesus*, for example, there is a heavy stress on the transcendent origin of speech about the Kingdom of God. Certainly Jüngel emphasises, as we saw, that the Kingdom of God is really present in the parables, in such a way that the parables are quasi-sacramental signs which effect that which they signify. But such an emphasis should not be confused with ideas of the immanence of the Kingdom in the resources of worldly speech. The Kingdom *comes* to speech. Here, as elsewhere, the idea of 'coming' is highly significant, functioning as a focal metaphor in the resolution of problems concerning 'the difference of God from the world'.[8] To say that the Kingdom 'comes' to speech is, at this early stage in Jüngel's theological work, to retain a fundamental distinction between God and the world. Thus, for example, he writes that the truth of Jesus' proclamation 'cannot be perceived directly'[9] for it is an 'eschatological event'[10] whose time is asymptotic with respect to the time of the world. As an eschatological reality the Kingdom cannot be identified with any state of affairs; consequently, the language of the Kingdom is tangential to worldly language.

There is much, indeed, in *Paulus und Jesus* which might stand under the famous maxim of the early Barth: 'We are human...and so cannot speak of God.'[11] And because Jüngel underlines that the language of the Kingdom is a strange intrusion upon the language of the world, he tends to neglect the ordinariness and naturalness which constitute a most striking feature of Jesus' parables: 'It is the nature of the parable that it advertises the unfamiliar by the

familiar.'[12] Indeed, it could be said that a persistent weakness of
Jüngel's parable theory in *Paulus und Jesus*[13] is that he passes over
the almost obstinately commonplace character of Jesus' parables
in which 'we encounter a religious idiom which...has been
rigorously "desacralized"'.[14] We must wait for a second treatment
of the parables in *Gott als Geheimnis* before Jüngel takes greater
account of the way in which the Kingdom comes to speech in
essentially worldly narratives. He will later express a conviction
that the world and its stories *in their very ordinariness and
naturalness* do *become* parables of the Kingdom. In *Paulus und
Jesus*, the Kingdom's world-relation remains ambivalent, and an
inadequate valuation of its human form is not entirely avoided.

Many of the same problems recur in Jüngel's presentation of
Barth's thought in *Gottes Sein ist im Werden*. He focusses on how
for Barth discussion of the possibility of human speech about God
is not to concentrate on the potential within human language but
on the demand which comes to language as the divine realities
themselves press the need for speech about God. Again, language
about God goes against the grain: man's speech has to be
'captured' by the Word of God which it may *interpret* but not
illustrate.[15]

Jüngel insists that this 'capturing' of language is to the benefit
of human speech: 'Where such "capturing" of language through
revelation happens, there occurs a *gain to language*. This consists
in the fact that God comes to speech *as God*.'[16] Yet once again the
statements fall short of a full affirmation of the humanity of speech
about God. Indeed, Jüngel appears to be close to suggesting that
only language taken captive by God is 'true' language: the Word
of God *brings* language to its true essence;[17] or again, 'Language
must be taken captive by revelation in order to be brought to its
true essence.'[18] It is difficult to see how this process can be a 'gain
to language' when the corollary is that language which does not
'bring God to speech' has somehow failed to attain its essence. For
all Jüngel's concern to validate human speech from the prevenient
divine Word, there is a real danger of absorption of our language
into the divine speech-act, or at least of the implication that a purely
'natural' language is a bastard form of speech.

'Metaphorical Truth'

Jüngel's early treatments of the problem of human speech about God result only in a dialectical maintenance of both the priority of the divine Word and the authenticity of human language. A more effective resolution is first achieved in the 1974 essay 'Metaphorische Wahrheit' which develops a theology of metaphor of considerable sophistication.

His essay can best be appreciated from the direction of parallel work in literary theory and the philosophy of science which reinstates the cognitive significance of metaphor.[19] Such proposals insist that metaphor cannot be reduced to 'a sort of happy extra trick with words'.[20] For an understanding of metaphor as mere stylistic embellishment works with too narrow a view of the referential relationship between language and reality, and is insensitive to the significance of 'non-literal' language in the exploration of the world. Max Black, for instance, suggests that metaphor is irreducible, its cognitive content lost if it is translated into terms other than itself. Metaphor is not simply a process of 'substitution' in which a metaphorical word is used *instead of* a literal one, so that 'understanding a metaphor is like deciphering a code or unravelling a riddle'.[21] Rather, metaphor is the application to one system of language from another system in a way which is semantically expansive: the focal word of the metaphor thereby gains 'a new meaning, which is not quite its meaning in literal uses, nor quite the meaning any literal substitute would have...The new context...imposes extension of meaning upon the focal word.'[22] This expansion of meaning precludes the resolution of metaphors into literal speech; literal paraphrase 'fails to be a translation because it fails to give the insight that the metaphor did'.[23] 'Translation' not merely loses a rhetorical embellishment but an insight into what is the case which is inseparable from its metaphorical form.

Perhaps the most significant work in this area is Ricoeur's study *The Rule of Metaphor*. One of Ricoeur's central observations is that the referential relationship found in literal discourse breaks down in literary language: 'the strategy of language proper to poetry... does indeed seem to consist in constituting a sense that intercepts reality and, in the limiting situation, abolishes reality'.[24] This disruption of literal reference is, however, only the negative condition for the emergence of a more fundamental form of reference which describes reality only by exploding the view of reality which is the referent of literal discourse: 'By drawing a new semantic pertinence out of the ruins of the literal meaning, the metaphoric interpretation also sustains a new referential design, through those same means of abolition of the reference corresponding to the literal interpretation of the statement.'[25] Ricoeur introduces the notion of 'metaphorical truth' in order to identify the cognitive status of metaphors as linguistic forms in which new aspects of reality are expressed: 'In service to the poetic function, metaphor is that strategy of language by which language divests itself of its function of direct description in order to reach the mythic level where its function of discovery is set free.'[26] Metaphor is thus no mere decoration, but a form of language which traces the emergence of new reality, straddling two systems of reference and unfolding from the *epoché* of 'ordinary' reference a new reference which 'seems to mark the invasion of language by the ante-predicative and the pre-categorial, and to require a concept of truth other than the concept of truth-verification, the correlative of our ordinary concept of reality'.[27]

Ricoeur's proposal is in many respects similar to that which Jüngel makes. For above all Jüngel stresses that metaphor is only properly understood when we call into question the finality of literal reality and the modes of discourse which express it. Fully to assimilate the irreducibility of metaphor demands an expansion of the semantics of reference; only in this way can metaphor be recognised as a linguistic device in which discoveries about the substance of reality are made. For Jüngel this demands the elaboration of a theological ontology in which the primacy of the referent of literal discourse (in Jüngel's terminology, 'actuality') would be questioned in order to do justice to that which is disclosed in metaphor ('possibility'). It also shows the need to develop a concept of truth which is capable of embracing the fact that metaphor is cognitively freighted. Metaphor expands the horizons of the world by bringing to expression new reality; as heuristic fiction it pushes back the limits of the world as well as those of language.

Jüngel's work on metaphor takes its rise from a conviction that religious discourse makes language perform functions beyond those of literal reference to 'actuality': 'The truth of what faith has to say manifests itself...not least in the fact that the language of faith does not correspond to actuality in any simple way.'[28] And because the language of faith does not fully correspond with actuality, such language 'must appear to be erroneous, if not deceptive'.[29] In response to this, Jüngel canvasses the centrality of metaphor as a form of religious language: 'he who states that actuality is what it is not, is...not lying if he is speaking metaphorically'.[30] For whilst faith's language is not literally descriptive of actuality, because it is metaphorical it is not thereby referential to *less* than actuality but to *more* than actuality. The suspension of literal reference enables us to articulate a state of affairs beyond the actual.

If we are fully to grasp Jüngel's concerns here, we need to appreciate two moves which he is making: first, his proposal that metaphor is ontologically charged, in the sense that it discloses what is the case; and second, the explanation of this by the use of the ontological categories of 'actuality' and 'more than actuality'.

First, Jüngel insists that metaphor cannot be defused as a rhetorical luxury, educationally useful but heuristically super-fluous. Metaphor is irreducible as language which articulates states of affairs for the articulation of which literal language is less than adequate: 'Through metaphor a gain occurs. The horizon of meaning is linguistically widened. And so metaphor is an admirable form of linguistic dealing with that which exists.'[31]

This leads to the second move, in which Jüngel goes on from such assertions to fashion an ontology and a theory of truth in order to identify the metaphorical disturbance of the dominance of literal speech and to demonstrate that metaphor is ontologically (and so cognitively) freighted. To do this, he deploys the contrast between actuality and possibility. The distinction is of considerable significance in Jüngel's more recent writing; as we shall see, it occurs in his account of God and transience in *Gott als Geheimnis*, as well as in his elaboration of a theological anthropology out of the doctrine of justification.

Jüngel seeks to expand the category of 'being' to cover both actuality and possibility: 'Being does not exhaust itself in the actual...More is possible.'[32] The statement here is laconic, but can be elucidated from the programmatic essay 'Die Welt als Möglichkeit und Wirklichkeit'. This piece offers a sustained critique of the ontological priority of actuality over possibility. 'From the beginnings of metaphysics actuality is given priority over possibility. Being was and is identified with actuality.'[33] Over against this, Jüngel suggests that possibility is properly included in the realm of *to on* (that which is): being includes possibility within its scope. And possibility 'comes to speech' in language which breaks the pattern of reference to actuality. Because 'being' is a more inclusive term, comprehending both actuality and possibility, literal speech does not delineate the limits of language. And so metaphor is not the abeyance of realism, of concern for what is the case. On the contrary, to take metaphor seriously is to demand a realism capable of embracing the ontological force of possibility. Metaphor discloses new aspects of what is the case so that 'the metaphorical mode of speech has ontological relevance, in that through it a new context of being is disclosed, grounded in a gain to language. The new (metaphorical) use of a word gives this word a new meaning and with this new meaning brings new being to speech.'[34] Metaphors 'contradict...actuality and yet are...true'.[35]

The word 'true' there is highly significant, for it is Jüngel's conviction that if metaphor is the disclosure of new being, then it requires for its identification a concept of truth which – like the concept of 'being' – is sufficiently flexible to embrace the ontological reference of metaphorical speech. He claims that 'in the tradition of Western thought "truth" is understood as the correspondence of the judgement of the mind (*intellectus*) with actuality (*res*), as *adaequatio intellectus et rei* in the sense of *adaequatio intellectus (humani) ad rem*. In the context of this understanding of truth religious language seems to be the opposite of true language.'[36] What Jüngel rejects in the correspondence theory of truth is not its realism but rather its literalism – its orientation towards actuality and so towards literal speech. 'Truth', however, must be located not only in actuality but also in the disturbance of actuality, linguistically identified as metaphors which 'participate in the truth, in that they take actuality beyond actuality, without asserting anything false about it'.[37]

The thrust of Jüngel's theory of metaphor and the attendant categories of 'actuality', 'possibility' and 'metaphorical truth' is to offer a resolution of the difficulty detected in his earlier work, namely a hiatus between the divine realities and man's linguistic capacity. For metaphor is authentically human language, drawn from the speech of actuality; but it is also the disclosure of the possibility of 'bringing God to speech'. The split reference of metaphor straddles both actuality and possibility, so that metaphor is a 'dialectic of familiarity and unfamiliarity'.[38] 'It makes both a state of affairs and a use of language unfamiliar, in that it uses an unaccustomed word to signify a state of affairs and uses this word in an unaccustomed sense. Equally, however, metaphor begins by bringing this unfamiliarity within the familiar world, so that it is a matter of the *expansion* of the familiar world.'[39] The *epoché* of reference to actuality does not negate that actuality. Rather it takes it beyond itself, so that 'actuality is neither overlooked nor passed by. Rather it is enhanced.'[40] By setting 'two horizons of meaning in relation to each other',[41] metaphor thematises actuality and so traces the emergence of new possibilities without detriment to the worldliness of the language of faith.

In 'Metaphorische Wahrheit', then, Jüngel has moved significantly beyond the antithesis of God and the world's discourse, putting less emphasis on the 'capturing' of language by God's Word. By focussing attention on *metaphor* (rather than on the transcendent Word of God which must come to speech in the essentially unsuitable form of human language) Jüngel makes the human component of talk of God much more fully thematic. This does not mean that he neglects the catachrestic elements of language about God. But catachresis does not now result from the incommensurability of human language and divine reality, but from the metaphoric bridging of a primary (human) and a secondary (divine) system of reference in a way which enhances the value of the first by allowing it to speak for the second. God's 'coming to speech' in metaphors drawn from the language-stock of the world discloses hitherto-unseen potential granted to that world.

The analogy of advent

We turn finally to Jüngel's latest full-dress treatment of questions concerning language about God, the section on the 'analogy of advent' in *Gott als Geheimnis*. His treatment here takes us to the heart of his concern to explore the character of the relationship between God and man. For he views analogical language – like metaphor – as a form of predication which corresponds to the proper distinction between God and the world. It is this deeper dogmatic concern which lies beneath the surface of his treatment of analogy. Its *Leitmotiv* is the following question: 'To what extent

may we say that human language brings God to speech?...How
can one speak of God in a human way without falling short of his
divinity?'[42]

Jüngel is again seeking a mode of speech which will be both fully
human and also 'bring God to speech'. He describes his proposal
thus: 'Analogy is to be understood as an event which allows the
One (x) to *come* to the Other (a), with the help of the relation of
a further Other (b) to one more Other (c). It is a matter of an
analogy of advent, which brings to speech God's coming to men
as a definitive event.'[43]

The analogy of advent, it should immediately be noted, is an
analogia relationis,[44] comparing relations in a way which Jüngel sets
out schematically as $x \rightarrow a = b:c$.[45] God and the world are not
compared directly. But this stress on the indirectness of analogical
language is not born of scepticism about the ability of a worldly
relation to enlarge our understanding of the relations which God
bears towards the world. Rather, it is maintained precisely in order
that the naturalness and substantiality of the worldly relation does
not recede from view. Jüngel is not asserting that the worldly
relation (b:c) only attains true significance as a pointer to God.
Much more is it a matter of maintaining how that worldly relation,
complete in itself, comes to be something which – without prejudice
to its proper worldliness – also speaks of God: 'The worldly
relation (b:c), which of itself can give absolutely no pointer to God,
now begins to speak for God, not as a *natura* brought to the peak
of perfection by God, but as a self-evident piece of the world
speaking in the service of something even more self-evident.'[46] The
analogy of advent is thus the linguistic equivalent of the proper
relation of God and the world. The divine and the human are not
confused, either by envisaging divine immanence within the
human or by resolving the human into a sign whose value is
exhausted in pointing to God. Divine and human are substantial
in themselves; but by coming to the world God allows the human
and worldly to speak of him, and so grants it new and further
significance.

For his examples, Jüngel once again returns to the parables. His
earlier interpretations suggested that the parables are an eschatological form of speech narrating the derangement and dispossession
of human language which occurs when the time of the Kingdom
intercepts the time of the world. In *Gott als Geheimnis*, however,
much less weight falls on the parables as eschatological discourse,

and much more on their narrative worldliness. God's coming to speech in worldly narratives does not supplant their worldliness but preserves and, indeed, enhances it, making such narratives interesting in new ways. 'The parables of Jesus,' Jüngel now proposes, 'certainly do not speak of God as a man. But they speak of God in such a way that they tell about the world of men.'[47] Earlier concerns are not, of course, entirely laid aside. He still asserts as in *Paulus und Jesus* that the Kingdom comes to speech 'in parable as parable',[48] and that 'the Kingdom of God cannot be *brought* to speech as itself without *coming* to speech, without x→a. The *secundem modus recipientis recipitur* presupposes a *secundem dicentem deum*. God *comes* to speech.'[49] Thus part of the force of the word 'advent' is the refusal to allow the coming to speech of the Kingdom of God as a possibility intrinsic to the resources of worldly discourse. Yet here the purpose is simply to protect the divine originality of language about the Kingdom: in this sense alone are we dealing with a *potentia aliena*, whose distinctiveness over against the world is not abstract, but concrete as a presence within the world. Here, too, Jüngel is concerned with new possibilities occurring within reality rather than with reality's abolition.

Reflections

Contemporary discussions of the nature of religious language frequently entertain a low view of imaginative language in general and of metaphor in particular. This view tends to be associated with a high evaluation of 'literal' language as the appropriate means of articulating objective states of affairs. Many of the contributions to *The Myth of God Incarnate*, for example, are informed by a suspicion of the cognitive status of anything other than literal discourse.[50] Certainly one of the weaknesses of that symposium was its failure to identify with sufficient acuity the peculiar characteristics of Christological language, a failure which led to many misconceptions of what such language might in fact be attempting to do.

If such misconstructions are to be avoided, attention to the kind of issues which Jüngel raises in his later work on religious language would be very greatly beneficial. For by close scrutiny of the referential systems of religious language, Jüngel is able to resist pressure to reduce such language to 'mere metaphor' expressing only, for example, ethical intention or subjective emotion. He is instructive in his attention to parts of the grammar of religious discourse and in his concern not to allow its peculiarities to be eclipsed by 'positivist' or 'literalist' assumptions about the operations of reference. Jüngel shows himself to be closely akin in this respect to Ian Ramsey's unwillingness to follow 'the craze for straightforward language' and to his concern to suggest that 'there is an important place for odd language...odd language may well have a distinctive significance, and we might even conclude that the odder the language the more it matters to us'.[51] And moreover, there are noteworthy overlaps between recent theological attempts to reinstate the heuristic function of the imagination and the kind of semantic analysis which Jüngel offers.[52]

Yet if Jüngel's sensitivity towards metaphor is one of the strengths of his presentation, it also proves to be its most persistent weakness. For he tends to elevate metaphor, parable and analogy to the position where they become the only appropriate modes of Christian speech. Once again, he compresses the multi-level, pluriform nature of Christian religious language, and so fails to be alert to the range of its possibilities. Certainly Jüngel's account of the semantics of metaphor offers a valuable protest against the hegemony of literal speech and the ontology underlying such a hegemony. Yet the price of such a protest may be a similar attempt too swiftly to resolve all religious language to one particular mode. 'The speech of faith is constituted through *metaphora* [metaphor].'[53] To claim that in such unqualified terms is to elide distinctions between the varieties of language which are appropriate for the expression of the Christian faith.[54]

One of the reasons for this is that Jüngel's discussion, however valuable, is generally prescriptive rather than descriptive, controlled by a dogmatic quest for a right account of the relationship between the human and the divine, and insufficiently attentive to *examples*. This emerges very clearly in the critique of Aquinas in *Gott als Geheimnis*.[55] Here Jüngel works with a frequent but to some degree at least questionable assumption that Aquinas is offering a systematic theory of analogy based on dogmatic principles rather than a logical analysis of particular examples of religious discourse.[56] If Jüngel were himself to furnish a greater variety of examples, his case would be more persuasive because more nuanced and more alert to particular usage.

A final question concerns the way in which Jüngel concentrates on *language* to the virtual exclusion of other ways in which the

Christian faith is articulated and embodied. He envisages the crisis
of Christian faith in the present as a crisis about the plausibility
of its speech. But what is demanded of Christian faith is not only
language which 'brings God to speech' but also patterns of
thought and strategies of action, both ritual and ethical. It would
be quite wrong to underestimate the critical potential of language
about God as a way of undermining the dictatorship of the actual:
in this way, Christian speech about God is profoundly creative of
hope. But 'there is a mediation in action also which can speak
clearly here and now'.[57] The Christian faith is not first and
foremost a message, a word, but the transformation of the world
of persons. Jüngel is entirely correct to emphasise the formative
function of language in the social world.[58] But language needs to
be placed within the context of a whole range of human symbolic
and cultural activity. Language is only one of many human projects
of meaning, and utterance cannot be divorced from decision and
deed.[59]

5. God the mystery of the world (2): thinking about God

The scope of the theme which Jüngel treats under the rubric 'Zur Denkbarkeit Gottes' in *Gott als Geheimnis* is not easy to formulate. His treatment covers not only strictly epistemological issues but also a range of much broader questions concerned with the disposition of the human subject in intellectual engagement with the reality of God. Consequently, *Gott als Geheimnis* offers not only a sketch of a theological theory of knowledge but also an essay on the distinction between God and man as it emerges in the relationship between the divine self-declaration and the manner of its assimilation by the human mind.

Jüngel's purpose is to outline an understanding of 'thinking' as a receptive rather than a primarily creative exercise. He offers, that is, a powerfully realist account of human knowing, in which the thrust of the mind in self-transcendence is caused by the movement of the transcendent towards the mind. 'Thinking' is the shape which human intellectual activity assumes under the pressure of external reality. But more immediately, Jüngel seeks to trace how this understanding of 'thinking' has been hidden from view in the 'metaphysical tradition',[1] a tradition which has consequently found itself in the situation of inability to think of God.

As we shall see in the course of the following discussion, the breadth of its engagement proves to be a besetting problem in this section of *Gott als Geheimnis*. The historical survey which Jüngel offers, whilst often sharp in its perceptions, is highly selective, covering only Kant, Fichte, Feuerbach and Nietzsche – Marx and Freud, for example, are glaringly absent. And because, moreover, the discussion is conducted at a level of wide generality, it lacks analytic edge. Indeed, it is difficult not to conclude that the identification of and concentration upon fewer and smaller problems would give greater purchase on the larger issues to which Jüngel constantly returns. In looking at his argument, therefore, it may be helpful to keep in mind a remark of Wittgenstein: '"Thinking", a widely ramified concept. A concept that compasses many manifestations of life. The phenomena of thinking are widely scattered.'[2]

Cartesianism

Jüngel's presentation orients itself by a critique of 'the Cartesian organisation of the modern human self-understanding'.[3] His writing on Descartes, here as elsewhere[4] is seen in its best light when regarded not so much as close interpretation of the Cartesian texts, but as a way of focussing dissatisfaction with the cognitive strategy which he feels Descartes best exemplifies. In common with a number of recent theologians and philosophers,[5] Jüngel is concerned to shift the centre of attention away from the knowing subject. In Jüngel's case, his critique of Descartes is also properly to be understood in the context of his doctrine of man, which challenges and offers sophisticated alternatives to an anthropology oriented towards human self-realisation and self-understanding.

He identifies three elements in the structure of the cartesian 'undermining of certainty of God'.[6] First, Descartes' thought represents a decision in favour of the doubting ego as the indubitable foundational truth. For Jüngel, this decision transposes the question of knowledge of God into a radically subjective mode: through it, the doubting ego becomes 'absolute presence'.[7] The ego, that is, is the absolute nodal point from which, as it were, the vibrations of history radiate outwards. Thus 'he who dares to direct himself, letting himself be led by no-one and nothing, is completely referred to himself, and, indeed, to himself as a being completely present to itself'.[8]

The second structural element concerns Descartes' concept of God, which Jüngel feels to be shaped by the initial decision in favour of the '*subiectum*...as *hupokeimenon* [that which is fundamental].'[9] God becomes the guarantor of the continuity of the successive moments of certainty which are afforded in the ego's self-reflection. Without some principle of coherence, the certainty which takes its rise from the doubting ego would be merely punctiliar, lacking in extension across time; Descartes' account of God functions as this principle of coherence. The consequence of this is that 'God is a methodological necessity for the *res cogitans* which seeks to secure the continuity of its existence'.[10]

This leads to the third element. The very weakness of the *dubito* in its need for a divine guarantor is paradoxically a powerful agent in the overthrow of the 'Denkbarkeit Gottes'. For the logic of Descartes' proposal is that God's existence is contingent upon man, in that that existence is posited in the project of the *cogito*'s self-securing.[11] In this way, the necessity of God for the doubting ego becomes a means of rendering God contingent upon the ego which he secures: 'It was precisely the weakness of the ability to doubt which made the cartesian man powerful...the unconditioned independence of God could ultimately turn out to be the absolute dependence of God on man.'[12]

Ernest Gellner has characterised the epistemological tradition stemming from Descartes as one in which there occurs 'the transfer of ultimate legitimacy inwards, to man, to human cognitive powers'.[13] In this tradition, knowledge is not 'in the world' and under the authority of objective orders of being, but rather the world is 'in knowledge', 'i.e. constructed by our cognition and its principles'.[14] It is precisely this shift towards human cognition and its principles which Jüngel disputes, because it invests the subject with a distinction which ill accords with the subject's being referred beyond the self to others and to God. It is only, indeed, by such reference that the subject is constituted. His critique of Descartes thus furnishes Jüngel with a background against which to propose the primacy of certain ontological and anthropological commitments as the only effective guard against subjectivism or even solipsism.

The sharpness of Jüngel's recommendation derives, however, in large measure from a false dichotomy. Whatever view be taken of Descartes' idealism and of his relation to Kant,[15] both Jüngel's critique and his counter-proposal are suffused by a confusion between ontological and epistemological issues. That is to say, he does not distinguish between the claim that God is contingent upon the world and the claim that *knowledge of* God is dependent upon *knowledge of* the world (that is, the self-knowledge of the *dubito*).[16] Certainly Jüngel is correct to suggest that the claim that God is known in (and thus that a concept of God is to a degree moulded by) the situation of the ego may lead to a severely restricted account of the divine being. But this is not identical with, nor does it necessarily lead to, the claim that God is *ontologically* dependent upon man. Here, as often, Jüngel assimilates formal to substantive issues where their careful separation would be more fruitful. But however impatient of such distinctions, the main features of

Jüngel's critique are clear, as is their place in formulating his own alternative epistemology: 'Theology is the location of a dispute of thinking with thinking, insofar as, from the perspective of God, it obliges thinking to call into question the self-grounding of thinking in the *cogito*.'[17]

Thinking as 'Entsprechung'

In opposition to 'Cartesianism', Jüngel's overriding concern is to dislodge the *cogito* from its position of centrality, and to emphasize what has been called the 'decentred subject'.[18] He does not do this by emphasising the dependence of knowledge on the resources of corporate tradition,[19] but by stressing that the thinking subject is evoked and constituted by that which comes to it from beyond itself: it is not of itself fundamental. Jüngel thus seeks to commend a way of knowing which is repentant of those habits of mind whose subjectivity obscures the proper concern of thinking with its object. The moral and religious connotations of the word 'repentant' are particularly helpful here, emphasising how for Jüngel theological thought demands an engagement with the divine reality which can only be described in terms of obedience and faithfulness to the solicitude of the Word of God to think in a certain way.[20] He is concerned to lay bare the necessity of choosing between the 'ascent...of the self-securing *cogito* into the concept of God, storming the gates of Heaven',[21] and the emergence of a 'thinking which identifies itself as *creaturely*'.[22] That this contrast is so sharply drawn is the root both of the cogency of Jüngel's work here and of its deficiencies in precise analysis. But before expanding upon this point, we set out the main features of his appeal for responsible theological thinking.

His first move is to emphasise that problems about thinking of God are inseparable from problems of speech about God: 'The problem of whether we can think of God leads back to the problem of whether we can speak of God.'[23] Such a comment may seem simply to echo a familiar claim that 'thinking is not an incorporeal process which lends life and sense to speaking, and which it would be possible to detach from speaking'.[24] Its background, however, is not in analytical philosophy but in the later work of Heidegger, and Jüngel is fielding decisions about the relationship between 'being' and language. When he claims that 'language has its own sovereignty',[25] he stands self-consciously in a tradition which understands language as the sacrament of reality. That is to say, he views the event of language as that event in which 'being' becomes actual: 'what does language do?...It permits being to be "present", it makes being into an event.'[26] Because language is the primary mode of the presence of 'being', thinking is constantly referred back to that mode. Thus Jüngel disputes any notion that 'before God can come to speech, reason must have arrived at a concept of God',[27] proposing rather that 'language calls thinking, and thinking follows language'.[28]

Jüngel's stress on the primacy of language over thought is intended to evict from the place of supremacy the calculative and objectifying mental representations of the *cogito*.[29] But there is more here than simple reiteration of motifs from the work of Heidegger and Fuchs. Jüngel is also bringing into play anthropological decisions about man as 'a being ordained for hearing'.[30] As such a being, man is definitively moulded by what lies beyond him: he is not ultimately the fashioner of his own subjectivity. The vocabulary of 'hearing' is carefully chosen, for the ego is constituted by what Jüngel calls *Anrede*, by words of address. In being addressed, man discovers that the continuity of his life and the coherence of its structures are interrupted. In terms of how we are to think of God, this means that Jüngel commends an attitude of receptivity towards the divine Word over against cognitive strategies which privilege the intentionality of the thinking subject. Thinking is referred beyond itself, provoked by the self-declaration of God; and so theology 'asks, since it has heard'.[31]

Jüngel's idiom here is alarmingly loose, and he tends to cover large tracts of ground at great speed. But the general drift of the basic assertion is unambiguous: because 'the location of the possibility of thinking of God is a Word which precedes thinking',[32] the *cogito* is displaced.

Having established this, Jüngel moves on to emphasise that thinking of God is reflexive upon faith. This because faith is the primary manner in which the divine address is appropriated by man. Faith, we might say, is the shape taken by human subjectivity when it is interrupted by the divine Word of address: 'Faith is the anthropological realisation of the fact that God has revealed himself.'[33] Because it is referred to the Word of God, and because that Word is realised as faith, thinking is a reflection of faith. And so the precise way in which thinking is determined by the Word is in its relation to faith: 'it is a matter of *thinking* what we *believe*'.[34]

Jüngel, in other words, envisages a view of thinking as structurally similar to faith, in that both deflect attention away from the ego onto the prevenient divine reality which draws man out of himself. Faith is a mode of *ekstasis*, the displacement of self-affirmation by abandonment to determination by God: 'To believe means to allow oneself to be interrupted by God in such a way that I forget myself in favour of God and in such self-forgetfulness ... am certain of myself.'[35] And thinking, similarly, involves a species of self-renunciation. The ego 'must fix upon that which it perceives as something other than and over against the ego in such a way that that other can be followed in its own order, structure and movement and in this following can be recognised as itself'.[36]

Thinking is *Nachfolge*, intellectual discipleship contoured by the objectivity of that which is thought. All along the line Jüngel is concerned to develop a theological rationality which is not 'sachfremd' but 'sachgemäss', appropriate rather than foreign to the object.[37] This introduces a third move: the deployment of the concept of *Entsprechung*, analogy or correspondence. The term is a key one throughout Jüngel's work, especially in his later work on the doctrine of man and natural theology. In the present context, *Entsprechung* denotes the proper relationship of subject and object in thinking. Thinking as *Entsprechung* is the activity of the thinking subject whose mental representations are moulded by the object of thought in such a way as to express its own inherent character.

His use of the concept of *Entsprechung* once again highlights the consistency of his realism. Jüngel refuses to abstract epistemology from ontology, to divide that which is thought from that which is. Thinking is fraught with reference to realities beyond itself, which it must express 'in the correspondence of thinking (*noein*) and being (*einai*)'.[38] Thinking as *Entsprechung* must, moreover, be appropriate to its object. There can be no independent epistemological strategy, no inquiry into the nature of thought in abstraction from the actual claim of the object. Theologically this means for Jüngel that 'It is essential that any thinking which sets out to learn to think of God can go along no other way than God's way, that is, along the way of revelation.'[39] The metaphor of 'following a path' is significant. Thinking follows the object of thought in that it does not establish preconditions for what can or cannot be thought but rather allows itself to be cast in the form appropriate to its object. And as always, Jüngel frames the matter in terms of a sharp contrast, pressing the need for decision between 'a conceptuality which *decides about* the being of God' and 'a thinking which *expresses* that being'.[40]

The result of this concept of *Entsprechung* is a radical shift in the situation of the *cogito*. Descartes, on Jüngel's analysis, sees the *cogito* as that 'place of presence' before which all being is present and by which all being is validated.[41] This Jüngel seeks to reverse: 'it is characteristic of the act of thinking of God...that the thinking subject experiences itself in the execution of this thinking to be an object known by God'.[42] The creativity of thinking as a human project is firmly subservient to the fact that the thinking subject is an object of divine knowledge: we know because we are known. Jüngel here owes much to Barth: in *Gottes Sein ist im Werden* he emphasises that Barth's notion of divine objectivity is 'not an objectifying of the being of God in the sense that the knowing subject could itself make God available as an object which may be, or has been, known'.[43] Divine objectivity is not validated from the *cogito*; rather, God is object because he makes himself to be such in an act which equally makes man the subject of the knowledge of such objectivity: 'Man *is* the subject of knowledge of God only because and in that he *becomes* (*fit*) this subject.'[44] In *Gott als Geheimnis* Jüngel takes up this train of thought in a passage which takes us to the heart of the concept of *Entsprechung*: 'That thinking experiences itself in the moment of perception as already having been perceived, is the expression of a prevenient ontic binding of thinking to its object, which only becomes able to be experienced in the act of thinking'.[45] What is most remarkable here is the proposal that the relation of subject and object established in the act of thinking is a realisation of some more primal relation – the prevenient *Bindung* (the word has overtones of 'commitment' and 'subordination') of thinking to the object which allows itself to be discovered by the subject. Thinking is a response to prior donations of meaning; it is not an act in which the matter of thought is inseparable from the manner of its organisation by the mind.

Reflections

Jüngel's account of thinking of God is an attempt to spell out some epistemological consequences of a Protestant doctrine of grace. That is to say, his chief motive in thrusting the imperious ego from the position of centrality is to reinstate the prevenience of the reality of God. This is why he urges that thinking, properly understood, is 'phenomenological': it is an activity which, as he wrote earlier, 'lets that which is be manifest insofar as that which is allows access to itself'.[46] The point is illustrated by his reflections on *questioning* in theological procedure. Questions do not arise from within the questioner's situation but under pressure from external reality:[47] 'Questioning takes place because a word occurred which makes God accessible for his own sake. Moreover, questioning takes place because something is there and makes its presence perceptible. Consequently we ask: *qu'est-ce que c'est que ça*? what is it that is there? Such questioning is called thinking'.[48] In terms of theological questioning, this means that God rather than man is the questioner: man cannot be extracted from the position of subsequence,[49] so that 'it is out of his being addressed that man begins to question'.[50]

The persistent problem for any theology of grace is that a stress on the divine priority may threaten to become a disqualification of the human and natural. Jüngel's sensitivity towards issues in the area of the relationship between God and man has made him acutely aware of this difficulty, and it is one which he avoids skilfully. His epistemology does not suspend all intentional mental acts, making the human mind into a *tabula rasa* upon which the reality of God impresses itself. Scope is left for the activity of the subject. Certainly Jüngel presses hard upon the point that 'thinking can only begin if it begins with something which is already there independent of all thinking'.[51] Nevertheless, in its response to the prevenient realities, thinking is genuinely creative: 'the formation of concepts is the creative act of thinking, initiated by the object, certainly, but derived solely from the power of reason'.[52] From within the perspective of his own concerns, then, Jüngel offers a theological objectivism which – at an initial and somewhat confined level – allows the subject its own proper strategy of intention.

But whilst Jüngel's 'objectivism' is not at the expense of the thinking subject, it does maintain itself only by a failure at a certain level to attend to the specific. Jüngel elaborates a theory of thinking without adequate regard for the particular: consequently, the central concepts involved in the theory are not fully analysed, and insufficient attention is paid to the nature of thinking as a human project in a particular situation. Two areas can be drawn out for special mention.

The first concerns the concept of thinking itself. Jüngel's proposal exemplifies an intellectual manner described by Wittgenstein as a tendency 'to sublime the logic of our language'.[53] Insufficient attention, that is, is accorded to the fact that 'thinking' is a polymorphous concept whose significance can only be understood when it is situated. The later work of Wittgenstein is no doubt a most striking example of one way in which such 'situating' may be affected by analysis of our linguistic and conceptual dealings with the world. Naturally there are other ways, notably those which have been suggested in the course of debates concerning hermeneutical problems or the relationship of theory and practice. A sensitive use of all such strategies is incumbent upon theology. This is not simply in the interests of intellectual crispness and rigour; it is also part of coming to terms with the historicality of theology as an enterprise engaged upon in *this* (and not *that*) situation in which *this* (and not *that*) operation is being performed. This recognition that theology is 'situation-specific' should lead to an unwillingness to determine what is or what ought to be happening in a particular piece of theological activity by reference to much larger judgements about the nature of the theological task.[54]

'If we study the grammar, say, of words such as "wishing", "thinking", "understanding", "meaning", we shall not be dissatisfied when we have described various cases of wishing, thinking, etc.'[55] And Wittgenstein goes on: 'The idea that in order to be clear about the meaning of a general term one had to find the common element in all its applications has shackled philosophical investigation; for it has not only led to no result, but also made the philosopher dismiss as irrelevant the concrete cases, which alone could have helped him understand the usage of the general term.'[56] The close student of Jüngel's writings can hardly evade the sense that he has not 'studied the grammar' of the concept of 'thinking' with sufficient attention. Because his account is again weighted towards the prescriptive (in its opposition to 'Cartesianism'), he fails at the level of attending to the scope of usage. The theory of thinking which he marshals is not rooted in examples, and so remains excessively abstract and a-historical.

The concept of thinking as *Entsprechung*, for example, may be helpful in stating the correspondence of the mind to the reality with which it is engaged. But it is not a very sharp tool with which to work out in any great detail what is taking place in a particular piece of thought or to determine how a particular theological job is to be tackled. Indeed, the concept tends to confuse a general recommendation about theological 'realism' with a specific methodological device. In the case of 'questioning', for example, Jüngel's proposal of the priority of 'being questioned' over 'questioning' as a theological procedure simply obscures the fact that in some – not all – situations, questioning may not necessarily be reductive or objectifying, and that to limit its employment may be unnecessarily to restrict the range of theological activities.[57] Or again, Jüngel tends to construe everything which comes to man from outside as *Anrede*, address. By so resolving that which lies beyond man into a basically revelational mode, the mind's response is codified as one of obedient hearing. There is here little sense that external reality may present itself in a variety of guises – as a problem to be solved, a hint to chase up, even as something as vague as a sense of unease about our accustomed traffic with the world, and that the response which the mind gives to these various situations must accordingly be manifold and adaptable. Gilbert Ryle once wrote that:

There is no general answer to the question 'What does thinking consist of?' There are hosts of different sorts of toilings and idlings, engaging in any one of which is thinking. Yet there need be nothing going on in any one of them such that something else of the same species or genus must be going on in another of them.[58]

There is need, then, for a more explicit awareness of the 'situation-specific' character of thinking. This leads to a second reflection. Part of the task of discovering what 'thinking' amounts to in a particular situation is an analysis of the thinking subject, of his place within a whole economy of discourses and of the place of his thinking of God within a complex of other events in the history of his subjectivity. In one passage, Jüngel acknowledges that 'in reflecting upon the ways of God the situation of the *cogito* does not become alien to the thinker'[59] – thinking is not a form of alienation. Such an admission, however, is not developed in Jüngel's account, remaining peripheral to the main line of his proposal. There is, then, need for a more thorough analysis of the insight that 'who reflects upon God, if not a man?'[60] Simply to ask that question commits Jüngel to furnishing an account of the thinking subject, oriented to the complex interplay between determinants upon man – historical, social, political as well as linguistic and revelational – and the multiplicity of human projects which engage with such determinants. And such analysis would remain abstract unless located through examples of particular acts of thinking in specific situations.

6. God the mystery of the world (3): the human God

Introductory

It would not be difficult to come away from a superficial reading of *Gott als Geheimnis*, especially on the formal issues discussed in the previous two chapters, with a sense that Jüngel attempts consistently to shift attention away from the human knower and speaker of God. Such a reading, indeed, might lead to criticism that his emphasis on the derivative nature of human knowledge and speech implies that man is an insignificant reality. This kind of line of criticism has already been forestalled to some degree, especially in looking at Jüngel's work on parable, metaphor and analogy. If it is more fully to be countered, it will have to be by attention to Jüngel's doctrine of God, one of whose chief themes is the correlation of divine and human subjectivity.

Because *Gott als Geheimnis* is in many ways a difficult and diffuse book, with little in the way of a sustained statement of its main proposals, the centrality of this theme may not be immediately apparent. It does, however, provide an underlying structure to the book, focussing on two particular concerns. First, Jüngel offers a theological statement of the confession that God's divinity is actual as his humanity. God is neither aloof nor tyrannous but reveals himself as the human God who safeguards the authenticity of man: in being *pro se* God is equiprimordially *pro nobis*. But, second, Jüngel also seeks to show that as *our* God, God does not cease to be himself. In becoming man and giving himself up to death, God is eminently himself, and his nearness to man in the crucified Jesus is the actuality of his freedom and sovereignty. By thus identifying God's aseity and his being for man, Jüngel tries to elude any polarisation of divine and human freedom.

It will readily be seen that this account of the identity of *pro se* and *pro nobis* in God builds on Jüngel's interpretation of Barth's doctrine of the Trinity. And as we shall see, his account forms a firm riposte to some recent criticisms of Barth. There is, however, another all-pervading influence throughout the book's presentation of its theme: the philosophy of Hegel. The thrust of Jüngel's interpretation of key Hegelian texts is to demonstrate that in his work above all can be found a metaphysic retaining the moments of self-affirmation and self-loss in the history of the absolute. In Hegel, he writes, 'the ideas of absolute freedom and absolute suffering are bound together, since God himself gives himself up to annihilation, and so in absolute freedom chooses absolute suffering'.[1] The role played by Hegel's metaphysics in Jüngel's doctrine of God is, in other words, very closely parallel to that played by Barth's doctrine of election and his trinitarian account of the identity of essence and essence in the divine being. Both offer Jüngel ways of stating how God can be supremely himself in giving himself up.

The death of God

'Christian faith in the crucified Jesus Christ leads to the heart of Christian belief. Christian theology is thus essentially *theologia crucifixi*.'[2] The statement is characteristically prescriptive, offering no detailed supports, exegetical or otherwise, for its proposal.[3] Indeed, Jüngel takes for granted that the heart of the Christian confession is the death of Christ – interpreted chiefly through the categories of Paul and Luther, a confession which expresses itself in 'the foolish and scandalous word of the cross'.[4] This characterisation of the distinctively Christian is undoubtedly excessively tight, even reductive. But its implication for the doctrine of God is that it is the *crucified* who defines God: 'the crucified is as it were the material definition of what is meant by the word "God"'.[5] Indeed, the definition of God is so bound up with the cross that an inevitable concomitant of confession of God's identification with Jesus is language about the *death* of God. As he writes elsewhere 'Faith in the identity of the Son of God with the crucified necessitates the confession that in and with the man Jesus God himself has suffered and died.'[6]

Consequently, one of the main themes of the treatment of the 'death of God' in *Gott als Geheimnis*, as well as of the essays 'Vom Tod des lebendigen Gottes' and 'Das dunkle Wort vom "Tode Gottes"', is that talk of the divine death does not simply denote an 'experience in intellectual history'.[7] Rather, its proper origin is faith's confession about Jesus. Language about the death of God does not describe the cessation of belief in God; it follows from the attempt to specify the nature of the being of God by reference to Christ and particularly to Calvary, and contains 'a deep insight into the peculiar ontological character of the divine being'.[8]

That last point is highly significant, for it opens into one of the paradoxes which Jüngel's doctrine of God seeks to explore, namely that 'death' can function as an ontologically positive attribute of God. It is partly the exploration of this theme which makes *Gott als Geheimnis* such an arresting book as well as one which frustrates the reader unprepared for the complexities of Jüngel's argument and for the range of reference which it exploits. His proposal is that the appropriate theological response to language about the death of God is inquiry into the nature of God who *can be* in such a way: the theologian's task is to ask 'Where is God, if he exists in such a manner?'[9] Language about the death of God does not so much render problematical assertions of the divine existence as specify the nature of the divine essence.

This specification of God's being as loving self-renunciation has, moreover, anthropological value. For Jüngel replaces the concept of God 'above us' with that of the 'near' God who comes to the world of men:

The God who is in heaven because he cannot be on earth is replaced by the Father who is in heaven in such a way that his heavenly Kingdom can indeed come to the world, that is, therefore, by a God who is in heaven in such a way that he can identify himself with the poverty of the man Jesus, with the existence of a man put to death on a cross.[10]

Sustaining this proposal, however, introduces into Jüngel's doctrine of God a problem which it is one of its chief concerns to seek to resolve. Language about the divine death is anthropologically exceedingly valuable in that it demonstrates a refusal to characterise God as an impassible despot. But it is equally deeply problematical as an account of the aseity and coherence of God. This is because such language seems to threaten the freedom of God from external constraint, to subject him to extrinsic necessity. Oeing-Hanhoff, for example, in an apposite criticism, asks whether Jüngel's doctrine of God not only calls into question so-called 'metaphysical' accounts of divine transcendence but also fails to offer adequate safeguards against the total collapse of divine freedom: 'does not Jüngel here throw out the baby with the bath-water, in that in dismissing the idea of an arbitrary divine despot he also dismisses the idea of the almighty God who is the creator and perfecter of the world?'[11]

There are certainly passages which might be criticised along these lines. Jüngel writes, for example, that God 'allows the continuity of his own life to be interrupted through the death of Jesus Christ',[12] allows himself to be broken up by the possibility of non-being.[13] Yet close attention to these and other passages shows how keenly Jüngel has seen the difficulty and how energetically he strives to elude it. It is especially important to notice his care in stating that God *allows* his life to be interrupted or imperilled. God retains his freedom in self-renunciation, because his submission to the cross is voluntary, the exercise of his will. In giving himself up to the cross, God actualises, and does not deny, his freedom: 'God's self-surrender [*Selbstpreisgabe*] is not God's self-abandonment [*Selbstaufgabe*].'[14]

The roots of this exposition lie in Barth's recasting of the notion of divine sovereignty in such a way that it becomes *the inner possibility of loving action*. The whole of Jüngel's discussion of the doctrine of God, indeed, is virtually incomprehensible without an understanding of Barth's reformulation of the idea of divine aseity in positive terms as God's freedom to love.[15] In proposing the commensurability of God's being for us and his aseity, Jüngel's argument is structurally similar to Barth's: like Barth, he shifts the issue away from a fundamental incoherence between divine absoluteness and human authenticity, suggesting that divine freedom is actual in such a form that the world is not denied its own proper reality. Assertions of divine sovereignty provide an answer to the question of what God *can* do, and so of God's ability to suffer death in such a way that death is the freely-chosen mode of his life and not its negation. Such assertions do not prescribe limits for the divine mode of being. Thus the divine 'ability' is defined, not from general considerations of what is appropriate to divinity, but by attention to the specific ways of God in Christ.

Clearly, then, the way in which the divine freedom is understood is of very great significance. Jüngel unfolds his reflections under the rubric of the 'non-necessity' of God. 'The proposition "God is necessary" is,' he writes, 'a shabby proposition, not worthy of God.'[16] The point is exceedingly obscure until we grasp the concept of necessity which Jüngel is rejecting. He regards necessity as fundamentally a relational state of affairs, in the sense that that which is necessary presupposes another being for which it is necessary and by which its freedom is curtailed. 'A necessary being always appears to presuppose in its very necessity another being whose consequence it is. Were there no other being beyond it, there would be no necessary being.'[17] The argument that necessity is in effect contingency may well trade upon the confusion of ontology and epistemology noted in the previous chapter, as well as upon a failure to distinguish intrinsic and extrinsic necessity.[18] But within Jüngel's purpose, divine necessity is clearly rejected as a species of *theologia gloriae*. In its place he offers the alternative of divine non-necessity, negatively defined by the proposition that 'God is unconditioned',[19] and positively by the notion of God as self-determining freedom. The strong voluntarist tone of *Gottes Sein ist im Werden* emerges again, and as the solution to a very similar problem, namely that of demonstrating how the *kenosis* of God on the cross is at the same time the *plerosis* in which God is true to himself. God's freedom is actual in his election to come near to man in the crucified.

A doctrine of God which takes its bearings from the man Jesus must...have a two-fold emphasis. First, God comes indeed from God and only from God; he is determined by no-one and nothing other than by himself alone...But, second, in his self-determination God comes to be himself precisely in coming to man...God comes from God; but he does not wish to come to himself without us. God comes to himself – but with man.[20]

We now look at several motifs in *Gott als Geheimnis* and elsewhere which Jüngel deploys in order to develop a concept of divine aseity fully congruent with God's self-renunciation in the death of Jesus.

Presence

The first of these motifs concerns the nature of God's presence. 'God is present as the absent One.'[21] Jüngel's intention here is to spell out a concept of divine presence which is able to embrace the fact that the specific mode of that presence in the world is withdrawal and hiddenness at the cross: 'God is near to us as the One who is withdrawn.'[22] Here, of course, he is drawing upon a classical theme in Lutheran theology, that of the dialectic of revelation and hiddenness which emerges when the cross is seen as the locus of God's self-manifestation. God reveals himself *sub contrario*, in the folly and weakness of the crucified. 'The hidden God is the crucified God. There on the cross, at this one place and cloaked in deepest darkness, God becomes visible.'[23] Jüngel makes use of this tradition of theological judgement as a lever against the 'theistic tradition': 'the fundamental problem of the metaphysical concept of God,' he writes, is that 'God has to be conceived as absolute presence'.[24] And it is precisely the application of the category of absolute presence to God which prevents this 'metaphysical tradition' from coming to terms with the mode of God's presence in the godforsakenness of the cross. In effect, to attribute 'absolute presence' to God is to exclude the moment of Calvary from his being. 'God's presence is as little real without the moment of a specific absence as his revelation without the moment of a specific hiddenness. And this specific hiddenness is the poverty of Jesus of Nazareth, the specific absence of divine omnipotence and omnipresence.'[25]

Here, as often, the suggestion is frustratingly brief and unanalysed. It may well be that Jüngel's recommendation derives some of its persuasiveness not so much from an explanation of its own features as from being set over against what he regards as an unsatisfactory 'traditional' alternative. Two issues in particular are left open. There is need for a more probing analysis of how it is that presence can be mediated by absence or hiddenness, of why 'that which is omnipresent is never present to us in its omnipresence'.[26] And there is also need for some account of how we are able to recognise that it is *God* who is hidden in the cross, of how the cross comes to be seen as God's revelation rather than simply a human tragedy in which no features of divinity can be traced.

But these points notwithstanding, the *function* of the concept of 'presence in absence' is clear: it serves so to specify (if not to analyse or explain) the mode of divine presence that the cross is not its negation but its actuality. God's 'omnipresence...is to be conceived out of the specific presence of God on the cross of Jesus and thus not without a christologically grounded withdrawal of God. The concept of God's omnipresence must pass through the needle's eye of the...death of God'.[27]

Transience

The concerns of this account of the divine presence are further explored as Jüngel turns to examine the notion of God's 'being'. He seeks to discover what account of the divine being is required if God's livingness is shown in the death of Christ and his self-identity is actual in self-renunciation. Considerable attention is devoted to fashioning a set of ontological categories to enable the theologian to speak of the cross as the location of God's being rather than as the occasion of its collapse. This he does most notably in the section of *Gott als Geheimnis* entitled 'God and Transience'.[28]

This section of the book is one whose sustained use of the broadest abstractions could easily lead to its being dismissed as the speculative imagination run riot. It is, indeed, a particularly good instance of how unfamiliarity with both the style and the underlying intentions of Jüngel's theology may make its sympathetic reception difficult. Partly this is because of his tendency to interpret ontological language as *descriptive of properties*, an interpretation submitted to damaging criticism at the hands of, for example, G. E. Moore.[29] Jüngel uses the language of 'being' to denote more than a judgement with respect to existence: his ontological statements are best construed as descriptive of the *nature* or *character* of states of affairs, not simply as assertions of their existence or non-existence. Thus in the case of language about the 'being' of God, Jüngel refuses to characterise that being as the plenitude of actuality, since God identifies himself with the crucified in the negation of actuality. Certainly his account is not attentive to questions of logic and grammar, as well as to the history of terms;[30] but its imaginative force should not be overlooked, nor should its wider dogmatic concerns be forgotten.

His work here, then, is best approached as an ontological redescription of the event of the cross. He is recasting into the language of substance the story of the end of Jesus' life, attributing that story to the life of God himself. This use of the language of substance may raise a second set of suspicions of his presentation, born this time of hostility to ontology in Christological discourse. Proponents of so-called 'functionalist' Christologies frequently suspect that the use of ontological categories inevitably abstracts from the detail of Jesus' human history. From Jüngel's account it is clear that his use of such categories has precisely the opposite intention: it seeks to take the history of Jesus with full seriousness, using the language of 'being' to state the identity between that history and the life of God. 'It is through the use of ontological categories that we are enabled to see precisely what it is that it may be confronts us in the person of Jesus.'[31]

The discussion of the divine being turns upon the same refusal of the ontological priority of 'actuality' that lay behind Jüngel's theology of metaphor. In the present context, the priority of

actuality is disputed precisely in order to give an account of how
God *can be* in identification with the crucified. For to deny
actuality's 'pretention to ontological prevalence'[32] is to call into
question certain ways of construing God's agency. God as agent
does not merely exemplify or embody that 'relationship between
act and actuality'[33] in which 'being' is characterised as self-
realisation through self-assertion. The theologian must always
return to the paradox that God's 'work', in self-identification with
the crucified, is that of delivering himself over to death. Since his
being is realised in this way, a concept of 'being' is required which
will be more extensive than the concept of actuality realised
through works (with which 'being' is frequently identified). The
development of such a concept will enable the theologian ontologically to identify God in the negation of actuality and the
absence of works – at the cross.

Accordingly, Jüngel develops a concept of the *positivity* of
transience in order to exclude assertions of the ontological
prevalence of actuality. If actuality is ontologically prevalent, then
the being of God cannot be located at the cross, since his plenitude
of being must locate him in the actuality with which being is
usually co-terminous. Transience is usually[34] evaluated negatively
as 'a lack of actuality',[35] so that God's relation to it is one of
contradiction, as 'pure actuality...the purest act of self-
realisation'.[36] Over against this, Jüngel seeks to suggest that
transience is 'in being':[37] it is not itself *nihil* but rather it
demonstrates 'a tendency towards nothingness'.[38] Transience as
it were straddles being and non-being: 'Transience is the struggle
between possibility and nothingness, the struggle between the capacity
of the possible and the maelstrom of nothingness...And insofar as
we have understood possibility as ontologically more primary than
actuality, we may also say: transience is *the struggle between being
and non-being*.'[39] If the negativity of transience is its 'tending
towards nothingness', its positivity consists in the possibilities it
contains; for possibility is not merely that which is *unrealised* (and
so lacking in 'being'), but much more 'the capacity of becoming'.[40]

Into this struggle between the positivity and the negativity of
transience, between being and non-being, God enters through
identification with the cross of Christ. Consequently, Jüngel insists
that an account of the divine being cannot be satisfied with a
definition of God as 'eternity in the sense of timeless immortality',[41]
as 'the actual and only actual'.[42] Whilst such accounts are attempts

to retain a sense of divine aseity, they tend to underplay the fact that God's aseity is maintained in his entering into transience and not in abstraction from it. The divine exclusion of *nihil* is achieved in identification with radical transience at the cross, by absorption of its chaos rather than by aloofness from it: 'When God identified himself with the dead Jesus, he made room for nothingness in the divine life...Suffering annihilation in himself, God shows himself to be victor over nothingness.'[43] The tone is unmistakably Hegelian; but behind these ontological statements lies a concern to avoid an incoherence between the concept of divine 'being' and the event of divine self-definition at the cross, by deploying ontological categories which enable a formulation of how God's life holds good at death. To refuse to interpret the transience of the cross as the absence of 'being' is to advertise how God's life holds good in the struggle between being and non-being, 'The positive meaning of talk of the death of God can be stated by saying that in the midst of the struggle between nothingness and possibility, God *is*.'[44]

God is love

Much of the foregoing argument is summed up in a phrase which echoes throughout Jüngel's more recent writing: God as 'the unity of life and death in favour of life'.[45] This leads to discussion of another central concept, that of God as love, for 'this living unity of life and death is the essence of love. As this unity God *is* love.'[46]

Jüngel's proposal is intended in a quite specific sense. To say that God is love is not simply to claim that love characterises the *opera dei ad extra*, God's act towards his creation: God does not simply *act lovingly*, but *is love*. Love is an ontological characterisation of God.[47] In particular, love is a way of so characterising God's being that he can be seen to be not foreign to himself but eminently true to himself in self-abasement. This emerges clearly in Jüngel's definition of the nature of love: 'Love is structurally to be described as – in the midst of ever greater self-relatedness – even greater selflessness, that is, as a self-relation, freely going beyond itself, flowing beyond itself and giving itself.'[48] It is particularly to be noted that he emphasises that love is not self-loss *tout court* but rather a form of self-relation: 'love is not identical with absolute selflessness'.[49] This is because 'the one who loves experiences at once an extreme distancing of himself from himself and a quite new mode of nearness to himself'.[50] Love embraces self-loss (death) and self-relation (life), in such a way that there is no abeyance of the lover's self-relation (in favour of life). Behind this definition lies a conviction that it is unnecessary to safeguard divine aseity by positing an essence of God behind his loving *pro nobis*, for his aseity takes form as loving self-renunciation. God's essence is 'a se in nihilum ek-sistere', to exist from himself in nothingness.[51] The God who is love is thus neither master nor victim. His self-love is not the antithesis of his self-gift, but its ultimate ground: in giving himself away, he does not lose but becomes himself.

The Trinity

We have already noted from *Gottes Sein ist im Werden* that one of the chief functions of the doctrine of the Trinity in Jüngel's theology is that of formulating the identity of God's being-for-himself and his being-for-us in the person of Jesus Christ. The doctrine of the Trinity offers a concept of God reconstructed in accordance with the Christian confession that the man Jesus is the actuality of the divine presence in the world. In particular, trinitarian formulae demonstrate how Jesus' history can be the actuality of God in the world *when that history ends in the negativity of death*.

At the heart of Jüngel's doctrine of God, then, lies the conviction that God's self-differentiated nature is revealed in the event of his self-identification with the crucified: 'Knowledge of God's identification with Jesus makes it possible and necessary for us to distinguish God from God.'[52] This conviction, however, introduces an element of potential disturbance of the divine coherence. For 'to distinguish God from God' may be to bifurcate God's unity; if this is not to take place, then trinitarian formulae need to be brought into play. Even though the distinction between Father and Son at the cross is one of 'absolute opposition',[53] because God is triune he 'remains at the same time related to himself in this opposition'.[54] Thus 'the distinction of God from God can never be understood as contradiction within God...God does not contradict himself. God corresponds with himself. And so we need the doctrine of the Trinity.'[55]

The doctrine of the Trinity is, accordingly, indispensable for Jüngel as the 'unity of life and death' which characterises the being of God is to be unity 'in favour of life'. Language about the 'unity of life and death' is an abstract formulation of the personal distinction between Father and Son. God is love in that he is 'in indissoluble differentiation...both lover and beloved. He is...God the Father and God the Son.'[56] This distinction is realised in the 'opposition between the God who makes alive and the dead man Jesus'.[57] To say that the unity of life and death is in favour of *life* is to formulate in abstract terms how the Spirit is that bond of love which prevents intra-divine conflict: to speak of God as Spirit is to say that 'in the midst of this most grievous separation, God does not cease to be the *one* and *living* God, but rather is precisely in this most completely himself'.[58] Trinitarian formulae thus prevent the explanation of God's being out of the concept of love from falling into problems with respect to the congruity of God with himself.[59]

This same function of trinitarian doctrine emerges in Jüngel's exposition of the divine triunity under the rubric 'God's being is in coming.'[60] Language about God's 'being-in-coming' formulates the congruence of the divine *a se* and the divine *pro nobis*, but only by presupposing a trinitarian account of the being of God. 'The proposition "God's being is in coming" means...that God's being is the event of his coming-to-himself.'[61] But this 'coming-to-himself' presupposes a three-fold modality in the being of God without which it would be insupportably difficult to weld together God's selflessness and his self-identity. 'God comes – from God. And God comes – as God. And God comes – to God.'[62] God comes *from* God as free, self-caused originality, the beginning of his own ways. As God the Father, that is, God 'is the absolute origin of himself'.[63] In God the Son God comes *to* God by descending to the depths in identification with the man Jesus: 'God comes to God...not without willing to come to another than himself, and in this way is the Logos who speaks out into nothingness and the Son who gives himself up to death.'[64] But in this descent, God comes to himself, 'even in the far country'.[65] This leads to the third mode: God comes *as* God, remaining entirely self-related, remaining a being-in-becoming in the separation of Father and Son: 'God's being *remains* in coming...and this is the third divine mode of being, this is God the Holy Spirit.'[66]

Jüngel does not claim to present a fully-ramified account of the trinitarian relations and distinctions. What he does offer is a sketch of how trinitarian formulae are particularly helpful in offering an account of the divine being in which the claim that 'God is completely defined in the crucified Jesus of Nazareth'[67] can be fully harmonious with the claim that 'God lives, and lives completely from himself.'[68]

Trinity and humanity

It should by now be clear that Jüngel presents a consistent amplification of his proposal that as God *pro nobis* God is equally *pro se*. Before moving on from *Gott als Geheimnis*, however, it may be helpful to consider the reverse side of this proposal which he is equally concerned to stress, namely that God's freedom takes form in Christ in such a manner that it does not constitute the negation of man.

One way of approaching this issue is to identify the significant differences between Jüngel's and Barth's (in many respects so similar) doctrines of the Trinity, since the burden of much recent criticism of Barth's doctrine has been its fundamental incoherence with the relative autonomy of the created order.[69] Recent work in the area has asked how far Barth's trinitarian dogma is fashioned out of the logic of God as absolute subject, and has sought to explore the adverse effects of that conceptual framework. Some claim that 'Barth shapes his account of the Trinity out of the idea of God's absolute subjectivity in self-revelation',[70] identifying an Hegelian background to this linking of subjectivity and revelation. Moreover, if, as Pannenberg suggests, 'Barth's doctrine of the Trinity is bound up with the concept of revelation, in the sense of God's self-revelation which is grounded in God's trinitarian self-unfolding',[71] then Barth is importing a concept of revelation which militates against understanding the trinitarian distinctions as fundamental to God's being. For if revelation is envisaged as the unfolding of a *single* subjectivity, then that subjectivity may become prior to the divine triunity: 'The construal of the Trinity as the self-unfolding of a divine subject inevitably does damage to the co-eternity of the divine persons, diminishing their plurality to mere modes of being subordinate to the divine subject.'[72] Consequently, the force of Barth's rough handling of talk of three divine persons as 'tritheistic', and his preference for the language of 'modes of being' is to strengthen the conviction that the divine persons become in Barth's work simply moments of the *Deus dixit*, 'moments of the self-unfolding of this Ego'.[73] Such close restriction of the divine plurality is, moreover, claimed to have serious repercussions in the sphere of the Christian doctrine of man. Conceived as absolute subject, God becomes a closed order over against man, a self-identical and almost monadic subjectivity to which man has no access. On this reading of Barth, 'what results...is a conception of the Trinity as a closed circle in a timeless realm, and not as an open circle in which man constantly participates through grace'.[74]

As an alternative to Barth, four lines of development are often suggested. First, it is argued that a concept of 'person' be developed in which the leading motif would be *relation* rather than *subjectivity*. On the basis of such an understanding of trinitarian personality, God would be conceived to be a person in his trinitarian relatedness and not in his subjectivity anterior to such relations. 'The thrust of the doctrine of the Trinity is precisely that the one God is not a person apart from the three persons, but only in the person of the Father and the Son, and also in the form of the Spirit.'[75]

Second, such renewed emphasis on divine relationality could partly be achieved by stressing the significance of the history of Jesus for our apprehension of the Trinity. In his essay 'Barth on the Triune God',[76] R. D. Williams suggests that as the *Church Dogmatics* develops and the emphasis shifts away from the inner structure of revelation towards the history of Jesus, the contours of Barth's earlier trinitarian doctrine are distorted: 'as soon as the *history* of Jesus...is allowed a place of genuine salvific import, the unity, clarity, and security of a scheme based upon a single and compelling act or event of revelation is put in question'.[77] Because in the Christological passages of IV/I Barth stresses the 'displacement'[78] between Father and Son at the cross, then the divine plurality is intensified: 'God's otherness to himself in his Word is the existence in him of response, mutuality, not simply a "self-expression" of some sort. He is not, in short *a self*.'[79] The clarification and extension of these developments, it is argued, would do much in moving beyond the problems discerned in Barth.

Third, if in the area of trinitarian personality we are dealing with 'a unity consisting in a system of relations',[80] then it is the concept of *love*, and not that of self-expressing, self-unfolding subjectivity, whose inner logic offers a more appropriate explanatory framework for the divine triunity. In the concept of a trinitarian society of love 'the plurality of the persons is not derivative, but primordial, *and the unity of God is only actual in that plurality*'.[81]

This leads to the final suggestion. To conceive of the Trinity as an irreducibly plural society is to begin to resolve at least some of

the problems which arise concerning the anthropological consequences of a concept of God as absolute subject. If God is
inherently something akin to a society of mutually open persons,
then he is able to demonstrate 'a threefold openness to the world
and particularly to man'.[82] And such 'openness is due precisely
to the fact that God is open in himself; God is not a closed monad,
but a community of loving interaction'.[83]

However we judge the justice or otherwise of this body of critical
engagement with Barth, it raises a question to which much of
Jüngel's theological writing has directed itself, namely how a
doctrine of the triune God must be framed if it is not to issue in
the depotentiation of the human and worldly. There is much to
suggest that Jüngel has dealt with the issues in this area in such
a way as significantly to advance beyond some of the problems some
discern in Barth's account. He himself criticises an inadequate
emphasis on the history of Jesus in Barth's doctrine of the
Trinity,[84] and, as we saw, in his own work he lays special emphasis
on maintaining the assertion that 'the doctrine of the Trinity is
christologically grounded'.[85] Moreover, the main thrust of his
doctrine of God pushes against any idea of God as absolute and
self-identical subject, since God's being is viewed as 'a going-
beyond-himself into nothingness'.[86] Consequently, his use of the
logic of the concept of love enables an account of divine personality
as essentially related, and presses towards a refusal of any notion
of an essence of God behind his trinitarian existence. Further, his
use of the conceptuality of 'love' and 'relation' helps him retain
the stability and coherence of the divine being without recourse
to notions of divine egotism (which would collapse the divine
triunity into unity), and without sacrificing that sense of 'displacement' which is introduced into the being of God by its
Christological component.

If there is a weakness to be detected in Jüngel's account, it is in
the area of the doctrine of the Spirit. One of the significant
advantages of a sense of the distancing of God from himself in the
relation of Father and Son is that it may constrain the theologian
to attribute personal agency to the Holy Spirit and so acknowledge
plurality of operation in the Godhead. As Moltmann suggests, 'it
is only when the Holy Spirit is understood as the unity of the
difference, and the unity of the Father and the Son, that a personal
and active function in the trinitarian relationship can be ascribed
to him'.[87] Certainly we have seen how Jüngel develops his doctrine

of the Spirit in the context of the 'opposition' between Father and Son. He does not, however, make the further move of articulating with any clarity the personal agency of the Spirit. It is a commonplace that the metaphor of the Spirit as the *vinculum caritatis* between Father and Son may tend to binitarianism rather than trinitarianism, in that it presents the divine life as 'two subsistents linked by a quality'.[88] The problem remains unresolved by Jüngel: his account of the Spirit is not so much an account of a personal agent as a description of a state of affairs, of the fact, that is, that 'God's being *remains* in coming'.[89] Language about the Spirit as 'the relation between the relations of the Father and the Son'[90] simply serves to denote the quality of relationship between Father and Son at the cross.

This imbalance in respect of the Spirit does not, however, lead Jüngel into another, primarily anthropological, weakness common in theologies which give inadequate attention to the Spirit's personal agency: namely, that 'God at the deepest level of his mystery is not conceived as open to a reality beyond himself'.[91] Moltmann, for example, notes that the 'binitarian' account of Father and Son linked by the Spirit as *vinculum caritatis* often issues in a compromise of God's 'open unity'[92] in respect of the creation. The work of the Spirit as the outgoing of God into the world and the demonstration of the openness of the triune community are, in other words, frequently neglected when 'Spirit' is seen primarily as descriptive of the bond between Father and Son.

Jüngel has both isolated and avoided this problem; indeed, he explicitly proposes that it is the doctrine of the Holy Spirit which alleviates any suspicion of God as 'the most sublime egoist'.[93] 'The suspicion would be justified if the *vinculum caritatis* which defines God as the one who is love were not also – as Holy Spirit – the gift in which and as which God relates himself to man in such a way that man is effectively incorporated into the divine love.'[94] This line of thought is of particular significance in a doctrine of God which lays particular emphasis on the coherence of God with himself, for it prevents that coherence from becoming an exclusive self-identity: 'In the Spirit God binds himself to us and us to God.'[95] As the bond between God and the world (as well as between Father and Son), the Spirit ensures a community of future between God and his creation, since God's becoming is not merely the outworking of monadic self-identity.

Given this, there is much here of considerable usefulness for the fabrication of a Christian anthropology which does not shelter man from the attainment of freedom and reality in relative autonomy. Moltmann, again, has recently suggested that a theological account of human freedom is most effectively grounded in a pluralist account of the doctrine of the Trinity: 'the theological concept of freedom is the concept of the trinitarian history of God: God unceasingly desires the freedom of his creation'.[96] But before we turn to look at Jüngel's writing on the doctrine of man in greater detail, the next chapter traces some of the corollaries of the 'death of God' motif.

7. Atheism and the theology of death

There are two main areas in Jüngel's theology where the 'death of God' motif has provided a basis for reflection: his response to atheism, and his theology of death. We examine each one in turn.

Atheism

Simone Weil once noted that 'there are two atheisms, of which one is a purification of the notion of God'.[1] There are, of course, more atheisms than two. But behind Simone Weil's remark lies an awareness that atheism may be prophetic against the illusions of religious belief and behaviour, and that as such it may be cathartic. As Paul Ricouer remarked at the beginning of his lectures on 'Religion, Atheism, and Faith', 'atheism is not limited in meaning to the mere negation and destruction of religion...rather, it opens up the horizon for something else, for a type of faith that might be called...a postreligious faith or a faith for a postreligious age'.[2]

Jüngel's studies of atheism work within much the same kinds of parameters.[3] He attempts to show that 'atheism' offers an invaluable critique of the sub-Christian aspects of 'theism', and that in this way it points to a genuinely Christian concept of God 'beyond theism and atheism'. A contrast with Pannenberg's response to contemporary atheism may help make the point.

Pannenberg is quite strident in rejecting the approach to atheism which he finds in Barth's essay on Feuerbach.[4] Barth there accepts the validity of Feuerbach's critique of 'religion' but claims that the Christian faith, grounded in divine self-revelation, is improperly identified as a human religious project and is therefore largely immune from Feuerbach's critique. Pannenberg views Barth's argument as mere capitulation. For atheism is to be challenged on its own ground – in terms, that is, of its denial of 'the religious tendency of man'.[5] 'The world of religions, and the religious

attitude of man in general to which it bears evidence, is the field
in which theology must take its stand against atheism.'[6] Over
against this type of apologetic approach, Jüngel's treatment rests
on his very sharp sense of the divergence between the Christocentric
understanding of God which he advocates and the divinity of the
'tradition of metaphysical theism' which the atheist rejects. And
so the *Leitmotiv* of his treatment of atheism is his proposal that
'It is irresponsible *not* to conceive and define the essence of God
out of God's identification with Jesus.'[7] On such a proposal both
theism and atheism founder.

In *Gott als Geheimnis der Welt*, as well as in his essays on the
meaning of the death of God, Jüngel expounds a severely negative
(if often impressionistic) evaluation of the 'theistic tradition'. His
underlying concern Christologically to specify the nature of God
is set against a supposed notion in 'traditional dogmatics', the
notion 'that God is to be thought of in his *essence*, in his divinity,
without taking into consideration the identity of this being with
his concrete trinitarian subsistence, and even by ignoring the
identity of God with the concrete existence of a man, the man Jesus
of Nazareth'.[8] He is especially critical of the 'metaphysically
conceived notion of God',[9] for this notion imports into Christian
theology the idea that 'God remains in the dimension of a first cause
supra nos',[10] over us and not among us.[11]

These are clumsy historical remarks, but they are the backcloth
for his treatment of atheism. For on Jüngel's reading it is precisely
these 'theistic' affirmations which the atheist rejects. And so if
the incompatibility between 'theism' and a genuinely Christian
understanding of God can be demonstrated, the atheist's protest
loses much of its cogency as a response to the *Christian* faith. Like
the theism of which it is the shadow, 'atheism' has failed to
appreciate the thrust of a properly Christian account of the
character of God.

In Jüngel's critique of the adequacy of atheist interpretations of
Christian beliefs, the discussion once again gravitates towards the
theme of the proper distinction between God and man. He
criticises, as we have seen, 'theistic' accounts of the divine nature
because they posit an infinite hiatus between the transcendent and
the mundane. And his critique of the atheist thinkers he examines
turns on precisely the same theme: 'atheism' fails to discern that
in a properly Christocentric account of the relations between the
divine and the human, God and man cannot be so distinguished.

Feuerbach and Nietzsche are submitted to particular scrutiny in this regard, for in both can be found an unwarranted assumption of the identity of Christian theology and 'philosophical theism'. And so Jüngel claims, for example, that Feuerbach's atheism trades upon a misinterpretation of the Christian faith, in that 'God's divinity...is posited as a kind of counter-concept to that of the essence of man.'[12] This presupposition is shared 'with traditional dogmatics'.[13] Or again, Nietzsche is criticised for presupposing a concept of God as 'an alien height lying over human thought',[14] so that both Feuerbach and Nietzsche 'share the understanding of God in the metaphysical tradition which they criticise'.[15]

Jüngel's criticism of his selected atheist thinkers highlights their unreadiness 'to conceive the metaphysical essence of God as contrary to God's true divinity'.[16] Atheism fails as a critique of the Christian concept of God to the extent that it does not break loose from the language and conceptuality of the theism which it rejects. Because 'the unbelieving atheist evades the death of God on the cross of Jesus Christ',[17] theology stands equally between theism and atheism on its own exclusively Christological ground: 'The dual task of theology consists in...leaving behind the alternative of an unchristian theism on the one hand and an unchristian atheism on the other.'[18]

Ultimately, then, atheism is countered by appeal to the specific content of Christian affirmations about God's self-identification with the crucified, through which the depth of God's humanity is laid bare.

Theism fails God's divinity, in that it defines God as absolutely unrelated essence...Atheism, on the other hand,...also fails the true divinity of God, who has revealed himself in Jesus Christ as precisely not a supremely self-possessed and self-willing absolutely independent essence. Whoever thinks of God as such a being has precisely not thought of him as God, but as all too human and, indeed, diabolical.[19]

What can be learnt about Jüngel's programme from his reflections on atheism? The shape of a theological response to the phenomena of atheism is, quite naturally, moulded by the larger theological framework within which it occurs. In particular, convictions about the nature of the theologian's task will play a very significant role in determining how atheistic critiques of the Christian faith are construed and countered. Jüngel approaches this area with a characteristic refusal to engage in anything other than what he understands to be the specifically *theological* task. He refuses, that is, to allow the theologian's confrontation with atheism to be anything other than determined at every point, both substantively and methodologically, by the *concretissimum*, Jesus Christ. 'A piece of theological reasoning has...always to begin from the fact that theology is indeed nothing other than – theology.'[20] Theology is itself; the tautology of the definition expresses a conviction that theology is an autonomous science, free from the support of ancillary disciplines, responsible to no norms beyond itself other than the supreme norm of its responsibility towards the self-bestowal of God in Jesus Christ. And so 'an apology against atheism is...not a matter for Christian speech of God'.[21]

Before looking at some of the limitations which this understanding of the nature of theology imposes on Jüngel's critique of atheism, it should also be noted that Jüngel has a similarly tight definition of atheism. For, like any theological account of atheism, his response is conditioned not only by his conception of the *theologian's* task but equally by the way in which he construes the stance of the atheist.[22] Pannenberg, for example, tends to envisage atheism as the denial of the grounds of Christian belief within human historical experience, and so counters atheism by seeking to demonstrate that 'man is essentially referred to infinity'.[23] Others concentrate on different problems, such as questions of the intelligibility and meaningfulness of talk of God.[24] Jüngel construes atheism as antitheism. That is to say, he focusses on those atheisms which define themselves over against a particular set of theological doctrines, which he identifies as 'metaphysical theism'.[25]

What is most immediately apparent about Jüngel's way of construing atheism is that it tends to compress the rejection of God into a unitary phenomenon, collapsing many different atheisms into one.[26] Atheism becomes synonymous with the rejection of one particular tradition of theistic metaphysical doctrine. This kind of definition does, however, limit the scope of atheist positions with which Jüngel is able to engage. In effect, he makes the task of the theologian *vis-à-vis* atheism too easy. His understanding of atheism enables him to operate on familiar territory, in that he only has to engage with that antitheism which, as Merleau-Ponty remarked, 'contains within itself the theology which it combats'.[27]

And so the style of atheism which Merleau-Ponty himself exemplifies – one which has moved quite beyond the categories of 'theism' and 'antitheism' – cannot be caught within Jüngel's net. A very clear example here is Jüngel's interpretation of language

about the death of God. So concerned is he to spell out the
significance of such language for the formulation of a specifically
Christian doctrine of God that he almost ignores the way in which
such language may also express 'an experience in the history of
ideas'.[28] The effect of this is to eliminate from consideration that
large body of atheistic criticism which

> precludes the metaphysical mode of thought [and] involves an atheism
> whose implications are calculated pragmatically rather than meta-
> physically. Its contraction of the range of significant discourse to within
> empirical boundaries, combined with its remarkable practical control of
> reality thus envisaged, favours an unconcerned forgetfulness of the
> problem of God rather than an agonised dwelling upon the consequences
> of his non-existence.[29]

Masterson's remark leads to a further reflection on Jüngel's treatment of atheism. His discussions almost invariably centre on
conceptual issues, since it is the concept of God affirmed by the
theist and rejected by the atheist which he regards as the heart of
the matter. Behind this lies, of course, his broader understanding
of the relation of concepts to action and of theory to practice.
Because action is envisaged as the *implication* of faith, *subsequent*
to theory, such action cannot be a criterion of theological truth.[30]

 Jüngel's approach here is partly unsatisfying because it is
inattentive to complex questions concerning the interaction
between theological concepts and social reality.[31] But, more
importantly, his understanding of the primacy of the theoretical
puts him in a position where he cannot feel the weight of, for
example, Marx's massive critique of religious practice and
theological concepts. Jüngel seeks to develop a response to atheism
by specifying proper speech about God and his death, speech which
is Christologically constrained. Yet such an answer, valuable
though it is in identifying 'theistic' accretions to Christian
theology, may in the end merely reinforce contentions that
interpreting reality is a sorry substitute for changing it. For whilst
'discourse draws the map of our journey to emancipation' it 'does
not set our destination, nor provide the vehicle and the motive
power'.[32] Perhaps the largest question to be set against Jüngel's
critique of atheism is whether he stresses sufficiently that the
Christian faith offers not only a radically new concept of God but
also 'the entitlement and enablement to *act*'.[33]

For all that, there is strength in Jüngel's response to atheism, a
strength which comes from his readiness to allow certain atheist

thinkers to interrogate theological concepts and test them, sometimes, to destruction. 'As the denial of theism, atheism is a critical
moment of Christian theology, which is to be brought to bear upon
the doctrine of God itself':[34] there is no room here for styles of
apologetic which leave the substance of the inherited tradition
cosily intact. And that exposure to criticism of the central concerns
of Christian doctrine is for Jüngel a way of laying bare the
Christological reference of all proper talk of God.

Death and God's death

The death of God, in that it defines the being of God, changes death. In
the event of God's death, God *allows* death to define his being, and thereby
disposes of death. In the event of God's death, death is ordained to become
a divine phenomenon.[35]

The previous section explored some of the ramifications of Jüngel's
conception of the 'death of God' for the Christian response to
atheism. In this section we turn to the cognate topic of the
relationship between God's death and the death of man. The 'death
of God' defines both the divine being and the nature of death, for
God's identification of himself with the crucified is both the
culmination of his own ways and the ultimate disclosure of his
purposes for man.

Jüngel's writings on the theology of death[36] are not only of
interest for what they reveal of his own preoccupations and
methods of procedure, but also for their potential contribution to
recent debates on death and life after death in a variety of
theological and philosophical quarters.[37] Admittedly, at first
reading his work here is tangential to those debates: its most
frequent manner of persuasion is rhetoric rather than close
argumentation, its engagement with (say) philosophical questions
about the relationship of embodiment to existence or with traditions
other than the Christian, is negligible. This very obliqueness,
however, points to one of the most fundamental convictions of
Jüngel's theology, namely a conviction that theology evades its
peculiar responsibility whenever it strays from its Christological
base.

'This is a *theological* inquiry,' he writes at the beginning of *Tod*:
'Its possible answers are in the province of Christian dogmatics,
and thus in the province of a disciplined inquiry concerned with
faith in God.'[38] Underlying this concern to prosecute a *theology* of

death is again an understanding of theology as an autonomous discipline with its own methods of inquiry and norms of judgement. This concern surfaces, for example, in the curious detachment of the opening sections of *Tod*, which focus on material from the human, social and medical sciences, from the theological sections which form the substance of the book. The 'non-theological' material is poorly integrated into the whole argument precisely because it simply furnishes a problematic to which the Christian faith addresses itself, without being in any way bound to its questions or expectations. And once again, this distinctiveness is sharpened by an appeal to the place of beliefs about the person of Jesus:

The Christian faith as a whole is in a way an answer to the question of death. The church proclaims 'the death of the Lord' Jesus Christ in the expectation that this same Lord 'is coming' (I Cor. 11.26)...Here there can be no doubt that the question of death is answered in a very definite, and characteristically strange, way...[39]

As an inquiry into the Christological dimensions of the Christian understanding of death, Jüngel's work is also an inquiry into the nature and conditions of appropriate *language about* death:

For theology – as talk of God – the question of death presents itself above all as a question about a language which defies death. Are there words which are a match for death? Or can we only properly keep silent about death, so that the most appropriate form of language about God is a silence made precise through speech?[40]

Death says nothing. Death alone has nothing to say in our world...When death comes it is dumb and makes us dumb.[41]

Theology has a particular responsibility to develop a language in which death is articulated and so given meaning. To *speak* of death is to defy it, to refuse its claim to paralyse language and so inhibit the discovery of meaning. 'He who speaks, lives. To speak means: to have time...Successful language as it were wins time, time to live.'[42] We will return at the end of this chapter to examine the inadequacy of this approach to a Christian search for meaning in death. For the present it should be noted that in construing the 'question of death' as the question 'how should and can one properly speak of death?',[43] Jüngel betrays significant aspects of his theology.

In particular, he understands Christian language about death as a 'word from beyond death'. For 'death is dumb, and so if we are to be able to speak about death, a word must come from beyond death. Christian faith claims to have heard such a word from beyond – indeed, it lives from it.'[44] Moreover, this 'word from beyond' can only be heard through disturbance of the settled structures of man's language about himself and the world. 'Our language changes, our speech as it were breaks out of itself, when we talk of death.'[45] And such renewal of the traditions of human speech in the face of death is for Jüngel one of the consequences of the resurrection of Jesus Christ. 'Faith, too, speaks the language of the world. But faith cannot speak this language without changing it. For in the language of faith the event of the resurrection of Jesus from the dead is at work. This event prevents language from becoming so fixed in traditions that nothing ever changes.'[46]

In order to identify this profound disturbance of traditions of language about death which is found in the New Testament, Jüngel makes much of the Old Testament material in which life is understood to consist in relationship to God. 'In the Old Testament...to live is to *have a relationship*. Above all, it means to have a relationship with God.'[47] To disturb this essential relatedness is to sin, for 'sin is the godless drive towards relationlessness'.[48] By rendering the self absolute through self-definition without life-giving relations, sin leads to death. 'The alien power of death encroaches upon the orderliness of creation and its life, thereby disturbing its orderliness and right conduct. When death actually occurs, then a man's life becomes completely relationless. The dead man is for ever alienated from his God. And without God everything becomes relationless.'[49]

The shift to which the New Testament testifies takes place in the death of Jesus. For the Old Testament, the criterion for relationship to God is life. For the New Testament, both life and death are the location of relationship to God. 'When the Son of God died a human death, God was incorporated into human history in such a way that man's life and death can be newly defined out of this event.'[50] Because God identifies himself with the crucified Jesus, death itself is changed: it is no longer 'gottfremd', alien to God. And thus death no longer spells the end of all relations; rather because death is not alien to God's own being, it is also the place of relationship to him. God reveals himself at the death of Jesus as 'the God who is there for all men':[51]

to be there for someone means to relate to him. But if God does not cease to relate to us in death, if he identifies himself with the crucified in order to show himself as gracious to all men, then out of the midst of the relationlessness of death arises a new relationship of God to man...Where relationships break off and connexions are brought to an end, even there God interposes himself.[52]

Jüngel is not offering a theory of human survival. Indeed, he would repudiate as misdirected any understanding of death oriented towards the maintenance of the human subject. Such an understanding would, indeed, run the risk of neglecting the extent to which man's identity is contoured by what lies beyond him. And so Jüngel seeks an understanding of man's death which is not concerned with his preservation but with the presence of God to man in death. The meaning of man's death lies not within himself and his survival, but beyond him, in God who is all in all. Death is 'an anthropological *passive*'.[53] It is in this light that we are to understand his characterisation of death as the *limit* of man's being.

'Man is only man within limits.'[54] The anthropology which underlies Jüngel's theology of death is, as might be expected, one which is imbued with a sense of the contingency of man upon that which is outside him. Man's humanity consists in his being limited: he is 'ein Wesen der Grenze', a being with limits.[55] Because of his perverse attempts to make himself absolute, man experiences this limitedness as a threat to his identity. Properly understood, however, man's limits are not the arbitrary truncation of his selfhood but the form of the relationships in which man is defined. Limits are 'the necessary forms which relationships take. As such, they are not an evil to be endured, but rather the orderliness of being which corresponds to the divine blessing of creation.'[56] Man is limited because he is related, indeed, 'constituted through relationships'.[57] And these relationships form human life: they define man, by putting an end to the chaotic, structureless urge of sin:

The limits which are set to man do not constitute a threat to him. They do not hem him in, nor do they rob him of anything; rather they give him the possibilities of being himself. Man has time, for example, between beginning and end; he has his space to live over against other men. The completely unlimited, on the other hand, would be equally the undefined and the undefinable. And its realisation would be chaos. Over against this, the limits which are set to man belong to the orderliness of being; to speak theologically, they are a blessing of the Creator. They only forbid insofar as they allow. The function of true limits is accordingly never primarily prohibition but rather consent, the opening up of a dimension within which the one who is limited is affirmed and able to exist as himself. Limitation is fundamentally an act of affirmation.[58]

From this perspective, death becomes an affirmation of man's being, and man's acceptance of this limit is part of his discovery of himself in that which lies beyond himself. 'To man's affirmation of his limitation by God belongs the affirmation of his finitude.'[59] To accept death as the final limit set to man, as the final way in which the Creator forms us, is to be properly human. And so the absolute abandonment of self in death is equally the ultimate confirmation of ourselves in God. For to die is to be subject to the creative, forming hand of God; death is the final form of creaturehood. We are, accordingly, to understand death as what Jesus Christ has made it to be: 'the limitation of man by God alone'.[60] Contemporary objections to the notion of life after death commonly focus on two sets of problems. One concerns the logical and philosophical difficulties attendant upon construing language about survival of bodily death;[61] the other concentrates on the counter-critical effects of belief in life after death in that such beliefs can stifle hostility towards intolerable conditions in present existence.[62] The roots of Jüngel's suspicion of the idea are to be sought more directly in his interpretation of the resurrection of Jesus.

Briefly, he suggests that the resurrection is improperly understood as a reversal of the events of Good Friday. Properly understood, the resurrection of Jesus is the proclamation that God has identified himself with the crucified and so is able to suffer death. 'The message of the resurrection does not cancel the *logos tou staurou* [word of the cross] but gives it its proper weight.'[63] For in Good Friday and Easter Day we have to do 'not with two distinct mysteries, but with two sides of one and the same mystery. On Easter Day there takes place nothing less and nothing more than the *disclosure* of the mystery of the death of Jesus.'[64] The content of that disclosure is that in the death of Jesus, the life of God is at work; in the relationlessness of death, God creates new relationships. God 'identified himself for time and eternity with this dead and godforsaken man. This identification of God with the dead man Jesus is called resurrection of the dead. It says that at the place where all relations end, God has interposed himself in order to create *new relations* in the midst of the relationlessness of death.'[65]

Jüngel is thus offering an interpretation of the resurrection without recourse to the notion of temporal continuity. The resurrection of Jesus is not an event subsequent to the events of Good Friday, and does not effect a continuation of his biography. Rather, the resurrection is a message about the death of Jesus. This is very clear in Jüngel's use of the language of 'message' and 'disclosure' about the resurrection: resurrection language is a way of *talking about* Jesus' death.

These Christological assertions shape the way in which Jüngel conceives of the final end of man. To share in the resurrection of Jesus Christ is not to be lifted out of finitude. 'One should not allow the Christian resurrection hope to obscure the fact that human life is temporally limited. Thus hope...cannot involve the expectation that life's temporal limitations will be lifted.'[66] This is above all because to envisage 'eternal life' in such a way is to espouse an eschatology oriented towards 'the religious subject'[67] rather than towards 'God...the measure of time'.[68] Its concern with the continuance of the human subject is mistaken in that the 'eternity' of man's life is neither its continuation nor its removal from the conditions of historical existence. Rather, man's eternity resides in the fact that his finite life is in communication with the eternal God. 'Insofar as man is eternally limited by God's grace, he *is* eternal.'[69] Man's life is eternal in the sense that as a finished, integrated whole, in all its limitedness, it is embraced by God and made part of his history with mankind: 'Our finite life will be made eternal in its very finiteness. But this will not be by endless prolongation: there is no immortality of the soul. Rather it will be my participation in God's own life...In this sense, the briefest form of the hope of resurrection is the statement: "God is my beyond".'[70]

Jüngel's understanding of eternal life is resolutely theocentric, oriented towards the fact that in death God is 'there for us', rather than towards any notion of human survival or continuance. Man's life is finished at death. But because 'God is my beyond', then 'the past which is redeemed is more than the past. The past which is redeemed is the past in the presence of God, made present by God himself and glorified...by God. The past in the presence of the living God cannot in any way be a dead past.'[71] Seen from this perspective, 'the ending of a life is quite different from its being

broken off'.[72] For 'the end is succeeded by God, and beyond that
which has ended is not merely nothing, but the same God who was
in the beginning'.[73]

Jüngel's theology of death is bound up with his particular
conception of man's nature as a fashioner of symbols. 'Man,' he
writes, 'is distinguished from animals as a semiotic being and thus
as a being capable of rationality. He alone can not only react to
signs but also create them and act through them.'[74] The emphasis,
however, falls very heavily upon *language* as the realisation of
man's semiotic nature: 'Man's capacity for symbolising and
speaking is never realised other than in one of the many different
systems of language and thus in a particular linguistic structure.'[75]
And it is for precisely this reason that Jüngel is so insistent on the
need to discover an authentically Christian language about death.
For man is a 'Sprachwesen':[76] 'theological anthropology has at
least this in common with philosophical anthropology, that it
considers language as constitutive of man's being. It is agreed that
man socialises himself in language and in that way is really
human.'[77]

This heavy emphasis on language, however, may blunt Jüngel's
alertness to the significance of other symbolic activities in man's
projects of meaning. Anthropologies of the symbolic act[78] have
sometimes sought to draw attention to the demise of ritual as the
atrophy of our ability to perceive and order the world through
non-verbal symbols. The establishment of an economy of meaning
is the establishment of an ordered, human world, a world invested
with meaning by and for human persons. This achievement of
meaning is inseparable from the manufacture of systems of signs.
Symbolic conventions both enable interpersonal communication
and also offer a means by which the world can be humanised and
appropriated. But such systems of signs are never purely verbal;
they include 'le langage du geste'.[79] 'Interpersonal language
assumes two distinct and complementary forms: articulate
language...and the silent language of gestures.'[80]

This personalist phenomenology of signs has been a particularly
rich resource for sacramental theology.[81] But its theological
ramifications are wider, and of particular relevance to a Christian
theology of death. For if man is not only a speaker but also 'a ritual
animal',[82] then it may be that experiences of liminality are
humanised and rendered meaningful as much through the language
of gesture and demonstration as through purely verbal articulation.

Here, too, 'the language of gesture is complementary to spoken language'.[83] And so the Christian response to death is not – as Jüngel suggests – only a message or a tradition of speech, but also traditions of action and rite, through which death is formed and humanised.

Jüngel's unease about the place of action in the theology of death surfaces again in his treatment of the death of Christ and its consequences for man's death. The idiom of his soteriology is not that of moral action. For in his theology what the cross accomplishes is not so much the pardoning of the sinner as his definition. We shall see when we come to look at his account of justification by faith that he construes the language of justification as *ontological* rather than moral. In justification man is distinguished from God and so restored to authentic humanity: 'To be justified means: for one's own good to be distinguished from God.'[84] Because, that is, justification functions as 'a definition of man',[85] salvation for Jüngel is not so much the imputation of righteousness as the attainment of being.[86]

The same idiom recurs in his theology of death. Death is understood to be the outworking of sin as relationlessness. Accordingly, the gulf between God and man is one which can be closed by man's being defined and limited by God. The human situation, that is, is such that man needs to be *formed* rather than *reconciled*, properly distinguished from God rather than redeemed by him. Through his self-identification with the crucified, God takes death into himself and so establishes relations in the relationlessness of death, in this way graciously forming and limiting the chaos of human self-definition. What is so conspicuously lacking here is any recourse to the language of judgement and forgiveness.[87] The past is not envisaged as an abiding reality for which atonement needs to be made, but rather as 'the life which we have actually lived, which will be gathered together, made eternal and made manifest'.[88] Sin is not seen as active hostility against God, but as an absence of relationship to which God responds by making himself present to man. Because the Christian faith is conceived to be a message – a message which can be condensed as 'the word of the cross' – then it is in definition through the word rather than in judgement and forgiveness through a moral deed that salvation is effected.

Man is 'wortbestimmt',[89] defined through the word. Such a definition of man – and the soteriology with which it is bound up – is to be judged idealist to the extent that it lays insufficient emphasis on the primacy of moral action in the Christian theology of salvation. '"Not a word but a deed." That is fundamental to the Christian understanding of the relation of God to the world.'[90] And in this our attention is again drawn to the importance of rite and liturgy: 'For liturgy is always thing done rather than thing said, action drawing its sense and power from the action of God in Christ, and by its very character as action preserving for the individual the sense that it is by deed that he is saved and held in the truth.'[91]

Something of the same movement away from historical action can be found in Jüngel's reflections on the nature of 'eternal life'. The whole movement of the book *Tod* is towards the notion of eternal life as achieved meaning. To have eternal life is to be limited by the gracious God in such a way that this limit forms and integrates the life we have lived. Put crudely, this means that what is ultimately significant is not my continued existence but the fact that 'God is my beyond': what matters is the eternal God before whom and by whom my life is finished.

The besetting problem in this suggestion is its emphasis on man's passivity. 'Man suffers death.'[92] This stress is clearly bound up with the theocentricity of Jüngel's theology of death; so strong is it that it is difficult to conceive of any sense in which death could constitute a *mutual* relationship between God and man. We are known, we are limited; but in no sense are we able to contribute to a reciprocal relationship with the God who is our beyond. There is 'no human life *after* death, no continued consciousness, no continued interaction with other people and with an environment'.[93] God does not cease to relate to us in death. But there is little sense in which we might be said to relate to him.[94]

8. Anthropology and justification

Introductory

The context of Jüngel's theological anthropology is his overarching concern to provide an account of the relation between God and man in which their respective realities are affirmed. The distinction between God and man, that is, is formulated as part of a larger strategy of excluding monism, whether it be a theomonism in which man and the world vanish as mere functions of God's self-affirmation, or an anthropomonism in which discourse about God can in the last analysis be reduced to discourse about the world. Properly to distinguish between God and man is to affirm that they constitute an irreducible duality in which neither is to be absorbed into the other.

Jüngel's anthropology is written with panache and not a little rhetorical flourish. If its presentation is at once markedly bold and defensive, this is because it is in many ways an apologetic exercise, directed to those who suggest that to give a Christological basis to anthropology may be to curtail the liberty and even the reality of man. Theo- or Christomonism, the absorption of man into the one divine reality, is, of course, a charge frequently levelled against Barth's doctrine of man. It is a charge which Jüngel's interpretations of some of the fundamental moves of Barth's anthropology, as well as his own essays in the area, have sought stoutly to deny.

Critics of Barth have raised questions about the status, dignity and freedom of man in his anthropology, and sought to discover whether in deriving and validating humanity from the humanity of Jesus, Barth is unable consistently to defend his work from the danger of reducing man to a mere shadow of the prior divine realities.[1] Roberts, for example, argues that Barth's manner of grounding man in Christ vitiates human reality, that 'in positing the contingent historical order upon the basis of a putative contingency and historicality of God, (Barth) attempts to recreate the natural order but by doing so effects a resolution and extinction of that order in the trinitarian abyss of the divine being'.[2] Both Barth's method and the substance of his doctrine are deemed by some students of his work to conspire to render man's being 'in Adam' ontologically and definitively inferior to his being 'in Christ',[3] so that the necessary duality of God and his creation is threatened. Jüngel seeks to show that the kind of Christologically-grounded anthropology so massively exemplified by Barth can retain an adequate sense of the substantiality of man as a free subject and agent, without having to abandon the initial decision to construct anthropology on the basis of Christology.[4]

At the close of his study of Barth, Bouillard remarks that in the *Church Dogmatics* 'the history of salvation has the appearance of a divine drama played out over the head of man. It is no use to repeat that it concerns us and that we are included in it; the discourse in which it is told often seems to float above us, a christological dream projected onto a platonic heaven.'[5] It is in the face of such criticism that Jüngel's recommendations about the distinction between God and the world come into their own, for it is his conviction that only a theology in which God and man are properly distinguished can adequately escape the danger to which Bouillard refers. At first sight the language of 'distinguishing' may imply the opposite, reinforcing suspicions of a divine world 'over our heads' in which all the significant decisions and acts have already been made and in the face of which any independent human reality is disqualified. That this is not the case can only be grasped by careful attention to the specific way in which Jüngel draws the distinction between God and man.

Certainly the charge of the extinction of the human would remain pertinent if the distinction were understood as an infinite hiatus between God and man. For in such an account, the divine is defined primarily in terms of its opposition to the human: God 'is conceived solely in terms of the *absoluteness* of his being and not in terms of the *relatedness* of his being to man from all eternity'.[6] Such a construction of the nature of God is not likely to offer a persuasive basis for a theological account of human freedom and authenticity, because in excluding from its definition of God the relations which he bears towards his creatures, it also excludes the substantiality of man as a reality over against God which is presupposed by such relations.

Against this, Jüngel commends a distinction between God and man which is 'not the difference of an even greater dissimilarity, but rather the difference within an ever greater dissimilarity of an even greater similarity between God and man'.[7] The distinction is made on the basis of God's self-identification with Jesus as that event which furnishes equally the definition of the humanity of God and the humanity of man. 'The *concrete* distinction between God and man must be oriented to that event which allows us to think of the *relation* of God and man as firmly as possible. And that event is...the event of the incarnation...God became man in order that God and man could be definitively distinguished from each other.'[8] The stages of the argument telescope at this point, and the precise line of argument is not easy to follow. But two positions are recommended. The first is that God is distinguished from man by his *humanity*.[9] By this, Jüngel seeks to exclude what he finds inadequate in the 'absolute hiatus' model of the distinction between God and man: the notion of an unrelated divine aseity which will not cohere with the authenticity of man. But divine aseity is not thereby cancelled out; rather, its form is specified as that humanity of God which is equally the affirmation of the humanity of man.

The second recommendation moves on from there to suggest that the humanity of God is an affirmation of the humanity of man insofar as its corollary is that man best images the divine in his humanity, and not in self-divinisation. 'That God is human in his divinity...excludes any idea that man is divine in his humanity... The Christian faith disputes the inhumanity of man.'[10] The incarnation discloses that God is in and for himself the human God, whose humanity spells the end of any picture of God as one who devalues man. To distinguish God and man by reference to God's becoming man is to affirm that God and his creation are complementary.

The next two chapters will be devoted to examining this argument in detail. In the rest of the present chapter we look at how Jüngel expounds the idea that man may only be said to be properly human when he is constituted *ab extra*: here we focus primarily on the motif of justification. The next chapter will then take up the question of how such a theological anthropology can be shown to be compatible with the authenticity of man.

Man defined 'ab extra'

'What God has intended for man is not discovered by thinking
through what man is and what properly belongs to him. Rather,
what God has intended for man is only discovered by thinking
through the *one* man...Jesus Christ.'[11] Jüngel's anthropology takes
its rise from the affirmation that Jesus Christ is the *ratio essendi
et cognoscendi* of true humanity. That is to say, because the
humanity of God in Christ is ontologically determinative for all
men, knowledge of the truth about man derives from knowledge
of Jesus Christ.

The claim here is partly methodological, identifying the procedural distinctiveness of *theological* anthropology over against
other kinds of reflection on the nature of man. In the discovery of
truth about man, theology does not attend to the range of human
history, but to one particular history. In this way, 'talk about...
the man who expresses God transcends hermeneutically that which
may be derived from analysis of his own being or from empirical
knowledge'.[12] It is not, however, exclusively a matter of a
distinctive method, but also of a distinctive content for theological
anthropology. For such an account of man 'is referred to a
secundum dicentem deum, a word which is to be measured against
the God who speaks, which theology calls the Word of God'.[13] This
'Word' determines not only its procedure but also its substantive
content. For the most significant emphasis of Jüngel's anthropology
is that the 'truth' of man's being is not to be discovered in
self-correspondence but in the event of interruption by God's
Word of address. Formally and materially, this divine address
informs theological doctrine about man.

Particular attention should be paid to Jüngel's stress on the *truth*
of humanity: 'When the Christian faith inquires into the definition
of human life, it is deeply concerned with the truth of life.'[14] If
we are to understand this stress, we should note his contention that
a Christian anthropology cannot be harmonised with a notion of
truth as *adaequatio intellectus et rei*. We have already seen in
discussing the concept of 'metaphorical truth' that what Jüngel
rejects in this definition is not its realism but what might be called
its conservatism, its resistance to the disturbance of actuality. In
an anthropological context, the *adaequatio* notion of truth is
rejected because its orientation to actuality includes an emphasis
on the works of man in which he corresponds with his fallen self.

This emphasis Jüngel counters by identifying the truth of man as something which *comes to* man as the disturbance of actuality rather than its realisation by man himself: 'Over against the understanding of truth as the correspondence of proposition and fact, truth is much more profoundly understood as that interruption of human life-connexions.'[15]

Jüngel's concern here is to shift the centre of gravity in an account of man away from the dominant modes of actuality onto those events in which man is exposed to critical scrutiny. In this way he underlines that, for the discovery of his humanity, man is referred beyond his self-realised actuality. Some specific examples provide an initial identification of this reference beyond the self: experiences of the death of other persons, for example, or of great beauty or pain.[16] In such experiences man is reminded of his essential relatedness to that which is beyond him, and of the social structure and constitution of his self, of which he cannot be said to be totally in possession. Such experiences emphasise that man is a 'related being'[17] whose 'life is something different from the possession of a human "I". My life is constituted through and through by relationships which do not belong to me. And so it is true to say that man lives by being dispossessed of himself. He is not his own lord.'[18]

Such characterisations of the way in which man is defined from outside play only a minor role in Jüngel's anthropology, however, and he is concerned to avoid presenting them as a kind of natural demonstration from within man's experience of himself and his world that he is surrounded and moulded by a transcendent reality. Much greater significance is accorded to *Anrede*, to the divine 'Word of address' in which man is disturbed out of self-identity and self-possession, released from dominance by works and freed from himself to become authentically human. Man is 'defined by the word'.[19] To explain this, we examine three basic determinations of human life (man as justified, man as believer, man as temporal), in the explanation of each of which Jüngel deploys the notion of the divine address to show how the truth of man's being is a gift and not a work.

Justification

The definition of man *ab extra* can be illustrated first of all from Jüngel's use of the concept of justification as a fundamental motif in anthropology. Noting that in the Pauline concept of *dikaiosunē theou* (the righteousness of God) righteousness is identified as the gift of God rather than as a reality realised through a human act, Jüngel extends the basic structures of the relationship between God and man which justification presupposes, so that the doctrine becomes a framework within which theological anthropology can be explicated. In terms of procedure, the doctrine of justification is thus extended beyond purely soteriological boundaries; it is not a clearly-circumscribed dogma to be set alongside others *seriatim*. Jüngel prefers to see it as a 'constructive criterion of truth',[20] a motif providing some of the distinctive features of a Christian account of man.

Most obviously, such a use of justification introduces an emphasis on man as the passive recipient of the work of God. In *Paulus und Jesus* Jüngel stresses the passives '*made* righteous' and '*declared* righteous', commenting that 'the being...of the justified sinner who participates in the being of God is an ontological passive'.[21] The point is developed by using a distinction between 'person' and 'works' drawn from classical Lutheran discussions of the nature of justifying grace and its relation to sanctification and human co-operation in the *ordo salutis*. The distinction needs carefully to be construed if Jüngel is not to be misunderstood. When he frequently claims that 'As a person I am...over and above all activities primarily a receiver',[22] he is not so much offering an exhaustive definition of human personhood as suggesting a manner of evaluating human worth, which is not oriented towards agency and performance, and which resists in its evaluations the 'drive to act'.[23] God's set of justification 'recognises' man without – indeed, despite – his works, entailing a distinction between the truth of personhood and the actuality of works. 'One's work is of course an outworking of one's personal being which cannot be separated from one's person. But in this undeniable connexion of person and work, man is addressed in his personal being in such a way that he experiences himself to be recognised *as man* not only without his works but in spite of them.'[24] In thus addressing and affirming man *chōris ergōn tou nomou* (without works of the law) God disturbs a relation of correspondence between works and the value of the person.

To elucidate his repudiation of models of man as artificer of his own being and its worth, Jüngel again returns to disputing the ontological primacy of actuality. Assent to such an ontology immediately privileges human agency and self-realisation, for 'with the ontological priority of actuality...*work* comes to have an unsurpassable significance'.[25] In an anthropology cast in such a mould, man 'is what he makes of himself',[26] and it is precisely this 'connection between work and actuality'[27] which will not cohere with the doctrine of justification, 'according to which we only come to act righteously when we have been made and become righteous'.[28] Thus human existence is, properly understood, 'existence out of the creative power of the justifying God'.[29]

This conception of man had led Jüngel to some contentious writing on the relationship between justification and man as social and political agent, where the apologetic strain noted above comes across with particular force. Jüngel disputes modes of theological rationality which place a high premium on political agency at the expense of reflective, theoretical work, claiming that such views presuppose a mistaken account of the relationship between person and works. Partly his plea is for a proper ordering of theory and practice so as to avoid impatience with theory: 'everything in its place and at its time!'[30] To Jüngel's mind the theoretical is a sphere of engagement not only separate from but prior to social and political practice. Practice is the consequence of theoretical activity, its forms entailed by reflection which should not be disturbed from its own concerns by the demands of practical activity. The deeper reason, however, for Jüngel's unease with 'political theology'[31] is that it works with a concept of truth which, in its orientation to the actual and practical, cannot cohere with his interpretation of justification, and which demonstrates an 'obsession with actuality'.[32]

The occasional, controversial character of Jüngel's writing here had no doubt led to statements and arguments lacking in precise analysis or qualification. But taken on its own terms, his work does reveal the depth of seriousness with which he takes the separation between person and works. Practice cannot be a criterion of theological truth[33] precisely because to accord it such a function would be to presuppose that 'man is concrete only in his acts'.[34]

Because Jüngel extends man's passivity before the divine work into a complete definition of humanity and its value, it is not surprising that he should canvass the fruitfulness of Luther's much maligned distinction between 'inner' and 'outer' man in his commentary on *Zur Freiheit eines Christenmenschen*. Jüngel defends the distinction in two ways. First, he argues that the 'portal' to man's being is not to be sought in his acts but 'in a word which

confronts him and makes him human'.[35] Second, he suggests that
the inner/outer distinction is improperly construed as a contrast
between an eternal inner man and a transitory outer man.[36] It is
more appropriately interpreted as the attempt to give a proper
order to the relationship of person (inner man) and works (outer
man). The refusal of 'pure externality' is made to release man from
dominance by works, so setting him in a proper relation to his
works as the subsequent expression of his person and not the
struggle for its realisation. 'It is the Word of God which makes
it possible for the inner man to go out of himself.'[37]

Faith

In justification, then, man is the passive recipient of the work of
God in which the 'truth' of life is granted by the disturbance of
its actuality. Jüngel's discussions of the nature of faith are to be
set in the context of this attempt to deflect attention away from
the self-realising subject or agent, and towards the divine Word
in which humanity is realised from outside. Something of this has
already been seen in the relation between thinking and faith; but
the ecstatic structure of the human response to God is extensive
beyond the noetic – it is, indeed, a fundamental characteristic of
human nature as such. Faith is exemplary of the orientation of the
whole man to the divine; it is that 'openness to God' which 'lets
God come'.[38] As such it is the renunciation of realisation of self,
for faith 'implies the demand to abandon oneself completely to
God. And one can only abandon oneself completely to God when
one gives oneself up. Truly to abandon oneself is to renounce any
attempt to establish oneself.'[39] Because of this, in common with
much Protestant theology Jüngel finds it extraordinarily difficult
to articulate a sense in which faith can be said to be a human
determination, act, or even response. Not only is faith 'oriented to
the outside',[40] it is itself a gift which comes to man: 'Faith *came*
(Gal. 3.25). It is the possibility of expressing God's righteousness
which is granted by righteousness itself.'[41] Faith is 'made possible'
by the Word which addresses man.[42]

Temporality

Staunch insistence on the constitution of man from outside is
nowhere more evident than in Jüngel's work on temporality, which

is that determination of human existence in which the fashioning of man by the Word is most clearly to be traced. Much of what he has to say here develops motifs learnt, as we have seen, from close engagement with the work of Barth and Fuchs. If it was Barth's emphasis that human temporality is realised and validated only on the basis of the prior historicality of God in Christ (so that 'real' time is not a natural *habitus* of man),[43] it was Fuchs' corresponding emphasis that time is structured linguistically, formed by those 'speech-events' which constitute its differentiation into past, present and future.[44] From both these thinkers Jüngel inherits a resolute exclusion of the self as the measure of time, in favour of a notion of temporality as a gift granted in the interception of self-identity through the Word.

Such an orientation of a theological account of temporality towards God as giver of time emerged, we saw, in Jüngel's early work on New Testament eschatology, where he urged an interpretation of the biblical material free from views of time as a measure of the subsequent moments of the ego's experience. 'God is the measure of time...Time is moved time.'[45] Time is 'moved' by God in his Word, so that the 'word of the Kingdom' in the parables of Jesus is the 'eschatological announcement of time',[46] the creative address in which the settled structures of human temporality are exploded as new time intersects the old.

The idiom here is heady, and opaque to those unfamiliar with Fuchs' style. The precise manner in which the Word constitutes temporality can be elucidated to a degree, however, by Jüngel's remarks on Descartes, concerning the 'securing' of the self against interruption which he feels to characterise 'Cartesianism'. This securing is to be countered by what Jüngel terms 'Entsicherung'. That last word primarily denotes the release of a safety catch, but here describes the release from temporal self-identity accomplished by 'words of address'.[47] Such words distance man from himself, disturbing the closedness of his temporal structures, and thus provoking 'the experience of a temporal alienation'.[48] Functioning as an interstice between past and future, the event of the Word breaks the domination of the past and so offers freedom.

In effect, Jüngel's work on time recasts into the language and conceptuality of temporality what he understands as the basic structures both of the relationship between God and man and of the constitution of man which are entailed by the doctrine of justification. The confession that man is justified *chōris ergōn tou nomou* (without works of the law) implies that man is radically contingent upon the divine Word, not only for his salvation but for the entire economy of his being, including his temporality.

Reflections

In looking at Jüngel's theology of death we have already noted that the idiom of his soteriology is ontological rather than moral: man is defined rather than forgiven and restored in justification. By abstracting the doctrine of justication from its forensic context, using it to answer the question of man's being rather than of man's salvation from ruin, Jüngel shifts out of a moral understanding of the relationship between God and man. Man's salvation is dealt with not so much by the alteration of his moral state before God accomplished through the death and resurrection of Jesus Christ, as by the hypostatic union: insofar as Jesus Christ is true Man, the truth of our humanity resides in him. And so in his person as true man united to God, Jesus Christ constitutes our proper humanity. Implicit, that is, in Jüngel's doctrine of justification is a conception of the vicarious humanity of Christ.[49] To talk of justification is to talk of the way in which our being lies beyond us in the true man Jesus. The doctrine of justification is thus at heart a doctrine concerning the person of Christ; in this sense 'the truth of the doctrine of justification lies in the fact that it uncompromisingly brings Christology to bear on the matter'.[50]

Two reflections are appropriate. The first concerns the adequacy of an account of justification which does not underline the primacy of the moral.[51] The most significant advantage of forensic accounts of justification is that they keep the character of the dealings of God and man firmly in the ethical realm. Certainly justification is not to be construed as forensic in any sense which would make the justice of God an abstract code external to his own self-determination, for justice is both intrinsic to his being and expressed in covenant relationships rather than in merely formal dealings with man. Nevertheless, by retaining the centrality of divine justice, justification does not allow the moral nature of reconciliation with God to recede from view. An ontological account of reconciliation would be analytic of the prior moral realities and in no way seek to sublate them.

A second question concerns the conception of the vicarious humanity of Christ which underlies Jüngel's account of justification. Stated very simply, the vigorous affirmation of *solus Christus* may well threaten rather than validate man. For such is the significance of Christ's fraternity with the human race that our humanity is already accomplished for us. As a consequence, any human response may come to be seen as a compromise of the all-sufficiency of Christ. As we saw, Jüngel finds it very difficult to state a sense in which faith may be said to be a determination of man, and at that point there surfaces one of the most characteristic problems of Protestant theology, namely that in repudiating synergism it may make faith into a merely formal ratification of prior divine decisions and deeds.[52] The question poses itself: does Christ's fraternity with the human race validate or invalidate our humanity? In order to answer this more fully, we turn to examine the role of analogy in Jüngel's doctrine of man.

9 Anthropology and analogy

Introductory

The place of analogy in theological anthropology has been one of the constant themes of Jüngel's work, from his early essay on Barth's anthropology[1] to his recent development of the concept of 'the man who expresses God'.[2] His concern with analogy, as we have seen, is broader in scope than simply observation of certain linguistic behaviour: it also focusses dogmatic issues about the way in which God and the creation relate to each other. In the context of theological anthropology, the term analogy denotes both a recommendation about procedure and a substantive proposal, since 'the being of the man Jesus is the ontological and epistemological basis for all analogy'.[3]

> In *theology*, analogy is pertinent:
> as the ontological structure of the relationship between God and his creation;
> as a hermeneutical model for formulating theological concepts, that is to say, as the condition of the possibility of appropriate human discourse about God;
> as the starting-point for an ethical theory of the Christian faith.[4]

This chapter picks up the first and third of the uses of analogy just mentioned, to try and show how his concept of man as the analogate of Jesus Christ helps him begin to offer a resolution of the problem identified at the end of the previous chapter – namely whether an anthropology constructed on a Christological basis can fully affirm the reality of man.

The basic characteristics of Jüngel's use of analogy in this context emerge in his account of the image of God in man. Once again taking his bearings from Barth,[5] he understands the image of God from within the horizon of the history of Jesus, and not from that of a relatively independent order of creation. 'The category of the *imago dei*...is identical only with the historical *name* Jesus Christ. The person called by this name is the man who expresses God.'[6] The image of God, that is, is personal, particular, nameable: it is Jesus. But precisely because the image is construed within this exclusively Christological perspective, it functions as a definition of mankind. This is not because it is a natural constant of human being, but because it is borne by Jesus Christ whose history is definitive for all men: 'On the basis of the reality of this one man who expresses God, it is true that the humanity of all men consists in expressing God.'[7] Thus man is the image of God insofar as he 'expresses' the history of Jesus: 'God speaks – man expresses. In this way he is the image of God.'[8]

It is important to grasp precisely what Jüngel intends by the claim that 'the humanity of all men consists in expressing God'.[9] The relationship of *Entsprechung* (correspondence, analogy) between God and man should not be cast in the idiom of an imperative: it is not that man properly becomes human when he responds to the divine call to image God. So to construe the divine – human relationship would accord a certain creative autonomy to the human response, and would introduce pressure to identify the *imago dei* as a natural possession independent of immediate divine determination. In this way its exclusively Christological grounds would be compromised. It is not, therefore, that man is called to a deeper realisation of his humanity by becoming 'one who expresses God', but more that only as such can he be said to be human at all. The Word constitutes man in addressing him; man's very humanity is the accomplishment of the divine speech-act. The mood, that is, is indicative rather than imperative. And so the analogy between God and man in which 'Gott spricht' and 'der Mensch entspricht' is 'an ontological repetition' in which man is contingent for his very being on Jesus Christ, the Word of God.[10]

In this use of the analogy motif we are taken to the furthest reaches of Jüngel's account of the constitution of man *ab extra*. We are also introduced to what is most deeply problematical in that account, namely its ambiguities in affirming man as a further reality beyond the divine on the basis of which he is posited. We shall see that these ambiguities do not arise in allowing that man *in Christ* is such a further reality, for the language of 'distinguishing between God and man' prevents the contingency of man in Christ from becoming his disqualification. The problems do arise, however, in respect of man *outside Christ*, and particularly in respect of the *universality* of the claim that the humanity of all men consists in 'expressing God'. Three sets of issues arise. First, there is a certain 'holism' or 'monism' in Jüngel's anthropology which threatens to compress to a single, self-consistent stratum the very many discordant and discontinuous levels of human reality. This compression expresses itself procedurally in a certain failure to render very large anthropological proposals in sufficiently concrete terms. Second, there are ambiguities with regard to the status of man outside Christ: if man is true man only insofar as he expresses God, difficulties are experienced in according full reality to man who does not so express God. And third, this latter problem comes across particularly acutely in according a definitive and ontologically significant sense to sin and unbelief as modes of being in which man refuses to be determined by God.

The authenticity of man in Christ

'Authenticity' is used here fairly loosely as a way of denoting the genuine reality of man. 'Authentic' man is man who is substantial in his own right, prototypical and not a mere repetition of some more primordial reality, possessed of a solidity proper to himself in which he stands over against other realities and through which he is able to relate to them. It is Jüngel's claim that to ground man beyond himself is not to deny that man is authentic in this sense, for a careful specifying of the nature of the divine determination shows that, grounded in Christ, man's authenticity is not contravened. In this, he takes a lead from Barth's last works, attending most especially to their characterisations of divine causality. In this way he seeks to resolve the problems just noted, not by calling into question his commitment to man's Christological grounding, but by further refinement of the theology of grace which it entails.

Jüngel has written widely in commentary upon Barth's last works, both the fragment on baptism[11] and the unfinished material edited under the title *The Christian Life*.[12] From this close engagement he has adopted many characteristic problems and solutions, discovering in Barth's texts an account of the relation of God and man fully alert to the realities of each.

Jüngel focusses on Barth's firm distinction between Spirit- and water-baptism as paradigmatic of a proper relation between God and the Christian in which human action does not usurp the divine and divine action does not obliterate the authentically human. Barth's doctrine of baptism is understood not simply as a piece of sacramental theology but as the basis of an entire theological ethics.[13] Crucial to its ethical intentions is an attempt to shift beyond either 'Christomonism' or 'anthropomonism', by envisaging the relation between God and man as one of analogy. Thus Jüngel places great weight on Barth's statement that 'the omnicausality of God must not be construed as his sole causality',[14] commenting that 'in the refusal of the thesis of God's sole causality a positive statement is made about man as the subject of himself ...Everything comes to the vital issue of allowing man to be subject *of himself* and *only* of himself, and so of allowing human activity to remain human.'[15] Because God's omnicausality is not construed as his sole causality, a space is left in which the Christian's acts can be accorded their proper, human significance. Such significance is not to be won by a human annexing of the divine work (thus compromising omnicausality), but rather by properly distinguishing between God and man, holding fast to their irreducible duality. This distinction is to man's benefit, in that it releases him from having to affirm his agency by performing what is properly the work of God. By distinguishing rather than confusing divine and human agency, each is allowed its inalienable sphere of operation, and Christian ethics are made possible.

Jüngel draws this positive affirmation of human agency out of Barth's denial of sacramental status to the human act of water-baptism. Only the exclusively divine work of Spirit-baptism may properly be called sacramental, as that divine act in which 'the history of Jesus Christ as it were reaches its soteriological peak'.[16] In Spirit-baptism, the effective agent is Jesus Christ '*the one and only sacrament of the Church*',[17] the one whose history is the '*mediating sacrament* between God and man'.[18] Yet to deny the appropriateness of sacramental language for water-baptism is not to render it insignificant but to accord to it the significance which belongs to it as that human act which interprets,[19] celebrates,[20] and answers[21] the exclusively divine act to which it 'corresponds'. The idea of the human act of baptism as 'interpretation' is especially significant. Whilst at first sight it may appear as a mere jealous defence of divine action to the exclusion of any sense of co-operation, it makes such a defence for man's sake, in order to prevent human reality from distorting its own features in attempting to perform the work which is properly God's. As interpretation, water-baptism 'gives and does the same thing in a different way'.[22] In this way, both the contingency and the inalienability of the agency of man are affirmed.

This distinction between Spirit- and water-baptism furnishes an account of the involvement of man as agent at the initiation of the Christian life: the act of offering oneself for baptism may properly be called 'the beginning of Christian activity'.[23] Similarly, Barth's exposition of the Lord's Prayer in *The Christian Life* offers a way of affirming man's continuing agency without loss to the grounding of his acts *extra se*. Jüngel writes that 'Amongst the most impressive accomplishments of Barth's theology is its grounding of ethics in Christology in such a way that...man's concrete activity is...not ideologically anticipated, but rather set free as concrete and – in its very concretion – obedient activity'.[24] Once again, Jüngel focusses his analysis of Barth with the concept of *Entsprechung*, in order to express a relationship in which God and man are distinguished in such a way that neither is otiose. Barth's use of the appeal 'Our Father' as an *ethical* motif is for Jüngel expressive of the dual agency of God and man, in which man's appeal both allows God to do his proper work and is itself an authentically human act. 'In his human way man has to perform a human activity, an activity in no way divine. But his human activity is good because "in its humanity" it becomes "an activity similar, parallel and analogous to the act of God"'.[25] The language of 'provocation' lays bare Jüngel's concern: 'No man...is theoretically violated through being christologically constructed. And the same is true of man's activity. It is not ethically constructed. It is not ethically deduced. Much more is it to be understood as provoked out of free responsibility, as activity called forth by God's good command, fully determined in complete freedom.'[26] God induces man, prevailing upon him freely to become himself. Whilst there can be no compromise of divine precedence, no establishment of human ethical agency apart from its Christological 'provocation', this precedence is an inducement to authenticity and not its devaluation. 'In the act of God's address, man appears as an agent who *expresses* the *active* God.'[27]

What Jüngel urges here was already expressed in his speech at the Barth *Gedenkfeier*: 'Without compromise Barth claimed to think of God himself: *autos*. But where God is concerned, only man himself can express God...*autos*, the free man himself.'[28] How far this represents a shift in the direction of Jüngel's theology can be gauged by comparison with the earlier ethical study 'Erwägungen zur Grundlegung der evangelischen Ethik'. Here ethics was grounded in justification in such a way as to shift attention from human onto divine activity, clearly making the question 'What has been done?' prior to the question 'What remains to be done?'[29] The two questions are distinguished in such a way as to render divine action the focal concern of Christian ethics, for 'a Christian doctrine of activity which is primarily oriented towards the action of man is disoriented from the outset'.[30] From the essay it is hard to avoid the conclusion that, on such a basis, man acts only in a Pickwickian sense, since 'God in his activity is the real subject of our activity'.[31] It is precisely such a conclusion which the concept of analogous action disallows. By supplementing the classical Lutheran grounding of ethics in justification with the Christology/ analogy motif, Jüngel is able to give a firmer account of the status of human activity. There is here no 'thumping of the mighty transcendentalist drum',[32] but rather a tough refusal of any Christian ethics in which human agency is idealistically resolved into its divine ground.

The authenticity of man outside Christ

Barth supplies Jüngel with a way of developing, without prejudice to the place of Christology in anthropology, a 'realist' account of human agency and subjectivity in Christ: man in Christ has an objective place as subject and agent over against his divine ground. We now move on to examine whether there is a similar 'realism' about Jüngel's account of man outside Christ. 'Realism', like 'authenticity', is used here in a rather flexible way. Partly it refers to an attitude to human history, to a sense of the substantiality and definitive significance of all man's historical acts rather than of a partial selection of them or of a realm entirely transcending human history from which alone that history derives its meaning. As Popper remarks, 'A concrete history of mankind, if there were any, would have to be the history of all men. It would have to be the history of all human hopes, struggles, and sufferings. For there is no one man more important than any other.'[33] But 'realism' also involves a certain manner of procedure in theological anthropology:

a willingness to allow concepts derived from larger decisions to be broken down, modified or even discarded in the light of the counterfactual, in order more adequately to explain the field of reference. 'Realism' thus involves a multiplication of the number of explanatory concepts involved, precisely because only such a multiplication is adequate to the manifold nature of the material.

Neither of these two characteristics just outlined – the sense of the significance of all particulars, the refusal to submit to the pressure of an unwarranted conceptual economy – can often be found in Jüngel's writing on man outside Christ. We shall seek to illustrate this lack, and then suggest that the reason for it is to be sought in his conviction of the universally definitive and explanatory significance of the history of Jesus Christ.

To see how Jüngel develops the theme in hand, we return to the concept of the non-necessity of God. From our earlier discussion of the doctrine of God, we have seen that he uses the concept of divine non-necessity to affirm God's freedom: to deny that God is a worldly necessity is to prevent the reduction of God to 'a result or a logical postulate of our reality'.[34] Non-necessity is also, however, canvassed for anthropological reasons. That is to say, it is a concept which enables the formulation of that correct distinction between God and man which alone, according to the now-familiar argument, furnishes an adequate sense of the reality of man. And so, 'As a statement about man in the world, language about the worldly non-necessity of God says that man can be human without God.'[35]

It is at this point that the argument begins to break down. For it is very difficult to see how the claim that man can be human without God can cohere with the claim that humanity as such consists in expressing God. To say that man can be human without God is to envisage 'humanity' as properly attributable to man independently of his status in Christ: to be human *with* God is not so much to become human for the first time but to become more human, human in new ways. From this perspective, God is 'a freely-offered plus',[36] a superadded reality for man, whose 'humanity consists in becoming ever more human'.[37] Here, if anywhere, is full recognition that both God and man are real. Jüngel draws the threads together in three theses:

1.   Man and his world are interesting for their own sakes.
2.   God is above all interesting for his own sake.
3.   God makes man – interesting for his own sake – interesting in a new way.[38]

The tension between this recognition and the universal claim that 'to be human is to express God' will form the theme of the rest of this chapter.

Freedom

For all his insistence that to ground man in Christ is not to indulge in some form of anthropological reductionism, there is a strand in Jüngel's doctrine of man according to which man is not free to reject God and remain fully human. The problem arises initially in his account of human freedom, where the coherence of God and human freedom is maintained only when that freedom is actual as response to and not denial of God. God is not the ground of human freedom in the sense that he grants man an – ultimately contingent but nevertheless irreducibly significant – autonomy, in the exercise of which man may reject God without ceasing to be God. Rather, those acts in which such rejection is externalised are accorded an inferior ontological status in Jüngel's anthropology.

In his celebrated essay 'Cartesian Freedom',[39] Sartre observes in Descartes 'an autonomous thinking that posits itself – in each of its acts – in its full and absolute independence';[40] such is the 'entire intellectual responsibility'[41] of the act of judgement that 'every man *is* a freedom'.[42] Yet it is precisely at this point that Sartre detects Descartes' failure: by grounding the continuity and coherence of the *cogito* in God, 'he hypostasized in God the original and *constituent* freedom whose infinite existence he recognised by means of the *cogito* itself'.[43] It is against such an argument as Sartre's – against, that is, the proposal that the existence of God is *per se* a curtailment of that absolute liberty which constitutes human authenticity – that Jüngel implicitly directs himself. This he does by deploying a concept of freedom as grounded beyond man, as the result of *being liberated*. Such an account of the structure of freedom, moreover, presupposes a view of the self as constituted by receptivity towards that which lies beyond the self rather than as asserting or maintaining its free selfhood in the absolutising of the ego.[44]

Most significantly, then, freedom is a divine gift: 'freedom as understood by faith does not in any way belong to man. It comes to him.'[45] Freedom is inseparable from the event of receiving liberty, and this gift of freedom involves a reorientation of attitude towards the self. Freedom is freedom from the drive to establish the self through works which is the antithesis of passive receptivity towards God's justifying word. This, of course, is why Jüngel refuses any concept of freedom as an assertion of the self-identity and underivability of the ego: freedom is not self-created but received in the dissolution of the tense self-striving which characterises actuality. And so freedom, properly understood, entails 'a temporary cessation of our existence as agents, a saving interruption of our working at building the world and establishing our own identity'.[46]

It is significant that this 'saving interruption' is accomplished in the word of address: it is 'as a hearer' that 'man is free for the future'.[47] The dialogical character of human freedom as created and sustained in intercourse between selves and between the self and God emerges above all in the linguistic structure of human existence; human freedom is inseparable from man's condition as one who is addressed. In an essay co-authored with I.U. Dalferth, Jüngel argues that man is free only on the basis of the ability to produce symbolic systems – of which language is the most significant – through which his actions can be prestructured and so through which he is released from dominance by immediate reflex activity.[48] In the present context, the particular way in which language is a bearer of liberty is especially important. The freedom offered by the possession of a symbolic system such as language is realised in interpersonal communication, that is, in those events in which the self is constituted in being addressed. Such address creates a situation in which the offer of meaning can be *refused*: 'This experience of "no", of the possibility of refusal, is the origin of the capacity for freedom which is made possible by the other.'[49]

The strength of the argument just outlined is its support of the compatibility of human freedom with the contingency of man upon the existence of other man or of God.[50] No doubt his argument does pass over those instances where man's contingency upon the other is experienced as a threat to his authenticity.[51] Yet the most telling weakness of the account lies elsewhere, that is, in its inability to support its intended notion of freedom as the *possibility of refusal of what is proffered*. For at this point there again surfaces the incoherence between the wish to maintain that man can be human without God and the wish to retain the universality of the humanity of Jesus Christ as ontologically definitive of all men. The definition of all men out of the history of Jesus Christ stifles the full development of an account of contracausal freedom, of freedom to reject God.[52] The difficulty can be traced at several points in Jüngel's anthropological writing.

In an exegetical context the imbalance can be noted in earlier writing on the relationship between old and new, law and gospel, Adam and Christ, where there can be discerned a certain reluctance to take with real seriousness the ambiguity of Christian existence between the sinful past of self-identity through works and the future granted by God: the relation between the old and the new is deeply asymmetrical. In *Paulus und Jesus*, for example, it is claimed that 'the law becomes thematic out of the gospel as a surpassed reality'.[53] In making the old man 'under the law' entirely correlative to its being overcome in Christ, Jüngel invites criticism for making the past real only insofar as it is that which is excluded by the 'eschatological announcement of time' which fills the present with reference to the future.

At a more systematic level, a similar asymmetry can be detected in his discussions of the relation between the 'truth' and the 'actuality' of the being of man. In the same way that 'old' is entirely relative to 'new' (from which it receives all meaning and significance), so the 'actuality' of man in his self-realisation is far outweighed in definitive significance by the 'truth' of man's being which is realised by God. One consequence here is that not to realise the truth of man's being is to exist in self-contradiction, in a disjunction between actuality and truth. Actuality is, indeed, disproportionately significant in the definition of man to the extent that, in the last analysis, man cannot not be what God has determined him to be. 'Man can deny the determination of his being...but cannot abolish it. When man for his part does not affirm his affirmation by God, his human nature is not disturbed, but rather there is a contradiction in the *accomplishment* of what man is.'[54]

Above all, the difficulties of Jüngel's account emerge in the question of the ontological status of sin, and hence of its status in the definition of man – clearly a matter of some considerable importance in an anthropology which locates the 'truth' of man with such sharp singularity at a level beyond that of human acts. The problem can be stated as follows: whilst Jüngel insists upon the authenticity and full significance of human acts when they *express* the divinely-constituted person, his emphasis upon the person (and not the person's works) as the most fundamental stratum of human being commits him to an effective denial of the definitive status of those acts which *contradict* the person. The acts in which God is rejected do not determine the person of the agent.

Sin, by consequence, remains a surpassed reality, for whose description only the language of negation is fully appropriate. 'Sin remains...an attempt which is not to be fulfilled';[55] 'sin makes nothingness into something'.[56] Sin, that is, is only a positive historical force insofar as 'under the appearance of being the sinner celebrates nothingness'.[57] To call attention to Jüngel's concentration upon the negativity of sin rather than upon its positivity as human action fraught with consequence is not, of course, to dismiss his anthropology for failure to attend to the reality of sin.[58] It is, nevertheless, noteworthy that the definition of all men out of the history of Jesus Christ entails assertions of the ontologically ambiguous status of man's manifest self-determination.

Pressure towards these assertions comes, clearly, from the direction of larger decisions about the manner in which theological anthropology is to be pursued. Hick observes that: 'The privative view of the status of evil...follows inevitably from various prior positions of Christian faith and is valid within this context...Only a wider metaphysical framework of belief impels us to believe that the true status of evil is that of negation and lack within a universe whose positive nature is good.'[59] It is, indeed, a wider framework (in this case, of certain Christological proposals) which lies behind Jüngel's definition of sin and evil: sin is 'identifiable only in the light of the analogy between God and man'.[60] It is doubtless true that the considerable strength of the privative view of evil is its avoidance of a final dualism, and its refusal to allow an irreducible surd-like element which would threaten the divine sovereignty. Yet Jüngel's account avoids *that* problem only by abstraction from the dispersion of human reality, ordering and unifying human history at cost to the significance of its variety. His work here is highly instructive about his intellectual manner; deeply impressed by the power and fruitfulness of the insight that man is determined by God as the analogate of Jesus Christ, it may so invest its entire attention in that insight that it passes over the range of human darkness.[61]

These problems come together in the distinction between the 'ontic' and 'ontological' strata of human existence, a distinction to which Jüngel often returns. He makes the characteristic claim that 'justification by faith defines man theologically. This theological definition concerns the whole of mankind and therefore all men.'[62] This claim is very similar to the claim that to be human as such is to be a 'man who expresses God', and the similarity is nowhere more evident than in its attempt to deal with those parts of human history where the external evidence of justification is not evident. The distinction between 'ontic' and 'ontological' is introduced to cope with just this counterevidence. All men are ontologically defined in the event of justification. Although this determination may not be realised at the explicit ontic level, its lack of realisation cannot count as its denial. For the ontological stratum, the 'truth of life', is primordial over against the ontic actuality of man: 'man is ontologically derived from justification by God which takes place in Christ' and realises this 'ontically, insofar as he believes. In faith man *exists* as what he already *is* in Christ.'[63] The inclusivity of the justifying act of God in Christ is such that there can be 'no ontological godlessness of man'[64] – atheism, disbelief, sin, are a failure to realise at the ontic, existential level the ontological truth of the human condition.[65]

Reflections

The Christological grounding of humanity can be shown to be coherent with the authenticity, freedom and dignity of man as a further reality beyond God when man *expresses* God. But there is much in Jüngel's anthropology which suggests that when man rejects God, he rejects his own authentic humanity. For if he remained authentically human in such rejection, the exclusive identification of authentic humanity with being a 'man who expresses God' would have to be revised. On Jüngel's terms, the absolute and undifferentiated generality of the definition of all men in Christ has to remain unaffected by those configurations of human history in which it is denied.

The undoubted attractiveness of Jüngel's work here is its conceptual economy in the explanation of the human condition:[66] contradiction and complexity are eschewed by offering an all-embracing framework, a vision of the determination of all out of the humanity of Christ. But it remains an attractiveness bought at a cost to sensitivity towards the discontinuities of human history, a more 'pluralist' account of which might, as William James suggested, have 'but a sorry appearance. It is a turbid, muddled, gothic sort of an affair, without sweeping outline and with little pictorial nobility.'[67] One of the effects of Jüngel's doctrine of man is to level out the differences in human history, giving the appearance of an overall evenness of tone into which the erratic is absorbed. This evenness is guaranteed by the heuristic function and doctrinal content of Christology.

In order to draw the discussion together, we look in greater detail at two more general aspects of Jüngel's doctrine of man. The first is primarily a formal matter, and concerns the abstractness of Jüngel's anthropology. Because the humanity of Jesus is accorded preponderant significance, Jüngel's account is constructed largely without reference to the infinite variety of human history. Above all, it is the singularity of Jüngel's rendering of the 'truth' of life which is most problematic. The impetus of his theology derives from commitment to the inexhaustible richness of the history of Jesus for all subsequent history. Yet to claim that Jesus Christ is in this way of universal significance is not to claim that he is significant in the same way at all times and in all places. Jüngel's analysis of fundamental human structures and 'constants' in the constitution of man (man as hearer, man as speaker, man as believer and receiver) does not always make that distinction clear. In looking at Jüngel's Christology we noted the need for fuller attention to the modes of human history in which the 'effectiveness' of Jesus is mediated. Issues of the same complexion also emerge in his anthropology: there is here, too, a similar lack of specificity concerning the forms of life in which the Christological determination of man could be discerned.

From this perspective, Jüngel's language about 'distinguishing between God and man' may be insufficiently incisive fully to perform the task for which it is invoked (the avoidance of 'theomonism'). For such language reaches the limits of its usefulness when it has established in general terms that the world and God may not be confused without threat to the authenticity of both. It cannot undertake the more detailed examination of the substantiality of the human unless it becomes more particular, less wide-ranging in its mode – perhaps by narrative. Appeal to 'narrative' may often prove to be a fashionable theological ploy of dubious utility, especially when it effects too easy a resolution of complex problems concerning the rationality of faith and theology or the historical content of their claims. Yet to pay attention to man's stories about himself and his world may nevertheless bear fruit in ensuring that those features of human history which are contra-indicative to highly generalised theories of human nature would not be forgotten.[68] For attentiveness to narrative introduces that sense of the sheer phenomenality of human history which can only be engaged with in the particular instance. As Schopenhauer noted, in story-telling, as in history, 'we see...the mind engaged with the particular as such'.[69]

The second more general point is closely allied to this and concerns the 'holistic' view of history which Jüngel's Christology introduces into his thought. The view that the history of man may, from a certain perspective, be interpreted as a meaningful whole, is one that informs his anthropology implicitly. Indeed, the conviction that in human history the last word is not contradiction but correspondence, is basic to the temper of his work. His understanding of the Christian vision is that of an historical pattern from which the discordant is excised. 'If there is something which holds the world together at its heart, it is the correspondence between God and his creation; this correspondence in its turn is the ground of the fact that within the creation, too, there are correspondences in which the world is not absolutely contradictory.'[70]

Jüngel's theology is imbued with a suspicion of the discordant, a deep-seated dissatisfaction with the erratic. The effect of this is, we have seen, a certain underrating of the consequence of discrete historical particulars, and the elevation of a general pattern. Of course, *one* discrete particular is accorded massive significance, which cannot be reduced to its instantiation of a more general trend: the history of Jesus. Yet if Jüngel is saved from one species of historical holism by making Barth rather than Hegel his intellectual master,[71] he inherits thereby Barth's stress that the *grandes lignes* of history can all be traced to one focal particular, and that in this focus their fundamental coherence is guaranteed. Scepticism about the epistemological and methodological basis[72] and the moral and political defensibility[73] of synthetic accounts of history is beyond our scope. It is perhaps sufficient to note that scepticism of this kind may also be theologically appropriate for a Christian account of man in which the discreteness of Jesus' history does not smooth over but accentuates the unevenness of the history of the world of which it is part. In this sense, 'Christianity has an instinctive distrust of systematic philosophies of history which would put in our hands the key of intelligibility.'[74]

10. Towards a theology of the natural

Introductory

If one were to seek a contemporary Protestant dogmatician in Germany engaged by the problems usually associated under the term 'natural theology', it would be to the work of Pannenberg that one would most readily turn. For more, perhaps, than any other, Pannenberg has sought in his dogmatic work to engage in dialogue with disciplines other than theology. His early work *What is Man?*,[1] for example, co-ordinates its theological affirmations with insights derived from philosophical and social anthropology, and from the human and natural sciences.[2] It would be a mistake, however, to interpret Pannenberg as merely envisaging Christian theology as concerned with religious implications drawn from our inspection of the world of nature and human history: his understanding of the relationship between the Christian faith and the natural order is more dialectical than such a characterisation would suggest, and he speaks of the '*confrontation* of the Christian faith with the contemporary experience of reality'.[3] Pannenberg is more properly understood from the direction of his understanding of revelation as an occurrence within man's experience of nature and history.[4]

Pannenberg's writing frequently orients itself by a resolutely critical departure from Barth's work,[5] and, indeed, it is not uncommon to find Barth presented as the determined foe of any search for signs of God in the natural order.[6] Detractors from Barth's work have tended to draw attention to his earlier repudiations of natural theology, most notably in the first series of his Gifford lectures[7] and in the caustic exchange with Brunner, in the penultimate sentence of which he wrote of natural theology that: 'Only the theology and the church of the antichrist can profit from it.'[8] Critics have less commonly considered the implications of a passage in Barth's mature work which make an unusually fruitful contribution to the matter, namely the few paragraphs on the 'parables of the Kingdom of Heaven' in *Church Dogmatics* IV/3. These parables, Barth writes,

are to be witnesses of something new to all men, and to be newly apprehended by them all...recounted by Jesus, these everyday happenings become what they were not before, and what they cannot be in and of themselves...the New Testament parables are as it were the prototype of the order in which there can be other true words alongside the one Word of God.[9]

Along with one or two other recent writers,[10] Jüngel has sought to exploit this somewhat meagre source in the search for a natural theology. And his work here represents some of the furthest reaches of his attempt to build out from Barth.

What has attracted Jüngel to Barth's reflections is their closeness to his own concern for maintaining the reality of both God and man. The parables 'bring before us happenings from everyday life and the familiar stories of human action and inaction'.[11] In this way they form a testimony to the imprescriptible naturalness and substantial reality of the natural order: they are an affirmation of the 'unequivocally everyday character'[12] of the natural world. Nevertheless, the parables also testify to the underivability of revelation from the same natural order, for these everyday stories only bear witness to the Kingdom of God as they are transformed: the potential to reveal the Kingdom does not lie within them. 'As Jesus tells them, the material is everywhere transformed, and there is an equation of the Kingdom with them' so that they 'become real testimony to the real presence of God on earth, and therefore to the events of this real presence'.[13]

Link sums up Barth's thought succinctly when he writes that: 'The world is not a parable of the Kingdom of Heaven. It can only become such.'[14] The world *is* not a parable of the Kingdom, because if it were, its naturalness would somehow be qualified, and revelation would be derivable from worldly sources. The world *becomes* a parable of the Kingdom because revelation cannot be deduced from the natural order; yet in that becoming, the world is enhanced and augmented.

Out of this material come two clusters of problems, which Jüngel identifies as central for a contemporary discussion of natural theology and for an appraisal of previous models. The first problem concerns the relation of the particular to the universal. Jüngel consistently refuses to envisage natural theology as a general framework within which specifically Christian affirmations can be located. For such a conception wins universality only at cost to the highly particularised base of Christian theology: it compromises the scandalous particularity of revelation in Christ alone. The second set of problems focusses on a dissatisfaction with 'traditional' natural theology because of its failure to engage with the *possibilities* of the natural order. Natural theology is in Jüngel's mind 'traditionally' conceived as the search for evidence of God in the *actuality* of the world; because it concentrates in this way on what the world *is* rather than what the world might *become*, it is inattentive to the possibilities in which actuality is both disturbed and renewed.

The universal and the particular

We look first at Jüngel's criticism of the relationship between the particular and the universal in 'traditional' natural theology. By offering a 'conceptual framework'[15] for the specifically Christian, natural theology, he urges, wins a degree of universality for theological claims in such a way that the particular event of revelation is threatened. There occurs 'the inversion of the claim to *universal validity* [*Allgemeingültigkeit*] of this highly particular event into the assertion of a *generality* [*Allgemeinheit*] under which the unique event is subsumed as a particular example of a more extensive relationship'.[16]

Jüngel is particularly concerned to undertake the scrutiny of the concept of 'universality' which is at work. The 'traditional' model on his reading construes universality in such a way that the specifically Christian becomes simply an instance of a more general and generally-available truth. Universality is here understood as 'generality'. One effect of this is to compromise the place of faith in knowledge of God, by seeking to discover grounds for faith's knowledge which are generally-available beyond faith. Hence Jüngel seeks to contradict Pannenberg (whom he views as a modern exponent of the error) by arguing that 'a truth which furnishes grounds for faith does not have to be known *remota fide* in order to be able to furnish such grounds...The logic of faith contests any assertion that the ground of faith and the certainty of faith can be attained *remota fide*.'[17] The notion of 'generality' also has a further consequence, namely that a wedge is driven between natural theology and the theology of revelation, by positing a knowledge of God prior to and more general than that derived from revelation: 'The cardinal error of so-called natural theology consists in the way in which it distinguishes itself from the theology of revelation.'[18]

Even from such a summary presentation of Jüngel's argument, it is immediately apparent that his critique of 'natural theology' is neither sharp nor searching. His presentation is historically undiscriminating and schematic. He tends to use the term 'natural theology' as a portmanteau designation, suggesting that it refers to a coherent set of problems which remain historically constant, and neglecting the very significant divergences in approaches, tasks and methods to which a closer study of particular examples might draw attention.[19] Furthermore, he tends to light upon only those features in the rejected model which differ from the one which he wishes to commend, describing and judging these in the light of his own presuppositions. Throughout his discussion of the relation of 'natural' and 'revealed' theology, for example, he makes no admission that there might be taken a broader view of revelation than his own which would immediately qualify the hiatus between the two models he contrasts so sharply.

Jüngel is attacking a straw man: but the attack is most instructive in indicating the nature of his alternative proposal. He wishes to replace 'generality' by 'general validity'. The grain of truth in previous attempts lies in their attempted demonstration that – as Jüngel puts it none too precisely – 'God' is a word with a universal claim,[20] a word 'whose *particular claim* at the same time has *general validity*'.[21] The rejected model imperfectly formulated its task by seeking to show the *universal availability* of the truth of faith, failing to attend to the fact that 'to the highly particularised event...there belongs an unconditional claim to universal validity'.[22] Not only does this mean that natural theology is for Jüngel a problem properly located 'within the dogmatic treatise, and therefore in the process of *fides quaerens intellectum*'.[23] It also means that a more effective correlation of the universal and the particular can only be achieved by firm adherence to the *concretissimum*, the punctiliar event of revelation in the history of Jesus. In his *Theology of Nature*,[24] G. S. Hendry draws a helpful distinction between the 'theology of nature' as the attempt 'to establish a knowledge of nature in the light of God' and 'natural theology' as the attempt 'to establish a knowledge of God in the light of nature'.[25] In terms of this distinction, Jüngel's work is much more a theology of nature: it is a theological account of the natural order, similar in presuppositions and method to, say, a theological account of man.

Nevertheless, it would not be wholly accurate to suggest that he envisages natural theology as nothing more than another part of dogmatics. Occasionally he proposes that, whilst natural theology may not demonstrate the grounds of faith outside faith, it may make statements about the natural order which are intended to evoke a degree of acceptance *remota fide*. And so, for instance, 'one must be able to formulate again every statement in theological anthropology in such a way that, without naming God, it is comprehensible, meaningful and profitable'.[26] *Deo remoto*, such statements are 'comprehensible and enlightening',[27] and can be 'acknowledged as true statements about the being of man',[28] even 'verifiable in the horizon of the analysis of human being [*Dasein*]'.[29]

Jüngel is not here drifting back into the notion of a generally-available knowledge of God apart from faith. He is simply suggesting that a theological affirmation does possess some validity apart from faith. But in such a context that affirmation changes from 'a statement of the gospel to a statement of the law, from an unequivocally beneficial statement to one that is ambivalent'.[30] Statements of faith function as law when 'the *specific* plus...of faith remains unformulated'.[31]

Clearly he has not yet undertaken a sufficiently detailed examination of the epistemological moves involved in the kind of natural theology which he wishes to prosecute. And the inattention to detail is exacerbated by a recurrent need for some particular examples to flesh out his rather skeletal and formal account. His writings on natural theology offer an almost exclusively theoretical vantage-point, from which it is not easy to envisage the detailed substantive content such a natural theology might be expected to have. But these points aside, it is clear that Jüngel has tried to bring out the *particula veri* of natural theology (the demonstration of the universal validity of theological assertions) by reversing its universal direction. Rather than working out the theological entailments of a general analysis of the order of nature, natural theology on Jüngel's model would undertake the analysis of the universal entailments of the particular event of revelation.

A more natural theology

In his approach to the second of the two problems identified above, Jüngel moves on to firmer ground; his writing gains in confidence and loses some of the conceptual flaccidity noted in the previous discussion.

The reversal of direction from the universal to the particular is partly undertaken to avoid a compromise of the Christological *concretissimum*. But behind it lies a further concern to draw attention to what he calls the 'capacity for enhancement' of the natural order,[32] in the light of which Jüngel presses for a revision of the procedure of 'traditional' natural theology. For a natural theology which simply scans the natural economy for 'signals of transcendence' is essentially conservative of the settled structures of the actuality of that economy.[33] It merely accepts the natural order as it is, and so inhibits the disclosure of ways in which it might be taken beyond its present state. There is none of that 'transformation' of the natural order which Barth noted in the parables of the Kingdom. Jüngel expands on Barth by envisaging natural theology as an enterprise which seeks out of the particular to cast light on the totality of the natural order, in which light its new and further possibilities are revealed and the order of nature enhanced: 'The Christian faith *draws attention to God* as the one who, over against all that is self-evident is ever more self-evident. The Christian faith speaks of God in such a way that it teaches the enhancement of the self-evident.'[34]

The drift of Jüngel's thought here can be caught most easily by looking at some of the central concepts and vocabulary involved. A recurring metaphor is that of the 'new light' shed upon the natural order by the event of revelation.[35] The combination of the ideas of novelty and illumination lays out Jüngel's main contention here, namely that of the *historicality* of the naturalness of nature. There is within the natural order a readiness to be deepened and enlarged, to become more than it is at present, by having its potentialities laid bare. In more conceptual terms, the same point is made by the notion of revelation as a 'critical comparative' which 'sets in a new light that which has been hitherto self-evident...This critical comparative could very properly be called eschatological, reminding us of Luther's Christmas hymn: "Das ewig Licht geht da herein, gibt der Welt ein neuen Schein".'[36] Revelation calls into question that which is self-evident, the actuality of the world, not by abolishing it but by demonstrating its historicality, its capacity for becoming and enhancement: 'The implication of this enhancement for the logic of the self-evident is that the self-evident is to be conceived as *historical*. The historicality of the self-evident allows the enhancement of the self-evident.'[37] Jüngel's natural theology views itself as a theory of this capacity for enhancement, and criticises the tradition it wishes to supplant for failure to accomplish this, accepting the actuality of the world and so inhibiting the emergence of new possibilities.

One way in which Jüngel does seek to earth his discussion is through deploying the concept of 'experience with experience', *Erfahrung mit der Erfahrung*.[38] He writes that: 'The Christian faith cannot be derived from any worldly experience. But of itself it is as it were an experience with experience, opened up by God: an experience in which all previous experiences and experience itself are re-experienced.'[39] Jüngel is not, it should again be noted, suggesting that natural experience of the world and of self is a kind of rudimentary experience of God. G. Green contends that 'experience with experience' 'functions for Jüngel precisely as the "feeling of absolute dependence" for Schleiermacher and "ultimate concern" for Tillich: it locates the anthropological point at which it becomes possible to speak of God'.[40] But his interpretation is only half correct, for the whole thrust of the notion of 'experience with experience' is to preserve a critical distance between faith and experience of self and the world. This critical distance is essential if faith is to push back the limits of the actuality of experience in order to further and renew rather than merely to conserve. For experience itself militates against its own historicality, and thus against the possibility of its own amplification. Past experiences, that is, tend to preside over the present and in this way to set limits to its possibilities. Faith is an experience *with* experience precisely because it is only at one remove from experience that it can counter the tendency of experiences to 'make themselves absolute'.[41] In faith's experience with experience, experience becomes an object of renewed experience,[42] of a critical appraisal which disturbs its dictatorship over the present and provokes the emergence of further potential. Here the structural parallels between Jüngel's account of human experience and his account of human temporality are illuminating. He sees the task of a theology of time as reflection upon the 'eschatological announcement of time' in which man is liberated from the past for a present heavy with reference to the future. Correspondingly, the task of natural theology is to reflect upon the 'experience with experience' in which the tyranny of past experience is broken by its becoming the '*object* of experience'.[43] Thus 'to take the problem of natural theology seriously means...*out of the event of God's revelation*...to lay bare a new possibility of experience, through which our everyday experiences are...opened to critical questioning'.[44]

Jüngel's natural theology is an attempt to formulate the liberation from the compulsions of actuality which revelation accomplishes by the granting of new possibilities. Thus natural theology is concerned, not so much with the availability of knowledge of God *remota fide*, as with the possibilities of the natural order, with what that order may become. Its concern is to show that here, too, 'more is possible'.[45]

We saw earlier that Jüngel feels the language of parable and metaphor to be most appropriate to express the occurrence of new possibilities in the world, for in the disturbance of the system of reference of literal speech there can be traced the presence of 'new being'. It is thus characteristic that in the present context he should speak of the world as the *parable* of God: 'in the light of grace, nature gains the new quality of becoming a parable of the One who comes'.[46]

We take the points of that last programmatic statement in reverse order. Jüngel emphasises that the world becomes a parable of God who *comes*. This is in order to underline that the new possibilities of the natural order with which natural theology concerns itself are not intrinsic to that order. 'God is to be conceived as the one who in Jesus Christ *has come* to the world and as such does not cease to come to the world.'[47] God, that is, is not a necessary part of the world's structure but rather a 'freely offered plus'.[48] It is only God's *coming* to speech which makes possible the 'gain to language' in which worldly discourse is given that new and further reference narrated in parable and metaphor. Similarly, it is only when God *comes* to the world from outside that the natural order becomes a parable of God. The possibilities of nature, like those of language, depend upon the creative *potentia aliena*, upon 'donations of the possible'.[49]

Jüngel stresses that nature becomes the parable of the God *who comes* in order to ensure the preservation of the gracious character of the world's possibilities. He stresses, second, that the world *becomes* such a parable in order to safeguard nature's 'capacity for

enhancement'. Parable leads 'to the disclosure of a new dimension
of actuality and to a making more precise of speech of the actual';[50]
nature becomes a parable of God when new dimensions – its
possibilities – are disclosed. It is the task of natural theology to
trace the process of that disclosure, showing how the world's
becoming a parable of God highlights 'the historicality of being'.[51]
In this way it overcomes the failure of 'traditional' natural
theology to appreciate 'not only the historicality and destructibility
of the self-evident but also its capacity for enhancement'.[52]
Moreover, by using the language of 'becoming', Jüngel also
underlines the free, 'playful',[53] indeterminate character of the
parabolic. This lifts the relationship of God and the world out of
the idiom of necessity. With regard to the synoptic parables, for
instance, Jüngel remarks that 'particular metaphors and parables
are as such never necessarily defined as such'.[54] Nature *is* not a
parable of God but *becomes* such, its naturalness freely enhanced.

But what of the central contention, that the world becomes a
parable? The category of parable, we have seen, condenses a large
number of Jüngel's convictions about the relationship between
God and the world, and the inalienable naturalness of nature which,
nevertheless, can be enhanced. Jüngel transfers to the order of
nature the attributes of parabolic discourse, most especially the way
in which such discourse discloses the emergence of new being.

The God who comes to the world (x→a) makes use of that which is
self-evident in the world in such a way that he shows himself to be even
more self-evident over against it. It is self-evident that for the greater value
of a treasure hidden in a field one would give up everything to gain that
greater value. This self-evidence appears in a completely new light when
it comes to speech as a parable for the Kingdom of God which lets itself
be found.[55]

Thus Jüngel's contention is that 'in the light' of grace, the whole
natural order may become a parable as its self-evidence is augmented
by the 'expansion of the familiar world'.[56]

This talk of the natural order as a 'parable' is more problematic
than Jüngel's account suggests. It is certainly clear how parabolic
language straddles two systems of reference in such a way that the
limits of language are pushed back. But when Jüngel attempts to
trace a similar movement in the natural order as a whole, the
argument becomes increasingly impressionistic. His claim requires,
for example, a sophisticated theory of the double meaning of
events, objects and persons in the world, and it is just such a theory

which is so far lacking. The concept of parable is thus over-freighted, and is unable adequately to perform the tasks for which it is invoked.[57] A clear instance of precisely how a worldly state of affairs might become a parable of God would be immensely useful in shifting the discussion beyond tantalisingly general references to 'die Natur' and 'die Welt'.

But however overstrained the concept may become in Jüngel's writing, and however much it may stand in need of sustained interrogation and clarification, the focus upon parable does help him to perform the task which occupies the centre of the stage in most of his work: an account of the mutually irreducible realities of God and man in which the advent of God makes man and his world ever more human and worldly. For as C. F. Evans suggests in an illuminating essay, parable 'performed within the strategy of the gospel as a whole the functions of a kind of natural theology',[58] using the term 'natural theology' 'to focus the appeal to the natural order which is of the essence of parable'.[59]

Jüngel seeks to show that one of the richest *dogmatic* resources which parable contains is its engagement with and demonstration of the potential within 'daily life and the observable world'.[60] This engagement Jüngel makes fruitful for the elaboration of a natural theology. If a concluding definition were to be offered, it would be that natural theology is 'a hermeneutic of the self-evident',[61] an interpretative theory of the enrichment of man and his world by the God who comes, a demonstration of the universally expansive scope of the particular. Such a natural theology is what Jüngel calls a 'more natural theology',[62] attempting in its formulations to catch the movement of nature as it becomes ever more natural. 'Over against so-called natural theology, theology of the Word of God...is *more natural theology*...In that it acknowledges that both God and man are interesting for their own sakes, such a more natural theology...gives each their proper honour.'[63]

Reflections

Jüngel's writings here are no doubt unsatisfying at a first reading: issues are tackled only in the broadest terms, and his characteristic firmness of line is at times blurred. Yet these features do not indicate a failure properly to address himself to the matter in hand. Rather, they show the inchoate state of his contribution (which has only recently been gathered together in the collection

Entsprechungen), as well as the lack within the fairly narrow span of his theological authorities of a major paradigm in natural theology by which his own discussions could be oriented. Jüngel is here moving into territory which is not familiar and in which there are not recognised areas of discussion or bodies of literature to act as landmarks. Because he is not so much entering into traditions of argument as creating them, and because his work is still in the process of maturation, we have only the outlines of a theory and not its detailed development and defence.

What is clear is that Jüngel's natural theology can only be properly understood from the context of his overall theological development and concerns. It is only from the context of his increasing emphasis on the need to correlate theological Christocentrism with a sense of the substantiality of the natural that his work on the 'naturalness of nature' comes into its own.[64] Because of this, his natural theology is a good barometer of the character of his present theological engagements, as well as of the areas where further work needs to be done. The foundational engagement, which furnishes his theology with both its overall framework and its constructive energy, we have seen to be two-fold: an affirmation of the universal significance of the history of Jesus Christ, and of the natural order as authentic and relatively autonomous.

These two concerns are most effectively dovetailed in his work on metaphor, analogy and parable, and in his theology of the natural: here a sense of nature's substantial reality is most effectively incorporated. The concept of the *historicality* of nature or language offers a means of affirming that nature and man are able to become ever more natural, interesting in new ways. And so the import of Jüngel's most recent writing is that the Christian vision is not the eschatological contradiction of the natural, nor even the perspective from which alone the natural can be said to be truly real and meaningful. Rather, that vision offers the renewal and furtherance of the natural, an augmentation of the value of which it is already indefeasibly possessed.[65]

Conclusion

Jüngel is already a weighty voice in contemporary continental theology, and promises to become a thinker of major importance in the history of twentieth-century Protestantism. Because his contribution is so wide-ranging, it is difficult to identify any one area in which his work is of overarching significance. His sophisticated work on the theology of language shows that in certain respects a good deal of English writing on religious discourse lacks a vigorously imaginative understanding of some key features of Christian talk of God. His work on the doctrine of God, and notably on the question of divine impassibility, is particularly fruitful in combining a richly dramatic and narrative account of God's suffering with an alertness to all-important questions concerning divine aseity. But it is perhaps above all in the area of anthropology and theological ethics that Jüngel has a uniquely creative contribution to make to contemporary theological reflection. He puts down a challenge to demonstrate *on the basis of a theology of grace* that human agency is interesting and important.

At present that challenge is one which Jüngel himself is only in the process of taking up. But it is for all that arguable that his most significant theological achievement may turn out to be that of putting back onto the theological agenda some very large questions concerning the relation of the gracious God to his human creatures. More specifically, he has sought to inquire after the kind of account of that relation which is entailed by understanding Jesus Christ as the starting-point for all Christian reflection about God and man. It is this question which forms the implicit theme of most of the areas which we have examined in previous chapters. It emerges in his attempt to characterise God's will or independence in such a way that suffering and death can be predicated of him without threat to his aseity. It emerges, too, in his various attempts to clarify the function of the doctrine of the Trinity in Christian theology, and above all in his writings on fundamental theological ethics. Crucially, it finds expression in the central concept of analogy or correspondence. And the keystone of the whole edifice is Christology. This concluding section seeks to draw together the various threads of the previous discussion by returning to two crucial areas of Jüngel's work: the function of Christology in his theological procedure, and its adequacy as a basis for his theological convictions concerning the complementarity between God and the world.

Christology and theological method

One of the real benefits of studying Jüngel's work is that it offers a worked example to show how the rather indefinite characterisation 'Christocentric' might be filled out.[1] It is clear that in Jüngel's case that term describes not only dogmatic commitments but also convictions about the way in which doctrine is to be constructed. Whilst the Christological framework of Jüngel's theology is everywhere massively apparent, he has undertaken little detailed examination of its underlying structure. In what follows, then, we are seeking to draw out methodological points from beneath the surface of the texts, tracing procedures which are usually implicit and rarely manifest themselves in self-conscious reflection.

Jüngel claims that a proper theology is one which 'allows Jesus Christ to be its starting-point'.[2] The metaphor of 'starting-point' is one which expresses the conviction that Christology is *the* foundational doctrine: not merely one *locus* alongside others but the basis upon which all *loci* are built. Jüngel's use of the metaphor is most explicit in remarks in praise of Barth's theological method. Noting that for Barth 'progress in theology meant...nothing else than starting afresh',[3] he goes on to explain that 'Barth had in mind a specific, concrete starting-point...and he called it concrete because the starting-point has a name: Jesus Christ. Upon this one concrete starting-point he reflected without compromise until the very end.'[4] It is noteworthy that Jüngel picks up in Barth not only the singularity of the 'one concrete starting-point', but also its personal specificity: theological assertions are measured, not by an abstract Christ-principle, but by the history of Jesus Christ – Barth 'was but little concerned with the general question of the *archē* [origin]'.[5]

This way of construing the procedural centrality of Christology is often implicit in Jüngel's own work. It emerges, for example, in his emphasis on theology as an activity free of support from ancillary sciences, its task that of uncompromising 'holding-fast to its subject-matter'.[6] The point is not simply that theology is not history or metaphysics; rather it involves the more elaborate claim that the 'subject-matter' of theology is Jesus Christ, whose history provides the starting-point for theological work on many different fronts and also gives theology its self-understanding, its distinctiveness *vis-à-vis* other disciplines, and its inner coherence.

At various points in the preceding analysis we have questioned the usefulness of the 'starting-point' metaphor as a prescription for theological procedure, asking whether it may not obscure the multi-level nature of theological discourse.[7] We shall also come to ask whether the implied method is, in fact, one which Jüngel follows consistently. We shall find that what sometimes takes place in his work is a more complex series of operations involving different levels of argument which are not properly accounted for in terms of the metaphor, which is thus both constrictive as a recommendation and descriptively imprecise.

Another aspect of the methodological centrality which Jüngel ascribes to Christology could be described by saying that Christology gives *direction* to his theology: it functions as a 'route-finding procedure',[8] helping him to find a way over the whole theological territory. This use of Christology can be seen in many instances, where substantive proposals (whether explicit or not) about the significance of Jesus Christ enable Jüngel to get purchase on particular problems in Christian doctrine. The nature of spiritual conflict is to be learnt from the experience of Jesus;[9] the material content of the Word of God as a Word of appeal addressed to mankind in the crucified Christ determines the character of its infallibility;[10] questions about the relationship between science and theology may not be answered in abstraction from 'the poverty of Jesus' which is to inform theological rationality.[11] Or again, the foundational structures of theological ethics,[12] or the contours of theological concepts of truth,[13] freedom[14] and language[15] (the list is not at all exhaustive) are all to be Christologically moulded, in the sense that Christology provides 'a basic interpretative structure for the explication of other areas of doctrinal material'.[16]

Accordingly, Jüngel's practice is often to approach theological problems with prior Christological assertions firmly in mind, and to test any resultant answers for coherence with those assertions. In this way, Christology offers a way of attaining theological consistency. This can be exemplified from his work on baptism, where he is especially concerned to establish a criterion to give a proper univocity to a theology of baptism. Such a criterion Jüngel finds in 'the doctrine of justification, whose truth lies in the fact that it lays uncompromising emphasis on Christology'.[17] There are two levels to Jüngel's point here. The first is that it is Christology which lies at the heart of the doctrine of justification, which is thus Christologically derived, and not simply a relatively independent theologoumenon. The second is that justification, understood out of Christology as 'Sachkriterium'[18] for a theology of baptism, helps attain 'a harmonious theology of baptism'.[19] In this way, Jüngel uses Christology to attain an ideal of inner harmony and consistency.

Because of the place afforded to Christology in the total theological context, the structure of theological argument on which Jüngel places considerable emphasis is, in a loose sense, that of inference, in that the direction of theological procedure is from Christology towards other theological *loci*. This inferential argumentation is a large part of what is involved in Jüngel's stress on analogy, without which, he writes, 'there can be no theology'.[20] In procedural terms, analogy is the formal expression of the foundational role of Christology. As we have seen, the way in which Jüngel sets about the construction of a theological doctrine of man exemplifies the point. 'Analogical argumentation' might at first sight seem to suggest a movement from the world towards the divine: we know (to some degree) how to think and speak of man, and need to learn how to think and speak of God in such a way that our concepts and words about him correspond to their more familiar use in articulating the world. But it is precisely against any such suggestion that the known realities of the world can function as the foundational principle that Jüngel's style of inferential argumentation directs itself. So staunch is his conviction of the ontological and epistemological priority of Jesus Christ that it is Jesus' history which forms the known, the foundational principle upon which all else is built. The history of Jesus Christ is the *analogans* whose significance is to be extended to the definition of man by arguing towards conclusions in anthropology *per analogiam* from conclusions about the history of Jesus. By inference from the humanity of Jesus the truth of the condition of all men is to be discovered.[21]

Out of this rather bald sketch of the place of Christology in theological method, three issues arise which in their different ways all converge on the question of the flexibility of such a restricted theological method.

(1) The first issue concerns Jüngel's use of the New Testament. We have seen how, for example, he makes use of the doctrine of justification (and so ultimately of the Christology of which it is a function) as a way of moving from 'the plurality of different and clearly distinguishable statements about baptism in the New Testament',[22] from a mere 'collection of baptismal theologoumena',[23] to a harmonious theology of baptism. This search for what Käsemann calls an 'interpretative criterion'[24] to unify or at least to stabilise the relationship between differing New Testament theologies is one which has been apparent from the start of Jüngel's work in *Paulus und Jesus*, where he sought to bring together Jesus and Paul as 'two speech-events which follow each other as events in a tradition of language'.[25]

Jüngel is, of course, correct to emphasise that the New Testament is given cohesion by the centrality for its authors of who Jesus Christ was and is and what he did and continues to do: the life, death and resurrection of Jesus Christ constitute that without which there would be no New Testament.[26] But its unity is one 'of direction and vision, and not of formulation'.[27] It is this which is not always clearly grasped in Jüngel's work: he tends to make one formulation the criterion for all others, and so to construe the unity of the New Testament on a rather cramped basis. Later work, as we have seen, shows particular evidence of this assimilation of the whole of Christology to one particular motif, the Pauline 'word of the cross'. Jüngel does not always clearly distinguish between the centrality of the person and work of Christ for the New Testament and the centrality of one particular formulation of the significance of that person and work. 'Christology should not be narrowly confined to one particular assessment of Christ, nor should it play one off against another, nor should it insist on squeezing all the different New Testament conceptualisations into one particular "shape", but it should recognize that from the first the significance of Christ could only be apprehended by a diversity of formulations which though not always strictly compatible with each other were not regarded as rendering each other invalid.'[28]

(2) Moving from the exegetical area, there is a further question which concerns Jüngel's claim to be using Christology as a foundational, pivotal or focal doctrine, inference from which

constitutes the basic mode of theological argument. Despite the method explicitly located in Barth and often implied in his own writing, there are also pieces of argument in Jüngel's work which are more 'field-encompassing'[29] than the metaphor of 'starting-point' would suggest. As an initial example, we might look at the relation of Christology to the doctrine of God. At one point Jüngel suggests that Christological factors simply *purify* and *specify* speech and thought about God, so that 'in faith in Jesus as the Christ, faith in God is brought to truth and purity':[30] one-directional inference is not envisaged. Elsewhere, however, he denies that there can be any 'non-Christological' doctrine of God, and that such a concept of God is 'the general anthropological presupposition of the Christian faith'.[31] Because 'God has become... accessible in and through Jesus',[32] all true knowledge of God is in him alone. The difference between the two proposals shows that Jüngel is unclear as to whether the relationship between Christology and the doctrine of God is one of linear, inferential argument or whether the two *loci* interact in a more complex way. If it is the latter, then a more subtle account of theological procedure is called for than the simple metaphor. If it is the former, then it is difficult to see how God could be recognised in the history of Jesus without some minimal knowledge of the divine. A minimal knowledge of God is a prerequisite if the observer is to interpret the history of Jesus as divine in origin and content: 'Only if "God" is a meaningful term to him, can he attribute what he experiences to God as its source.'[33]

There are, in short, passages in Jüngel's work which display a tendency to oversimplify the nature of theological discourse by making Christology into an exclusive heuristic device with regard to other areas of doctrine. As Wingren puts it, 'talk about *the* theological method obscures the situation'.[34] In the course of our exposition we have sought to show that Jüngel is not always alert to the fact that the different *loci* in theology are mutually informative, interpretative and corrective. There is much truth in Pannenberg's remark that 'the relationship between Christology and anthropology, as also that between Christology and the doctrine of God, is one of mutual grounding, in the same way that the fundamental Christological affirmation of the unity of God and man presupposes a knowledge of God and man and yet alters their relationship on both sides'.[35]

(3) A final question seeks to discover whether the way in which

Jüngel focusses on Christology tends to promote a hermeneutical deficiency, namely underemphasis on realities other than Jesus Christ. We will return presently to the substantive issues which arise here, especially in the area of human agency. In the present hermeneutical context it is necessary to ask whether Jüngel's work displays sufficient interest in 'the practical and theoretical mediations of meaning and truth in history'.[36] There is a sense in which his account of the 'effective history' of Jesus is excessively abstract, in that it does not contextualise its discussion of 'present-day faith in Jesus Christ'[37] or render such faith in sufficiently concrete terms. Certainly Jüngel accords a formal place in his hermeneutics to the thematisation of the present situation of all talk about Jesus Christ.[38] But his actual practice often suggests that the move from early Christian narration of the saving significance of Jesus to contemporary language about him is relatively unproblematic. Often he seems to assume that once the 'effectiveness' of historical being has been established, the hermeneutical task is well on its way to completion. But the task in fact only begins there, for it is not at all obvious what would constitute a re-telling of Jesus' story, or how the effectiveness of that story could be recognised, appropriated or articulated in language, thought or action. Re-telling Jesus' story in a meaningful way involves doing justice not only to Jüngel's criterion of reference back to the life and ministry of Jesus but also to the contexts of such narration.

In a review of Ernst Fuchs' *Marburger Hermeneutik*, Jüngel observed that 'human talk of God...must be comprehensibly translated into those situations which befit speech of God...It must be correctly placed'.[39] If this placing is not adequately accomplished in his work, the reasons are primarily substantive. That is to say, they are to be sought in Jüngel's insistence that the history of Jesus Christ far outweighs all other histories in significance, since it is definitive and 'the definitiveness of the divine revelation and the singularity of the God who reveals himself means that God's history cannot be reduced to other histories'.[40] It is telling that in attempting to safeguard the irreducibility of Jesus' history, Jüngel is led to polarise the one, definitive history of God and all other histories. Not only is such a polarisation insensitive to the necessary mediations of God's history; it is also born of a refusal to allow that Jesus Christ is in some sense imitable, a refusal which rests on a clear delineation of the boundaries between Christ and the church.

Many English readers will feel that Jüngel goes so far so quickly because he pursues one line of inquiry without attending to other, equally pertinent, possibilities. One of the most significant issues which his work raises for an English audience, then, is that concerning the character of theological pluralism. It is true that pluralism has by now acquired the status of orthodoxy; Gellner is to a degree just in seeing this state of affairs as faddish *laissez-faire*, indulged in by those who have ceased to regard 'monism' as an attractive alternative.[41] That monism *is* an attractive alternative, whether as the rigorous adoption of one intellectual strategy,[42] or as an overall vision of the coherence of human history, the student of Jüngel's writings cannot fail to note. But neither can he fail to note an intellectual manner which might benefit from at least some sense of the erratic nature of historical sequence or of the frequent unhelpfulness of general procedural recommendations when faced with a particular problem. Nor, indeed, can he ignore the way in which a vision of such totalities as 'humanity' and 'history' may suppress the counterfactual.

Theodor Adorno once suggested that a style of intellectual engagement which exalts the general may evacuate the contra-evidential of some of its power to contradict. For Adorno, the essay is the literary form most appropriate to articulate a vision which refuses the synthetic, for the essay 'thinks in breaks, in the way that reality is broken, and finds its unity through the breaks rather than by smoothing them out'.[43] Adorno's collection of brief studies, *Minima Moralia*, illustrates 'the disconnected and non-binding character of the form, the renunciation of explicit theoretical cohesion'.[44] If Jüngel resists pressure towards such a renunciation (and he does indeed resist, massively), it is above all because the motif of *Entsprechung*, 'correspondence', outweighs all paradox and dialectic.[45] It is in refusing to lose sight of the correspondences that both the strength and the weakness of his theology lie.

Distinguishing between God and man

At the beginning of the posthumous fragment on *The Christian Life*, Barth wrote that

The Word of God, with which dogmatics (and consequently theological ethics) is concerned at every point as the basis, object, content, and norm of true church proclamation, is...Jesus Christ in the divine – human unity

of his being and work. In God's Word, then, we are dealing both with
God and with man: with God acting in relation to man and with man acting
in relation to God...At every point in true church proclamation it must
and will be a matter of both.[46]

Barth's words would form a fitting epigraph to Jüngel's most
substantial dogmatic achievement, which is that of elaborating a
theology of the complementarity of God and man through the use
of the notion of the 'correspondence' between God and the human
self. Earlier chapters have tried to explore the adequacy of Jüngel's
Christology as the basis for the kind of account of the relation
between God and the world which he wishes to make, and have
observed that at certain points – notably over the reality of human
sin and rejection of God – there are signs of strain. What is needed
is not so much a qualification of the concept of 'correspondence'
as a much more explicit and extended treatment of the shape taken
by human lives which 'correspond to' God. Above all, Jüngel's
theology needs to devote more space to exploring the nature of
human agency. He has perceived very acutely that it is in the
account they offer of human action that Barth's last writings give
substantial ground for the refutation of the charge of 'Christomonism'. Nevertheless, it is in just this area that Jüngel's own
thinking stands in need of extension and specification. How might
his initial mapping of the area be done in more detail?

First, there is need to inquire more closely into the character of
grace, and especially into what might be called its *imperatival*
aspects.[47] Jüngel most commonly speaks of grace as a gift which
presents man with a prior accomplishment on his behalf, with
status achieved. Consequently his anthropology gives great weight
to passivity, receptivity, and 'hearing'. Only occasionally does he
complement the 'gift' notion of grace with that of grace as a call
which evokes or invites a response (as in the account of 'address'
as 'meaning preferred for acceptance or refusal' in 'Sprache als
Träger der Sittlichkeit'). He generally subsumes the imperative
under the indicative: the call is heavily outweighed by the gift.
Behind this, of course, lies a denial that the stature of man as agent
can be achieved independently of the vicarious accomplishment of
human reality in the person and work of Christ.

And so in a recent essay on the nature of peace, for example,
Jüngel argues that what is most distinctive in a Christian understanding of peace is its 'indicative...way of speaking' which 'is in
striking contrast to the existential dimension of striving'.[48] This

indicative is, moreover, a Christological indicative: 'Jesus Christ is our peace...The indicative of peace is...constituted and guaranteed in the one person in whom God became a man for men'.[49] The result of this characteristic emphasis on the indicative is to leave unexamined how peace can properly be attributed to man when its accomplishment involves neither his consent nor his agency. Because in effect Jüngel divorces 'peace' from 'peacemaking', he does not specify how the creation of peace might involve human action in response to grace.

There are indications in his very positive reception of the last fragments of the *Church Dogmatics* that Jüngel would be open to the concept of grace as elicitation, as that which calls as well as that which states and accomplishes.

Grace elicits rather than invades in that the agent must actively respond, not just passively receive. Grace elicits rather than infuses in that nothing fundamentally non-human is introduced as an extension of given human powers. The creaturely response considered in itself is never more than creaturely. Elicitation also differs from acquirement in that virtue is evoked and sustained from without: it is not simply self-activated and self-directed. The agent is drawn to do what he cannot do by himself. The relation between grace and human love may be called interpersonal, but it is also asymmetrical.[50]

Deeper inquiry into the imperatival aspect of grace would of course by no means deny the validity of envisaging grace as a gift over and above merit or achievement. But it would enable greater elaboration of the human response of moral action, whilst retaining a full acknowledgement that such action is precisely that: *responsive*, reactive, initiated and sustained from without and not purely self-directed or self-realised.

To use the language of call, invitation, elicitation in order to describe grace is to spell out what humanity distinguished from God might look like. It is, in other words, to say that human response to God is theologically interesting (interesting, that is, because of who God is). This might be developed by opening up a second line of inquiry in which Jüngel's theology has so far evinced little interest, but one in which it has a stake if the idea of man as 'one who expresses God' is to have real resonance. This area is that of the analysis of moral deliberation. Like both Barth and Bultmann,[51] Jüngel probably shies away from detailed work in this area because of a characteristically Lutheran suspicion of human sanctity as a possession or attribute of the believer rather than as that which is located in the holiness of Christ.[52] But without at least some attempt to describe how the indicative is transformed into a chosen policy by a human agent, talk of man as real over against God runs the risk of lacking substance. Jüngel's insistence that such is the nature of God's self-revelation that the reality of man is affirmed needs to be given greater edge by some elaboration of morality as a human project, in which the agency of the self and its duration in moral discrimination and choice have a distinctive place.

Understanding grace in this way means that questions of moral choice, and of character and virtue, become more interesting than Jüngel's account of the distinction between God and the world generally allows. But it also means that we need to ask whether his very clear account of the separation between Christ and the human self offers the best grounds for the moves which he wishes to make in the doctrine of man. The burden of much of Jüngel's recent writing is, in effect, to raise important questions about the sense in which the Protestant affirmation of 'solus Christus' is to be sustained. That affirmation frequently has the effect of separating Christ and Christian existence, sometimes elevating the former at the expense of the latter. Jüngel's most recent studies in theological ethics offer some valuable protests against such moves. At the very least there are indications that he has found in Barth's last writings the possibility of a Christology in which Jesus Christ is intrinsically to be understood out of his character as one through whom the transformation of human existence is accomplished, and so whose effectiveness needs to be taken into account in any dogmatic account of his person.

To suggest all this is by no means to qualify Jüngel's Christo-centrism, but rather to suggest ways in which his refusal of Christomonism could be given greater profile. Talk of the impe-ratival aspect of grace, of theological interest in moral deliberation and of the effectiveness of Jesus Christ in human renewal, is intended to flesh out Jüngel's fundamental assertion that God makes the world interesting in new ways. It is in his perception of that issue, and in his uneasiness with ways of addressing it which compromise either term in the analogy of God and man, that the weightiness of his theological work lies.

Notes

Introduction

1. See S. W. Sykes, 'Germany and England: An Attempt at Theological Diplomacy' in *idem* (ed.), *England and Germany. Studies in Theological Diplomacy* (Frankfurt/M, 1982), 146–70. For a recent attempt the other way, see D. Ritschl, *Theologie in den Neuen Welten* (Munich, 1981).
2. E.g. PJ, preface to 3rd edition: GS 123–5; KS 434f.
3. A. König, 'Le Dieu crucifié' (*Hok* 17 (1981) 73–95).
4. L. J. O'Donovan, 'The Mystery of God as a History of Love' (*ThSt* 42 (1981) 251–71).
5. J. A. Bracken, 'Process Philosophy and Trinitarian Theology' (*PS* 8 (1978) 217–30) 220.
6. TC A.2.113f.
7. RVG 476.
8. DUC 299.
9. K. Barth, *Letters 1961–8*, (ET, Edinburgh, 1981), letter 239.
10. Ibid. 234.

1 Paul and Jesus

1. For a survey of works on the theme, see J. W. Fraser, *Jesus and Paul* (Abingdon, 1974).
2. See ch. 3.
3. This period produced two *New Frontiers in Theology* volumes edited by J. M. Robinson and J. B. Cobb: *I: The Later Heidegger and Theology* and *II: The New Hermeneutic* (New York, 1963, 1964), and R. W. Funk's *Language, Hermeneutic and Word of God* (New York, 1966). The only major ET of Fuchs' work, *Studies of the Historical Jesus* (London, 1964) came from this period, as did the important articles by J. C. Weber, 'Language-Event and Christian Faith' (*ThTo* 21 (1964) 448–57) and P. J. Achtemeier 'How Adequate is the New Hermeneutic?' (*ThTo* 23 (1966) 105–11). Later surveys include P. J. Achtemeier, *An Introduction to the New Hermeneutic* (Philadelphia, 1969) and A. C. Thiselton, 'The New Hermeneutic' in

I. H. Marshall (ed.), *New Testament Interpretation* (Exeter, 1977) 308–33.

4. See, for example, J. Crossan, *In Parables* (New York, 1973); E. Linnemann, *Parables of Jesus* (ET, London, 1966); N. Perrin, *Jesus and the Language of the Kingdom* (London, 1976) 89–193; S. TeSelle, *Speaking in Parables* (Philadelphia, 1975) 66–89; D. O. Via, *The Parables* (Philadelphia, 1967); A. N. Wilder, *Early Christian Rhetoric* (Cambridge, Mass., 1971) 71–88; *idem, Jesus' Parables and the War of Myths* (London, 1982). See also F. Kermode, *The Genesis of Secrecy* (London, 1979).

5. Perhaps the most helpful first taste of Heidegger is *On the Way to Language* (ET, New York, 1971). A good introduction is G. Steiner, *Heidegger* (London, 1978) 122–50. For fuller accounts see W. J. Richardson, *Heidegger* (The Hague, 1963) and A. C. Thiselton, *The Two Horizons*, 327–42.

6. R. N. Soulen, *Biblical Hermeneutics and Parable Interpretation in the Writings of Ernst Fuchs* (Ph.D. thesis, Boston University Graduate School, 1964) 20.

7. See DSZ 122 n. 8; GS 8 (ET xviii).

8. See J. B. Brantschen's study of Fuchs, *Zeit zu verstehen* (Zürich, 1974).

9. E.g. F. Hahn, *The Titles of Jesus in Christology* (ET, London, 1969); I. H. Marshall, *The Origins of New Testament Christology* (Leicester, 1976); C. F. D. Moule, *The Origin of Christology* (Cambridge, 1977).

10. E.g. J. Blank, *Paulus und Jesus* (Munich, 1968); D. L. Dungan, *The Sayings of Jesus in the Churches of Paul* (Oxford, 1971); F. F. Bruce, *Paul and Jesus* (London, 1974); G. N. Stanton, *Jesus of Nazareth in New Testament Preaching* (Cambridge, 1974).

11. Cf. PJ v.

12. 'eine phänomengeschichtliche Methode' – this (virtually untranslatable) phrase is rich in Heideggerian overtones. See also Jüngel's early study UA.

13. PJ 5.

14. As we shall see, this proposal opens out into a much wider rejection of 'calculative' thinking in, e.g., M. Heidegger (*Discourse on Thinking* (ET, New York, 1966)) and H.-G. Gadamer (*Truth and Method* (ET, London, 1979²)).

15. PJ 87.

16. A. Jülicher, *Die Gleichnisreden Jesu* (Tübingen, 1899, 2 vols). See PJ 88–102.

17. PJ 92, 95.

18. Ibid. 94.

19. *Die Gleichnisreden Jesu* 196.

20. PJ 101.

21. Ibid. 135.

22. Ibid. 202.

23. Ibid. 135.

24. Ibid. 292.
25. Ibid. 135.
26. Ibid. 128.
27. Cf. ibid. 128–35, which makes the debt explicit.
28. Fuchs, *Studies of the Historical Jesus* 207.
29. The implications of this for Barth's reading of biblical narrative have been shrewdly noted by D. F. Ford in *Barth and God's Story* (Frankfurt/M, 1982) and in his essay 'Barth's Interpretation of the Bible' in S. W. Sykes (ed.), *Karl Barth. Studies in his Theological Method* (Oxford, 1979) 55–87.
30. PJ 33.
31. His discussion is indebted to Barth, *CD* II/2, 733–81; IV/1, 514–642, esp. 520–8. See also E. Käsemann, *Perspectives on Paul* (ET, London, 1971) 73.
32. PJ 263.
33. Ibid. 266.
34. Ibid. 268.
35. Ibid. 273.
36. Ibid. 277.
37. Ibid. 279.
38. Ibid. 140.
39. Ibid. 141.
40. Ibid. 206.
41. Ibid.
42. Ibid. 149–51.
43. Ibid. 151.
44. See Fuchs, 'Jesus' Understanding of Time' in *Studies of the Historical Jesus* 104–66.
45. See PJ 288f n. 2, with *CD* III/2 437–640.
46. *CD* III/2 525.
47. PJ 265.
48. On this, see now J. D. G. Dunn, *Unity and Diversity in the New Testament* (London, 1977). See also J. L. Houlden, *Patterns of Faith* (London, 1977), 25–46, and J. Charlot, *New Testament Disunity* (New York, 1970) esp. 39–97. For an excellent worked example, see C. F. Evans, *Resurrection of the New Testament* (London, 1970).
49. This point is well made with reference to others by A. C. Thiselton in e.g. *The Two Horizons* 352–6; 'The New Hermeneutic' 323–9; 'The Parables as Language-Event' (*SJT* 23 (1970) 437–68, esp. 462–8). See also G. B. Caird, *The Language and Imagery of the Bible* (London, 1980) esp. 7–36; J. Verhaar, 'Language and Theological Method' (*Cont* 7 (1967) 3–29) and Weber, 'Language-Event and Christian Faith'.

2 God's being is in becoming

1. ET of the second edition: *The Doctrine of the Trinity: God's Being is in Becoming*. Quotations are from this translation, with fairly frequent alterations. Page references are given to both German and English texts.

2. See Braun's articles, translated as 'The Problem of a New Testament Theology' (*JThCh* 1 (1965) 169–83) and 'The Meaning of New Testament Christology' (*JThCh* 5 (1968) 89–127), along with 'Gottes Existenz und meine Geschichtlichkeit' in E. Dinkler (ed.), *Zeit und Geschichte* (Tübingen, 1964) 399–421, and *Jesus* (ET, Philadelphia, 1979).

3. H. Gollwitzer, *The Existence of God as Confessed by Faith* (ET, London, 1965). The debate is continued in H. Symanowski (ed.), *Post Bultmann Locutum* (Hamburg, 1965, 2 vols). See also H.-G. Geyer, 'Gottes Sein als Thema der Theologie' (*EvTh*, Beiheft 1966) 3–37.

4. Braun, 'The Problem of a New Testament Theology' 182f.

5. GS 35 (ET 23).

6. GS 35f (ET 24).

7. GS 82 (ET 68).

8. GS 107 (ET 92).

9. Braun, 'The Problem of a New Testament Theology' 177.

10. Jüngel's term here (*Gegenständlich-Sein*) is chosen to contrast with 'objectification' (*Objektivierung*).

11. GS 54 (ET 42).

12. GS 57 (ET 44f.).

13. GS 69 (ET 56).

14. It is this which distinguishes Jüngel very sharply from any version of 'process' philosophy or theology. See GS 113f. n. 48 (ET 100 n. 151), and C. Gunton's use of Jüngel in *Becoming and Being* (Oxford, 1978). See also J. J. O'Donnell, *Trinity and Temporality* (Oxford, 1983).

15. GS VII (ET vii).

16. GS 113 n. 148 (ET 100f. n. 152).

17. GS VII (ET vii).

18. Ibid.

19. GS 99 (ET 85).

20. GS 101 (ET 87).

21. Ibid.

22. BSV 10.

23. Ibid. 9.

24. KMG 332.

25. GS 1 (ET xi).

26. GS 9 (ET xix).

27. H. Ott, *Faith and Reality* (ET, London, 1971) 56f. Similar comments can be found in the opening chapter of F. Buri's book *How Can We Still Speak Responsibly of God?* (ET, Philadelphia, 1968).

3 Christology: exegesis and dogmatics

1. See the two excellent pieces of historical analysis by R. Morgan, 'Non Angli sed Angeli: Some Anglican Responses to German Gospel Criticism' (*NST* 1 (1980) 1–30) and 'Historical Criticism and Christology' in S. W. Sykes (ed.), *England and Germany*, 80–112. See also L. S. Lawton, *Conflict in Christology* (London, 1947); J. K. Mozley, *Some Tendencies in British Theology* (London, 1951); L. B. Smedes, *The Incarnation. Trends in Modern Anglican Thought* (Kampen, 1953); A. M. Ramsey, *From Gore to Temple* (London, 1960); B. L. Hebblethwaite, 'The Propriety of the Doctrine of the Incarnation as a Way of Interpreting Christ' (*SJT* 33 (1980) 201–22, esp. 203–9).
2. *The Myth of God Incarnate*, (ed.), J. Hick (London, 1977).
3. Notably M. Green (ed.), *The Truth of God Incarnate* (London, 1977).
4. Morgan, 'Non Angli' 4.
5. Other examples would be W. Kasper, *Jesus the Christ* (ET, London, 1976) and (not German but largely from German sources) E. Schillebeeckx, *Jesus* (ET, London, 1979) and *Christ* (ET, London, 1980). For a rare English contribution, see R. Morgan, 'The Hermeneutical Significance of Four Gospels' (*Int* 33 (1979) 376–88).
6. JW 128 n. 10.
7. G. Ebeling, *Theology and Proclamation. A Discussion with Rudolf Bultmann* (ET, London, 1966). On Ebeling see A. Patriquin's study *Gerhard Ebeling's Programme of Hermeneutics for Biblical Interpretation* (Ph.D. thesis, Northwestern University, 1973) and more recently M. Ruokanen, *Hermeneutics as an Ecumenical Method in the Theology of Gerhard Ebeling* (Helsinki, 1982).
8. Cf. H. Ott, *Theology and Preaching* (ET, London, 1965).
9. Ebeling, *Theology and Proclamation* 23. See also the historical analysis in P. Stuhlmacher, *Historical Criticism and the Theological Interpretation of Scripture* (ET, Philadelphia, 1977).
10. VTD 0.
11. See, e.g., J. Barr, *The Bible in the Modern World* (London, 1973) 18–22, 179f.; M. F. Wiles, 'Christian Doctrine in the 1960's' (*ChQ* 2 (1969–70) 215–21), to which R. Morgan replies with positive suggestions about the category in 'The Word' (*Theol* 74 (1971) 213–22).
12. PJ v.
13. FT 3.6.
14. FT 5.41; cf. VTD 6.31.
15. FT 5.44; cf. VTD 6.34.
16. See Ebeling, *Theology and Proclamation* 22–31, with his *Kirchengeschichte als Geschichte der Auslegung der Heiligen Schrift* (Tübingen, 1947); *The Problem of Historicity* (ET, Philadelphia, 1967); *Word of God and Tradition* (ET, Philadelphia, 1968).
17. GS 25 n. 43 (ET 14 n. 43).

18. On the relation of historico-critical study and preaching, see the excursus to P (omitted in the 1979 reprint) 'Was hat die Predigt mit dem Text zu tun?' – with Barth's comments (*Letters 1961–8* 339).
19. VTD 5.
20. Ibid. 5.1.
21. Ibid.
22. Notably in the set of theses TC and in WE.
23. TS 43.
24. Ibid.
25. Ibid. For the distinction, see further SJ 5.2; TC B.2.22f.; VTD 4.2.
26. Jüngel regards the death of Jesus as the pivotal point of his history: see SJ 2.5; GUG 76f.; GG 308f, 312 (ET 227, 229).
27. T 132.
28. Cf. SJ 4–4.14; T 132f.
29. SJ 4.
30. Ibid. 5.2.
31. PJ 4.
32. Ibid. 2. Cf. 107–20.
33. Ibid. 4.
34. 'geschichtliches Dasein', WE 18.
35. Ibid. 26.
36. Ibid.
37. Ibid. 28.
38. Ibid.
39. Ibid. 29.
40. T 132.
41. PJ 81.
42. GG 420 (ET 306). Cf. SJ 3.2; TC B.2.221. See also H. T. Wrege, *Die Gestalt des Evangeliums* (Frankfurt/M, 1978) 29–38.
43. JW 127.
44. Ibid.
45. T 134, o 64f.
46. WE 29.
47. TC B.2.22.
48. TC B.2.221.
49. TC B.2.217.
50. Cf. WE 15f.
51. PJ 82. Cf. ibid. 2, 4f., 15, 296; DSZ 115f., n. 4.
52. GG 417 (ET 305).
53. T 131. Cf. SJ 2.2.
54. SJ 11. The ideas of 'identification' and 'identity' are not always clearly distinguished by Jüngel, and imprecision at this point may leave him exposed to W. Pannenberg's charge that 'The interpretation of the history of Jesus Christ as the history of the death of God is an inverted monophysitism' (*Christian Spirituality* (Philadelphia, 1983) 83).
55. For a recent survey of the area see W. Pannenberg, *Jesus – God and*

Man (ET, London, 1968) 337-44. For an older attempt to revitalise anhypostasia, see H. M. Relton, *A Study in Christology* (London, 1934).

56. Pannenberg, *Jesus – God and Man*, 338f.
57. Ibid. 338.
58. SJ 12.5f.; cf. T 126-30.
59. TWG 28.
60. SJ 12.6.
61. JW 129.
62. Ibid. 140.
63. Ibid.
64. Ibid.
65. SJ 10.6; cf. 5.3, JW 133.
66. WE 29.
67. SJ 4.
68. MW 145.
69. KMG 339.
70. GG 127 (ET 96f.).
71. JW 137, cf. 137f. n. 32.
72. JW 140.
73. Bonhoeffer, *Christology* (ET, London, 1978), 78f., 103.
74. Ibid. 103 (trans. slightly altered).
75. GG 315 (ET 231).
76. Cf. VT 113-15.
77. T. F. Torrance, *Theology in Reconstruction* (London, 1965) 148f.
78. E. F. Osborn, 'Method and Myth' (*Prud* 10 (1978) 37-47) 40.
79. See Osborn's exposition of 'problematic elucidation' in 'Elucidation of Problems as a Method of Interpretation' I (*Coll* 8 (1976) 24-32), II (*Coll* 9 (1976) 10-18), and his use of the method in *The Beginnings of Christian Philosophy* (Cambridge, 1981).
80. I. T. Ramsey, *Freedom and Immortality* (London, 1960) 60.
81. Three English-language works are notable exceptions: J. MacIntyre, *The Shape of Christology* (London, 1966); S. M. Ogden, *The Point of Christology* (London, 1982) and C. Gunton, *Yesterday and Today* (London, 1983).

4 God the mystery of the world (1): speaking about God

1. GG XVI (ET xii).
2. GG X (ET vii): having said that, the book's historical presentations are often decidedly impressionistic.
3. GWS 82.
4. Ibid. 81.
5. GG 2 (ET 3).
6. Cf. G. Ebeling, *God and Word* (ET, Philadelphia, 1966) and *Introduction to a Theological Theory of Language* (ET, London, 1973).
7. Cf. GS 16-27 (ET 5-15).
8. PJ 128.

9. Ibid. 129.
10. Ibid.
11. K. Barth, *The Word of God and the Word of Man* (ET, London, 1928) 186.
12. D. M. MacKinnon, *The Problem of Metaphysics* (Cambridge, 1974) 186.
13. See, e.g., PJ 142–74. Jüngel often abstracts from the ordinariness of the parables by redescribing them in formal temporal categories. An early sermon (GP 47–52) offers an interesting counter-example.
14. D. M. MacKinnon, 'Parable and Sacrament' in *Explorations in Theology* 5 (London, 1979) 174. Cf. F. H. Borsch, *God's Parable* (London, 1975) 45–71.
15. GS 23–6 (ET 11–15).
16. Ibid. 22 (ET 11).
17. Ibid. 26 (ET 14).
18. Ibid. 26 n. 45 (ET 14 n. 45).
19. For scientific work see M. Black, *Models and Metaphors* (New York, 1962) 25–47; M. B. Hesse, *Science and the Human Imagination* (London, 1954) 134–46; *idem*, *Models and Analogies in Science* (Notre Dame, 1966) 157–77); *idem*, *Forces and Fields* (Westport, 1970) 21–8; R. Harré, *The Principles of Scientific Thinking* (London, 1970) 33–62; A. Ortony (ed.), *Metaphor and Thought* (Cambridge, 1979). On literary and more general issues, see G. Lakoff and M. Johnson, *Metaphors We Live By* (Chicago, 1980); I. A. Richards, *The Philosophy of Rhetoric* (Oxford, 1936) 89–138; P. Ricoeur, *The Rule of Metaphor* (ET, London, 1978); P. Wheelwright, *The Burning Fountain* (Bloomington, 1954) 30–51; *idem*, *Metaphor and Reality* (Bloomington, 1962). On theological issues, see I. U. Dalferth, *Religiöse Rede von Gott* (Munich, 1981) 218–36; C. Ernst, *Multiple Echo* (London, 1979) 57–75; H. Rikhof, *The Concept of Church* (London, 1981) 67–121; S. Macfague, *Metaphorical Theology* (London, 1983).
20. Richards, *Philosophy of Rhetoric* 90.
21. Black, *Models and Metaphors* 32.
22. Ibid. 39.
23. Ibid. 46.
24. Ricoeur, *Rule of Metaphor* 222.
25. Ibid. 230.
26. Ibid. 247.
27. Ibid. 305.
28. MW 104.
29. Ibid.
30. Ibid. 105.
31. Ibid. 127.
32. Ibid. 103. By way of direct contrast see N. Rescher, 'The Ontology of the Possible' in M. K. Munitz (ed.), *Logic and Ontology* (New York, 1973) 213–28; *idem*, *A Theory of Possibility* (Oxford, 1975). See also M. J. Loux (ed.), *The Possible and the Actual* (Ithaca, 1979);

A. Plantinga, *The Nature of Necessity* (Oxford, 1974) 121–63; S. Sutherland, *God, Jesus and Belief* (Oxford, 1984) 73–86.

33. WMW 208.
34. MW 137 n. 85.
35. Ibid. 105.
36. Ibid. 104. Cf. Mary Hesse's interrogation of the correspondence theory in *Revolutions and Reconstructions in the Philosophy of Science* (Brighton, 1980).
37. MW 143.
38. Ibid. 154 thesis 4.
39. Ibid.
40. Ibid. 152.
41. Ibid. 132.
42. GG 313 (ET 230).
43. Ibid. 389 (ET 285). Further here see SAT, *passim*.
44. Cf. MTA 216f.
45. GG 390 (ET 286).
46. Ibid. 389f. (ET 285).
47. Ibid. 401 (ET 293).
48. Ibid. 403 (ET 295).
49. Ibid.
50. This is pointed out by N. L. A. Lash, 'Interpretation and Imagination' in M. D. Goulder (ed.), *Incarnation and Myth* (London, 1979) 19–26.
51. I. T. Ramsey, *Religious Language* (London, 1957) 48.
52. Here I have in mind such studies as J. Coulson, *Religion and Imagination* (Oxford, 1981); A. E. Harvey (ed.), *God Incarnate: Story and Belief* (London, 1981); T. W. Jennings, *Introduction to Theology* (London, 1977); A. Louth, *Discerning the Mystery* (Oxford, 1983). See also R. Williams' essay 'Poetic and Religious Imagination' (*Theol* 80 (1977) 178–87).
53. MW 110.
54. Jüngel may also be eliding distinctions between 'religious' and 'theological' language: see N. L. A. Lash, 'Ideology, Metaphor and Analogy' in B. Hebblethwaite and S. Sutherland (ed.), *The Philosophical Frontiers of Christian Theology* (Cambridge, 1982) 68–94.
55. GG 322–34 (ET 236–45).
56. See Lash, 'Ideology' 80–2; R. White, 'Notes on Analogical Predication and Speaking about God' in Hebblethwaite and Sutherland, *Philosophical Frontiers* 198–200; D. Burrell, *Aquinas. God and Action* (London, 1979). See also H. McCabe's note on 'Analogy' in *idem* (ed.), Aquinas, *Summa Theologiae* 3 (London, 1963) 106f.
57. D. M. MacKinnon, 'Prayer, Worship and Life' in *idem* (ed.), *Christian Faith and Communist Faith* (London, 1953) 255.
58. See, e.g., STS.
59. For some searching analysis of this theme see T. Rendtorff, 'Zum

ethischen Sinn evangelischer Theologie' (*ZEE* 26 (1982) 19–28), and his recent *Ethik*, 2 vols. (Munich, 1980–1).

5 God the mystery of the world (2): thinking about God

1. It should be noted that Jüngel tends to see this 'tradition' as a highly cohesive historical continuity.
2. L. Wittgenstein, *Zettel* (Oxford, 1981²) no. 110.
3. GG 147 (ET 111).
4. Cf. TL, GW.
5. Of particular importance here is Barth's account of Descartes in *CD* III/1, 350–63 (see also R. E. Cushman, 'Barth's Attack upon Cartesianism' (*JR* 36 (1956) 207–23). See further H. Thielicke, *The Evangelical Faith I*, (ET, Grand Rapids, 1974) 30–218; J. Baillie, *Our Knowledge of God* (Oxford, 1939) 147–54. For non-theological perspectives, see M. Heidegger, *Nietzsche II* (Pfullingen, 1961) 158–92, and H.-G. Gadamer, *Truth and Method* (ET, London, 1975) 59, 210f.
6. GG 161 (ET 122).
7. Ibid. 149 (ET 113). See the valuable essay by J. Harms, 'Sein und Zeit bei Cartesius' (*NZSTh* 18 (1976) 277–94).
8. GG 149 (ET 113).
9. GW 255.
10. GG 160 (ET 122). Cf. TL 234, GW 256.
11. See GG 163–5 (ET 123–5).
12. Ibid. 162f. (ET 123); cf. 29–44 (ET 23–35).
13. E. Gellner, *Legitimation of Belief* (Cambridge, 1974) 28.
14. Ibid. 29.
15. See E. Cassirer, *Das Erkenntnisproblem in der Philosophie und Wissenschaft der neueren Zeit I* (Berlin, 1922) 439–505 for a classic survey, with M. Heidegger, *Nietzsche II*, 31–256, and A. Zóltowski, 'Théorie cartésienne et théorie idéaliste de la connaissance' (*ConDes* 3 (1937) 75–80). The discontinuity between Descartes and Kant is stressed by V. Delbos, 'L'idéalisme et le réalisme dans la philosophie de Descartes' (*AnPhil* n.s. 22 (1911) 39–53).
16. Cf. J. Rohls, 'Ist Gott notwendig?' (*NZSTh* 22 (1980) 282–96) 295: 'Assuming that I can prove that God exists from the existence of the world, that does not mean that God is contingent upon the world. Rather, it means that my knowledge of God's existence is contingent upon my knowledge that the world exists.'
17. GG 239 (ET 177).
18. F. Kerr, 'Objections to Lonergan's Method' (*NB* 56 (1975) 305–16) 314.
19. Cf. P. L. Berger and T. Luckmann, *The Social Construction of Reality* (Harmondsworth, 1971); G. Gurvitch, *The Social Frameworks of Knowledge* (Oxford, 1971); J. Ziman, *Public Knowledge: The Social*

Dimension of Science (Cambridge, 1968); A. C. Thiselton, 'Knowledge, Myth and Corporate Memory' in *Believing in the Church* (London, 1981) 45–78.

20. For parallels, see T. F. Torrance's studies in theological rationality, notably *Theological Science* and *God and Rationality* (Oxford, 1969 and 1971).
21. GG 23 (ET 19).
22. DD 163.
23. GG 13 (ET 12); cf. 411 (ET 301).
24. L. Wittgenstein, *Philosophical Investigations* (Oxford, 1953) no. 339; cf. nos. 329f.
25. GG 345 (ET 253).
26. Fuchs, *Studies of the Historical Jesus* 207.
27. GG 343 (ET 252).
28. Ibid. 345 (ET 253).
29. The roots of this can be traced in such later works of Heidegger as *Discourse on Thinking* (ET, New York, 1966); *An Introduction to Metaphysics* (ET, New Haven, 1959) and *What is Called Thinking?* (ET, New York, 1972). Heidegger is reverently paraphrased by W. J. Richardson, *Heidegger* (The Hague, 1963) 577–620.
30. GEM 291.
31. GES 41.
32. GG 206 (ET 151).
33. Ibid. 309 (ET 228).
34. Ibid. 144 (ET 110). See further KS 439–41.
35. GW 262.
36. GG 223 (ET 166).
37. Cf. KB 20.
38. UA 78.
39. GG 225 (ET 168).
40. Ibid. 204 (ET 153).
41. Ibid. 164 (ET 124).
42. Ibid. 218 (ET 162).
43. GS 54 (ET 42).
44. Ibid. 57 (ET 45). On Barth see further J. Brown, *Subject and Object in Modern Theology* (London, 1955) 140–67 and H. W. Frei's astute characterisations of Barth in 'Niebuhr's Theological Background' in P. Ramsey (ed.), *Faith and Ethics* (New York, 1965) 9–64, esp. 40–53.
45. GG 218 (ET 163).
46. PJ 5.
47. Cf. GG 334–8 (ET 246–9).
48. Ibid. 338 (ET 248f.); cf. GS 9 (ET xix), GEM 295–7.
49. Cf. Barth, *CD* II/1, 21 on 'the position of grace, which is the position of faith'.
50. GG 337 (ET 248); cf. Gadamer, *Truth and Method*, 336f.
51. Ibid. 223 (ET 166).
52. Ibid. (ET 167).

53. Wittgenstein, *Philosophical Investigations* no 38. Cf. his comment that in our concept of 'thinking' 'we expect a smooth contour and what we get to see is ragged' (*Zettel* no 111). Compare also R. Bambrough's remarks on Aristotle and Wittgenstein in 'Aristotle on Justice' in *idem* (ed.), *New Essays on Plato and Aristotle* (London, 1965) 159–74, esp. 168–74.
54. On the matters raised here, see D. Tracy, *The Analogical Imagination* (London, 1981).
55. L. Wittgenstein, *The Blue and Brown Books* (Oxford, 1960) 19.
56. Ibid. 19f. Further on the grammar of thinking, see *Philosophical Investigations*, nos. 327–44.
57. See K. Rahner, *Spirit in the World* (ET London, 1968) 57–65; E. Coreth, *Metaphysics* (ET New York, 1968) 45–68; B. J. F. Lonergan, *Method in Theology* (London, 1972) 101–5; O. Muck, *The Transcendental Method* (ET New York, 1968) 190–4, 289–91.
58. G. Ryle, 'Thinking and Language' in *Collected Papers II. Collected Essays 1929–1968* (London, 1971) 261. Other papers in this collection ('Thinking'; 'A Puzzling Element in the Notion of Thinking'; 'Thinking and Reflecting') explore the same theme, which is also treated in his posthumous study *On Thinking* (Oxford, 1979).
59. GG 272 (ET 201).
60. Ibid. 273 (ET 201).

6 God the mystery of the world (3): the human God

1. GG 98 (ET 74). On Jüngel's use of Hegel, see recently R. Ahlers, 'Hegel's Theological Atheism' (*HeyJ* 25 (1984) 158–77).
2. SJ 2.5.
3. Jüngel was a member of the Theological Committee of the *Evangelische Kirche der Union* set up in the 1960s to study the theology of the cross in relation to the proclamation of the church. See F. Viering, *Der Kreuzestod Jesu* (Gütersloh, 1969) and the report on and translations of the committee's work in *Int* 25 (1970) issue 2.

   For recent exegetical surveys in the area, see G. Delling, *Der Kreuzestod Jesu in der urchristlichen Verkündigung* (Göttingen, 1972); K. Kertelge (ed.), *Der Tod Jesu* (Freiburg, 1976); H. Kessler, *Die theologische Bedeutung des Todes Jesu* (Dusseldorf, 1970); M. L. Gubler, *Die früheste Deutungen des Todes Jesu* (Göttingen, 1977). Sympathetic to Jüngel's staurocentric emphasis are, for example, M. Hengel, *Crucifixion* (London, 1970); idem, *The Atonement* (London, 1981); U. Luz, 'Theologia crucis als Mitte der Theologie im Neuen Testament' (*EvTh* 34 (1974) 116–41); P. Stuhlmacher, 'Achtzehn Thesen zur paulinischen Kreuzestheologie' in *idem*, *Versöhnung, Gesetz und Gerechtigkeit* (Göttingen, 1981) 192–208.
4. GES 42.
5. GG 15 (ET 13).
6. SJ 12.41.

7. GG 56 (ET 44).
8. Ibid. 81 (ET 62).
9. Ibid. 134 (ET 102).
10. Ibid. 284 (ET 209).
11. L. Oeing-Hanhoff, 'Die Krise des Gottesgedankens' (*ThQ* 159 (1979) 285–303) 292.
12. TL 235f.
13. Cf. WW 67.
14. Sak 57.
15. See especially *CD* II/1, 257–321, with C. Gunton, *Becoming and Being* (Oxford, 1978) 194–9.
16. GG 31 (ET 25).
17. Ibid. (This sentence is omitted in the ET.)
18. See J. Rohls' critique in 'Ist Gott notwendig?' (*NZSTh* 22 (1980) 282–96). More generally on God and necessity, see Plantinga, *The Nature of Necessity* 196–221.
19. GG 44 (ET 35).
20. Ibid. 47 (ET 37).
21. Ibid. 222, 246, 410, 478f. (ET 166, 182, 300, 349).
22. Ibid. 248 (ET 184).
23. W. von Loewenich, *Luther's Theology of the Cross* (ET Belfast, 1976). Further on the theme, see H. Bandt, *Luthers Lehre vom verborgenen Gott* (Berlin, 1958); H. Rückert, 'Luthers Anschauung von der verborgenen Gott' in *Vorträge und Aufsätze zur historischen Theologie* (Tübingen, 1972) 96–107; J. Dillenberger, *God Hidden and Revealed* (Philadelphia, 1953).
24. GG 246 (ET 182).
25. W 11; cf. ZF 31; QSN 239, 249f.
26. W 11. See also GG 82 n. 19 (ET 62 n. 19), where Jüngel refers to the contrast between 'personal presence' and 'presence at hand' drawn by W. Pannenberg in 'Speaking of God in the Face of Atheist Criticism' in *Basic Questions in Theology II* (ET London, 1973) 112.
27. GG 82 (ET 63).
28. Ibid. 248–306 (ET 184–225).
29. G. E. Moore, 'Is Existence a Predicate?' in *Philosophical Papers* (London, 1959), 115–26.
30. Cf. here especially G. C. Stead, *Divine Substance* (Oxford, 1977).
31. D. M. MacKinnon, '"Substance" in Christology' in S. W. Sykes and J. P. Clayton (ed.), *Christ, Faith and History* (Cambridge, 1972) 294. Cf. his essay 'Aristotle's Conception of Substance' in Bambrough (ed.), *New Essays on Plato and Aristotle* 97–119, esp. 113–8, and C. F. D. Moule, 'The Borderlands of Ontology in the New Testament' in Hebblethwaite and Sutherland (ed.), *Philosophical Frontiers* 1–11.
32. WMW 206f.
33. Ibid. 211.
34. Jüngel generally defines himself here over against Aristotle.
35. GG 290 (ET 214).

36. Ibid.
37. Ibid. 287 (ET 211).
38. Ibid.
39. Ibid. 294 (ET 217).
40. Ibid. 292 (ET 215); cf. ZF 43, 48.
41. GG 290 (ET 214).
42. Ibid.
43. Ibid. 294 (ET 217).
44. Ibid. 295 (ET 217).
45. Ibid. 409 (ET 299); cf. Trin 270; GL 201.
46. GL 201.
47. See R. Prenter's classic essay 'Der Gott, der Liebe ist' in *Theologie und Gottesdienst* (Göttingen, 1977) 275–91.
48. Trin 270; cf. GG 434, 444 (ET 317, 324).
49. GG 435 (ET 318). On this, see the remarkable book by S. Moore, *The Fire and the Rose are One* (London, 1980).
50. GG 435 (ET 318).
51. Ibid. 303 (ET 223).
52. TC B.5.2.
53. SJ 1.1.
54. Ibid. 1.11.
55. GG 474 (ET 346).
56. Ibid. 448 (ET 327).
57. SJ 1.1.
58. GG 449 (ET 328).
59. I have tried to show a similar function in von Balthasar's doctrine of the Trinity in 'Hans Urs von Balthasar: The Paschal Mystery' (*Ev* 1:4 (1983) 6–8).
60. GG 521–34 (ET 380–89); cf. Trin 8.1–4; WSF 174.
61. GG 521 (ET 380).
62. WSF 174.
63. GG 521 (ET 380).
64. Trin 8.3.
65. GG 525 (ET 383).
66. Ibid. 531 (ET 387f.).
67. SJ 1.14.
68. GG 522 (ET 381).
69. See especially T. Rendtorff, 'Radikale Autonomie Gottes' in *idem*, *Theorie des Christentums* (Gütersloh, 1972) 161–81, with F. W. Graf, 'Die Freiheit der Entsprechung Gottes' in T. Rendtorff (ed.), *Die Realisierung der Freiheit* (Gütersloh, 1975) 76–118; J. Moltmann, *The Trinity and the Kingdom of God* (ET London, 1981) 139–44; L. Oeing-Hanhoff, 'Hegels Trinitätslehre' (*ThPh* 52 (1977) 378–407, esp. 395–402); W. Pannenberg, 'Person und Subjekt' in *idem*, *Grundfragen systematischer Theologie. Gesammelte Aufsätze II* (Göttingen, 1980) 80–95; *idem*, 'Die Subjektivität Gottes und die Trinitätslehre' in ibid. 96–111; *idem*, 'Der Gott der Geschichte' in

ibid. 112–28; F. Wagner, 'Christologie als exemplarische Theorie des Selbstbewusstseins' in Rendtorff (ed.), *Die Realisierung der Freiheit*, 135–67, esp. 157f. I have analysed some of these recent critiques in 'Recent Work on Barth' (*Them* 7:3 (1982) 31–5).
70. W. Groll, *Ernst Troeltsch und Karl Barth* (Munich, 1976) 52.
71. Pannenberg, 'Die Subjektivität Gottes' 98. In defence of Barth, see L. During, 'Hegel, Barth, and the Rationality of the Trinity' (*KTR* 2 (1979) 69–81).
72. Pannenberg, 'Der Gott der Geschichte' 124.
73. Pannenberg, 'Die Subjektivität Gottes' 100.
74. P. J. Rosato, *The Spirit as Lord. The Pneumatology of Karl Barth* (Edinburgh, 1981) 135.
75. Pannenberg, 'Person und Subjekt' 95.
76. R. Williams, 'Barth on the Triune God', in S. W. Sykes (ed.), *Karl Barth. Studies in his Theological Method* (Oxford, 1979).
77. Ibid. 176.
78. Ibid. 181.
79. Ibid.
80. Ibid. 181f.
81. Pannenberg, 'Die Subjektivität Gottes', 108.
82. Rosato, *The Spirit as Lord* 141.
83. Ibid.
84. Cf. GG 77f. (ET 348f.).
85. Trin 356.
86. GG 303 (ET 223).
87. Moltmann, *The Trinity*, 142.
88. Williams, 'Barth on the Triune God' 182.
89. GG 531 (ET 387).
90. Ibid. 513 (ET 375).
91. Rosato, *The Spirit as Lord*, 136.
92. Moltmann, *The Trinity*, 90.
93. GG 513 (ET 375).
94. Ibid. 513f. (ET 375).
95. Ibid. 533 (ET 389).
96. Moltmann, *The Trinity* 218. Cf. HG 9–9.35 on the relation between the Holy Spirit and freedom.

7 Atheism and the theology of death

1. S. Weil, *Gravity and Grace* (ET London, 1952) 103.
2. P. Ricoeur, *The Conflict of Interpretations* (ET Evanston, 1974) 440.
3. Besides the full-scale treatment in GG, see also D, VT, WTG, KMG, and TGA.
4. Barth, 'Feuerbach' in *Protestant Theology in the Nineteenth Century* (ET London, 1972) 534–40. See also 'Ludwig Feuerbach' in *Theology and Church* (ET London, 1962) 217–37.
5. Pannenberg, 'Speaking of God' 105. See also 'Types of Atheism and

their Theological Significance' in *Basic Questions in Theology II* (ET London, 1971) 184–200.

6. Pannenberg, 'Speaking of God' 104f.
7. TC A.6.43.
8. D 289; cf. GG 193, 276 (ET 145, 203); KMG 333–5.
9. GG 276 (ET 203).
10. Ibid. 381 (ET 279).
11. Jüngel contrasts God 'über uns' with God 'unter uns' frequently: TC A.65, GG 62, 82, 136, 166, 252, 261f. (ET 48, 62, 103, 125, 187, 193). His – startlingly imprecise – remarks are probably directed against some of the Fathers and scholastics. For much more nuanced accounts, showing the revisionary effect of Christian beliefs about Jesus within the 'theistic tradition' see, e.g., A. Louth, *The Origins of the Christian Mystical Tradition* (Oxford, 1980) and W. Pannenberg, 'The Appropriation of the Philosophical Concept of God as a Dogmatic Problem of Early Christian Theology' in *Basic Questions in Theology* II, 119–83.
12. D 289f.
13. Ibid. Further on Feuerbach see GL, GG 188–95 (ET 141–6).
14. D 295. Jüngel is alert to Nietzsche's appreciation of the Christological alternative (GG 282 (ET 207), D 296). Further on Nietzsche, see GG 195–200, 279–83 (ET 146–50, 205–9), VT 108.
15. D 295.
16. GG 276 (ET 203).
17. WTG 38.
18. Ibid. 40.
19. KMG 344.
20. LG 372.
21. GG 344 n. 15 (ET 253 n. 15).
22. For typologies of atheism and histories of theological responses, see H. R. Burkle, *The Non-Existence of God* (New York, 1969); H. Döring, *Abwesenheit Gottes* (Paderborn, 1977); C. Fabro, *Modern Atheism* (ET Westminster, 1968); J. Figl, *Atheismus als theologisches Problem* (Mainz, 1977); W. Gent, *Untersuchungen zum Problem des Atheismus* (Hildesheim, 1964); E. E. Harris, *Atheism and Theism* (New Orleans, 1977); W. Kasper, *Glaube im Wandel der Geschichte* (Mainz, 1970) 103–56; H. Küng, *Does God Exist?* (ET London, 1980); W. A. Luijpen, *Phenomenology and Atheism* (Pittsburgh, 1964); W. A. Luijpen and H. J. Koren, *Religion and Atheism* (Pittsburgh, 1971); P. Masterson, *Atheism and Alienation* (Dublin, 1971); T. Molnar, *Theists and Atheists* (The Hague, 1980); W. Pannenberg, 'Types of Atheism'; H.-G. Pöhlmann, 'Der Atheismus, eine Selbsttäuschung?' (*KuD* 21 (1975) 13–48); J. Thrower, *A Short History of Atheism* (London, 1971); *idem, The Alternative Tradition* (The Hague, 1980).
23. Pannenberg, 'Types of Atheism', 191.
24. There is a good survey of this field in K. Nielsen, *Contemporary Critiques of Religion* (London, 1971).

25. For parallel readings, see J. Moltmann, *The Crucified God* (ET London, 1974) 207–27; H.-G. Geyer, 'Atheismus und Christentum' (*EvTh* 30 (1970) 255–74); Harris, *Atheism and Theism*, 29–46; J. Lacroix, *The Meaning of Modern Atheism* (ET Dublin, 1965) 55–7.
26. For a fine counter-example, see S. R. Sutherland, *Atheism and the Rejection of God* (Oxford, 1977) esp 3–24.
27. M. Merleau-Ponty, *In Praise of Philosophy* (ET Evanston, 1963) 43.
28. GG 56 (ET 44). This is specified against D. Sölle, *Christ the Representative* (ET London, 1967). On this issue, see W. Pannenberg's interesting essay 'The Absence of God in Theological Perspective' in *Christian Spirituality* (Philadelphia, 1983) 71–92.
29. Masterson, *Atheism and Alienation* 126.
30. Cf. WMW 227f.
31. See R. Gill's treatment of the issues in *The Social Context of Theology* (Oxford, 1975), *Theology and Social Structure* (London, 1977) and *Prophecy and Praxis* (London, 1981).
32. C. Davis, *Theology and Political Society* (Cambridge, 1980) 102.
33. N. L. A. Lash, 'Should Christianity be Credible?' in *Theology on Dover Beach* (London, 1979) 82.
34. GG 128 (ET 97).
35. VT 123.
36. In chronological order of publication: VT, WTG, TB, T, TV, TGL, RL.
37. From the mass of literature, see in particular: R. Aldwinckle, *Death in the Secular City* (London, 1972); P. Badham, *Christian Beliefs about Life after Death* (London, 1976); J. Hick, *Death and Eternal Life* (London, 1976); N. L. A. Lash, 'Eternal Life: Life "after" Death?' in *Theology on Dover Beach* (London, 1979) 164–82; H. Lewis, *The Self and Immortality* (London, 1973); J. Macquarrie, *Christian Hope* (Oxford, 1978); A. Paus (ed.), *Grenzerfahrung Tod* (Vienna, 1976); T. Penelhum, *Survival and Disembodied Existence* (London, 1970); D. Z. Phillips, *Death and Immortality* (London, 1970); J. Pieper, *Death and Immortality* (ET London, 1969); K. Rahner, *On the Theology of Death* (ET London, 1965); G. Schunack, *Das hermeneutische Problem des Todes* (Tübingen, 1967); J. Schwartländer (ed.), *Der Mensch und sein Tod* (Göttingen, 1976); S. W. Sykes, 'Life after Death: The Christian Doctrine of Heaven' in R. W. A. Mackinney (ed.), *Creation, Christ and Culture* (Edinburgh, 1976) 250–71; S. H. Travis, *Christian Hope and the Future of Man* (Leicester, 1980); H. Wohlgschaft, *Hoffnung angesichts des Todes* (Munich, 1977).
38. T 38 (ET 26).
39. Ibid. 40f. (ET 28).
40. TGL 327.
41. WTG 42.
42. TGL 327.
43. Ibid. 331.

44. T 7 (ET vii).
45. TGL 332.
46. T 109f. (ET 85f.).
47. Ibid. 99 (ET 77).
48. Ibid. 99 (ET 78).
49. Ibid. 100 (ET 78).
50. WTG 52.
51. T 139 (ET 109).
52. Ibid. 139 (ET 109f.).
53. TGL 344.
54. RL 9.1.
55. LG 372.
56. GM 1.
57. TGL 340.
58. LG 374f.
59. RL 10
60. T 171 (ET 136).
61. See e.g. A. Flew, 'Death' in A. Flew and A. MacIntyre (ed.), *New Essays in Philosophical Theology* (London, 1955) 267–72.
62. Lash, 'Eternal Life'; Moltmann, *The Crucified God* 169ff.
63. VT 121f.
64. O 66.
65. Ibid. 69.
66. T 150 (ET 119).
67. PJ 286
68. Ibid. 141.
69. GM 8.11.
70. T 152 (ET 120).
71. Ibid. 113 (ET 121).
72. Ibid. 115 (ET 90).
73. Ibid.
74. STS 460.
75. Ibid. 461.
76. GEM 310.
77. Ibid.
78. See, e.g., M. Douglas, *Natural Symbols* (London, 1973²); *idem, Purity and Danger* (London, 1966); R. Grainger, *The Language of the Rite* (London, 1974); V. Turner, *The Forest of Symbols* (Ithaca, 1967); *idem, The Ritual Process* (London, 1969); *idem, Dramas, Fields and Metaphors* (Ithaca, 1974); A. van Gennep, *The Rites of Passage* (ET London, 1960). See also T. W. Jennings, 'On Ritual Knowledge' (*JR* 62 (1982) 111–27).
79. F. J. Leenhardt, *Parole visible* (Neuchâtel, 1971) 21.
80. Ibid.
81. Besides Leenhardt, see, e.g., L.-M. Chauvet, *Du symbolique au symbole* (Paris, 1979); J. M. Powers, *Eucharistic Theology* (London,

1968); E. Schillebeeckx, *The Eucharist* (ET London, 1968) and especially *idem, Christ the Sacrament of Encounter with God* (ET London, 1975).

82. M. Douglas, *Purity and Danger*, 62.
83. Leenhardt, *Parole visible*, 21f.
84. ZF 26.
85. Ibid.
86. Cf. the similar remarks about Barth in G. Wingren, *Theology in Conflict* (ET Edinburgh, 1958).
87. A. Peters notes in Jüngel's account of the cross insufficient emphasis on 'the "no" of the holy God to our sin' ('Gedanken zu Eberhard Jüngel's These: Gott als Geheimnis der Welt' in H. Burkhardt (ed.), *Wer ist das – Gott?* (Giessen, 1982) 178–89, 187.
88. T 153 (ET 121).
89. KBT 272.
90. D. M. MacKinnon, 'Prayer, Worship and Life' in *idem*, (ed.), *Christian Faith and Communist Faith* (London, 1953) 246.
91. Ibid.
92. TGL 343.
93. J. Hick's remark about Hartshorne in *Death and Eternal Life*, 219.
94. Jüngel later notes that in T the question of continued personal identity was inadequately stated: GG 292f. n. 58 (ET 215 n. 58).

8 Anthropology and justification

1. See D. Bonhoeffer, *Act and Being* (ET London, 1962) 100–3; H. Bouillard, *Karl Barth* (Paris, 1957) vols. 2 and 3; *idem, The Knowledge of God* (ET London, 1969); W. Dantine, 'Der Welt-Bezug des Glaubens' in W. Dantine and K. Lüthi (ed.), *Theologie zwischen Gestern und Morgen* (Munich, 1968) 261–301; F. W. Graf, 'Die Freiheit der Entsprechung Gottes' in Rendtorff (ed.), *Die Realisierung* 76–118; K. Lüthi, 'Theologie als Gespräch' in Dantine and Lüthi (ed.), *Theologie*, 302–32; R. H. Roberts, *Eternity and Time in the Theology of Karl Barth* (Ph.D. thesis, University of Edinburgh, 1975); *idem*, 'The Ideal and the Real' (*NST* 1 (1980) 163–80); *idem*, 'Karl Barth's Doctrine of Time' in S. W. Sykes (ed.), *Karl Barth*, 88–146; R. E. Willis, *The Ethics of Karl Barth* (Leiden, 1981) 139–47, 202–72, 428–49; Wingren, *Theology in Conflict* 23–44. For more sympathetic accounts of Barth, see C. Frey, 'Zur theologischen Anthropologie Karl Barths' in H. Fischer (ed.), *Anthropologie als Thema der Theologie* (Göttingen, 1978) 38–69; S. McLean, *Humanity in Karl Barth's Thought* (Edinburgh, 1981); A. Quadt, *Gott und Mensch* (Munich, 1976), and especially E. H. Friedmann, *Christologie und Anthropologie* (Munsterschwarzach, 1972).
2. R. H. Roberts, 'Karl Barth' in P. Toon and J. Spiceland (ed.), *One God in Trinity* (London, 1980) 88.

3. See K. Barth, *Christ and Adam* (ET Edinburgh, 1956) with P. Lengs-feld, *Adam und Christus* (Essen, 1965) 162–216.
4. It is this decision which distinguishes Jüngel's anthropology from, e.g., J. Moltmann, *Man* (ET London, 1974) and W. Pannenberg, *What is Man?* (ET Philadelphia, 1970) and now *Anthropologie* (Göttingen, 1983).
5. H. Bouillard, *Karl Barth III*, 291.
6. KMG 342.
7. GG 393 (ET 288).
8. KMG 343.
9. Cf. TC B.2.284.
10. DUC 293. Cf. W. Kasper, 'Theonomie und Autonomie' in H. Weber and D. Mieth (ed.), *Anspruch der Wirklichkeit und christlicher Glaube* (Düsseldorf, 1980) 31: 'a man made absolute is no longer human'.
11. KM 234.
12. GEM 291.
13. Ibid.
14. WW 47.
15. ANR 330; cf. BP 61, GW 260.
16. Cf. TL 233, WW 62.
17. LG 373; cf. EC 188, GEM 298f.
18. TGL 340.
19. KBT 273. Jüngel takes up a common Protestant theme: see J. Calvin, *Commentary on John* (ET Edinburgh, 1847) vol. 1, 31f, with T. F. Torrance, *Calvin's Doctrine of Man* (London, 1949) and 'The Word of God and the Nature of Man' in *Theology in Reconstruction* (London, 1965) 99–116.
20. KSV 301 n. 10. On the use of justification as a principle of doctrinal coherence, see W. Dantine, *Justification of the Ungodly* (ET St Louis, 1968) 129–39; *idem*, 'Die Rechtfertigungslehre' (*EvTh* 23 (1963) 257–65); G. Gloege, 'Die Rechtfertigungslehre als hermeneutische Kategorie' in *idem*, *Gnade für die Welt* (Göttingen, 1964) 34–54; W. Härle and E. Herms, *Rechtfertigung* (Göttingen, 1979) 9–15; E. Wolf, 'Die Rechtfertigungslehre als Mitte und Grenze reformatorischer Theologie' in *Peregrinatio II* (Munich, 1965) 11–21. On the doctrine of man, see W. Lohff, 'Rechtfertigung und Anthropologie' in W. Lohff and Chr. Walter (ed.), *Rechtfertigung im neuzeitlichen Lebenszusammenhang* (Gütersloh, 1974) 126–45; and for an overview, H. Döring, 'Rechtfertigung Heute' (*Cath* 37 (1983) 36–70).
21. PJ 49.
22. ZH 17; cf. BP 66, ZF 100f., SGW 261, STS 473, TGL 352.
23. AM 319.
24. Ibid. 320; cf. GEM 314.
25. WMW 210.
26. Ibid. 217.
27. Ibid. 211.

28. Ibid. 217.
29. Ibid. 219.
30. GG XV (ET xi).
31. He uses the term loosely, without identifying specific practitioners – though he has engaged in sharp debate with Gollwitzer (WG), Marquardt (GS 130f – not in ET) and Sölle (WDK).
32. ZF 17.
33. WMW 227f.
34. ZH 20.
35. ZF 73f.
36. Ibid. 102, 105.
37. Ibid. 82, cf. 80.
38. WSF 173.
39. GG 243 (ET 181); cf. GW 262f.
40. WSF 165.
41. PJ 274.
42. Cf. TWG 23f, and G. Ebeling, *The Nature of Faith* (ET London, 1961).
43. See *CD* III/2 437–640.
44. See 'Jesus' Understanding of Time' and G. Ebeling, 'Time and Word' in J. M. Robinson (ed.), *The Future of our Religious Past* (London, 1971) 241–66.
45. PJ 141, cf. JW 130f.
46. Cf. JW 131.
47. GG 229 (ET 170). For the whole analysis see GG 227–48 (ET 169–84), and compare G. Ebeling's study 'Gewissheit und Zweifel' in *Wort und Glaube II* (Tübingen, 1969) 138–83.
48. GG 234 (ET 173).
49. On this doctrine, see J. B. Torrance, 'The Place of Jesus Christ in Worship' in R. S. Anderson (ed.), *Theological Foundations for Ministry* (Grand Rapids, 1979) 348–69; *idem*, 'The Vicarious Humanity of Christ' in T. F. Torrance (ed.), *The Incarnation* (Edinburgh, 1981) 127–47; T. F. Torrance; 'The Mind of Christ in Worship' in *Theology in Reconciliation* (London, 1975) 139–214. For Jüngel on substitution, see GST, *passim*, and KS 455.
50. KSV 301, cf. PJ 49–70. Further on this conception of justification see T. F. Torrance, 'Justification' in *Theology in Reconstruction*, 150–68, and U. Wilckens, 'Christologie und Anthropologie im Zusammenhang der paulinischen Rechtfertigungslehre' (*ZNW* 67 (1976) 64–82).
51. On this see P. T. Forsyth, *Positive Preaching and the Modern Mind* (London, 1909) 339–69, and H. Scott Holland, *Logic and Life* (London, 1885) 276f.
52. See, e.g., T. F. Torrance, 'Justification' esp. 159f., and G. C. Berkouwer, *Faith and Justification* (ET Grand Rapids, 1954). Jüngel's remarks on *fides adventitia* (HG 13.21) should be balanced against his skeletal account of faith as a human *existentiale* in HG 15.7–73; 15.82.

9 Anthropology and analogy

1. MTA.
2. See esp. GEM.
3. MTA 212.
4. SAT 3–3.3.
5. See *CD* III/1, 183–206.
6. GEM 297.
7. Ibid. 298.
8. MTA 226. The German reads 'Gott spricht – der Mensch entspricht'. The rather abstract formulation is fleshed out in the account of faith, hope and love in GG 534–43 (ET 389–96).
9. GEM 298.
10. MTA 214.
11. See KBT, KBTT, KSV.
12. K. Barth, *The Christian Life. Church Dogmatics IV/4. Lecture Fragments* (ET Edinburgh, 1981). The essay ANR is a commentary upon some themes in this volume.
13. On the ethical context of Barth's doctrine of baptism, see KBTT 1.3; 1.4; 2; KBT 254; ANR 316f. See also Rendtorff (ed.), 'Die ethische Sinn der Dogmatik' in *idem* (ed.), *Die Realisierung der Freiheit* 119–34. and R. Schlüter, *Karl Barths Tauflehre* (Paderborn, 1973) esp. 56–107.
14. CD IV/4, 22.
15. KBT 254f; cf. KBTT 2.23.
16. KBT 258.
17. Ibid. Cf. GS 65 n. 199 (ET 52 n. 51); KBTT 2.1; 2.12; WS 53; S 30.
18. KBTT 2.12.
19. Cf. KSV 304.
20. Cf. ibid. 310f.
21. Cf. KBT 258f.
22. KSV 310f.
23. Ibid. 311.
24. ANR 317. For what follows, see also W. Krötke, 'Karl Barth und das Anliegen der "natürlichen Theologie"' (*ZdZ* 30 (1976) 177–83).
25. ANR 319, citing Barth, *The Christian Life* 173 (I have altered the ET slightly).
26. ANR 317.
27. Ibid. 321.
28. KBE 49; cf. KB 21.
29. EGE 236.
30. Ibid. 237.
31. Ibid. 239.
32. Austin Farrer's description of Barth in *Interpretation and Belief* (London, 1976) 57.
33. K. R. Popper, *The Open Society and its Enemies II* (London, 1966⁵) 270.

34. WS 56.
35. GG 24 (ET 20); cf. EC 188.
36. WS 53.
37. EC 189.
38. GG 43 (ET 34).
39. J.-P. Sartre, 'Cartesian Freedom' in *Literary and Philosophical Essays* (ET London, 1968) 169–84.
40. Ibid. 170.
41. Ibid. 171.
42. Ibid. 172.
43. Ibid. 184.
44. For a response to Sartre along these lines, see J. L. Marsh, 'Freedom, Receptivity and God' (*IJPR* 6 (1975) 219–33).
45. FG 247.
46. AG 33.
47. PJ 62.
48. STS 456.
49. Ibid. 468.
50. The argument is familiar in much theological anthropology. For classic statements, see K. Barth, 'The Gift of Freedom' in *The Humanity of God* (ET London, 1961) 37–65; J. Macmurray, *Freedom in the Modern World* (London, 1935) and *Conditions of Freedom* (London, 1950); H. R. Niebuhr, *The Responsible Self* (New York, 1963). See also the interesting studies by E. McDonagh, *Doing the Truth* (Dublin, 1979), 24–31, 76–100; T. Rendtorff, 'Die christliche Freiheit als Orientierungsbegriff der gegenwärtigen christlichen Ethik' in A. Hertz *et al.*, *Handbuch der christlichen Ethik I* (Freiburg, 1978) 377–88.
51. See McDonagh, *Doing the Truth* 30; D. M. MacKinnon, *A Study in Ethical Theory* (London, 1957) 270.
52. Jüngel's account shares many features of Barth's rejection of contracausal freedom: see U. Hedinger, *Der Freiheitsbegriff in der Kirklichen Dogmatik Karl Barths* (Zürich, 1962) 159–97, esp. 172f.
53. PJ 29.
54. EC 191.
55. Ibid. Cf. GT 7.6; EV 7.
56. GG 305 n. 73 (ET 225 n. 73).
57. WMW 218.
58. Cf. J. Hick's comment that 'the doctrine of the negative character of evil does not entail that evil is other than a real fact and a grievously oppressive problem; and its major proponents have never supposed that it did' (*Evil and the God of Love* (London, 1966) 187).
59. Ibid. 186f.
60. EV 7.
61. In subsuming the doctrine of sin under Christology, Jüngel is again close to Barth. Similar conclusions to these reached about Jüngel are reached about Barth by K. Lüthi, *Gott und das Böse* (Zürich, 1961)

esp. 88–114, 260–5, 284–6. See also T. F. Torrance, *Divine and Contingent Order* (Oxford, 1981) 113–28.

62. EC 185. Cf. ZF 26; DD 117f.
63. DD 168.
64. KMG 346; cf. EC 191f.
65. Cf. GT 6.1.
66. On the attractiveness of the conceptual economy of deterministic explanations of man, see D. M. MacKinnon, 'Moral Freedom' in *idem*, (ed.), *Making Moral Decisions* (London, 1969) esp. 10–14.
67. W. James, *A Pluralistic Universe* (1909 = Cambridge, 1977) 26.
68. Cf. J. B. Metz, 'Erlösung und Emanzipation' in L. Scheffzyk (ed.), *Erlösung und Emanzipation* (Freiburg, 1973) 120–40.
69. A. Schopenhauer, *Parerga and Paralipomena* (ET Oxford, 1974) vol. II, 446.
70. EV 7.
71. There are, of course, students of Hegel who stress that in explaining contingency he does not explain it *away*: see, e.g., E. Fackenheim, *The Religious Dimension in Hegel's Thought* (Bloomington, 1967); D. Henrich, 'Hegels Theorie über den Zufall' (*KS* 50 (1958) 131–48); B. T. Wilkins, *Hegel's Philosophy of History* (Ithaca, 1974) 143–90.
72. See not only K. R. Popper, *The Poverty of Historicism* (London, 1960²) but also A. C. Danto, *Analytical Philosophy of History* (Cambridge, 1965), and the extension of Danto's work by, e.g., M. G. White, *Foundations of Historical Knowledge* (New York, 1965); J. Habermas, *Zur Logik der Sozialwissenschaften* (*PR* Beiheft 5, 1965) 161–7; H. M. Baumgartner, *Kontinuität und Geschichte* (Frankfurt/M, 1972) esp 249–343; F. Platzer, *Geschichte, Heilsgeschichte, Hermeneutik* (Bern, 1979).
73. See again K. R. Popper, *The Open Society and its Enemies*; I. Berlin, *Four Essays on Liberty* (Oxford, 1969).
74. P. Ricoeur, 'Christianity and the Meaning of History' in *History and Truth* (ET Evanston, 1965) 95.

10 Towards a theology of the natural

1. ET Philadelphia 1970.
2. Other examples include Pannenberg's *The Apostles' Creed* (ET London, 1972), and the massive *Theology and the Philosophy of Science* (ET London, 1976), with *Faith and Reality* (ET London, 1977) and the two essays 'The Question of God' in *Basic Questions in Theology II* (ET London, 1971) 201–33, 'Anthropology and the Question of God' in ibid. *III* 80–98. See also now *Anthropologie* (Göttingen, 1983).
3. *Faith and Reality*, vii.
4. Along with his sophisticated use of the human sciences, it is this which distinguishes Pannenberg from the kind of natural theology presented by E. L. Mascall in *The Openness of Being* (London, 1971) which is

pervaded by a clear distinction between natural and revealed knowledge of God.

5. Pannenberg, 'The Question of God', 207–9; 'Anthropology and the Question of God' 89.
6. See H. Meynell, *Grace versus Nature* (London, 1965). For more positive accounts of Barth, see A. Szekeres, 'Karl Barth und die natürliche Theologie' (*EvTh* 24 (1964) 229–42); T. F. Torrance, 'The Problem of Natural Theology in the Thought of Karl Barth' (*RelSt* 6 (1970) 121–35).
7. Barth, *The Knowledge of God and the Service of God* (London, 1938).
8. E. Brunner and K. Barth, *Natural Theology* (ET London, 1946) 128.
9. *CD* IV/3, 113.
10. Most notably Chr. Link in *Die Welt als Gleichnis* (Munich, 1976), and 'Das menschliche Gesicht der Offenbarung' (*KuD* 26 (1980) 264–76). Further, W. Krötke, 'Karl Barth und das Anliegen der "natürlichen Theologie"' (*ZdZ* 30 (1976) 177–83) and S. Daecke, 'Gott erkennen in der Natur' (*EK* 17 (1984) 181–4). For surveys, see H. Fischer, 'Natürliche Theologie im Wandel' (*ZThK* 80 (1983) 85–102) and J. Werbich, 'Der Streit um die "natürliche Theologie"' (*Cath* 37 (1983) 119–32).
11. *CD* IV/3, 112.
12. Ibid.
13. Ibid. 113.
14. *Die Welt als Gleichnis*, 302.
15. GG X (ET viii); cf. D 290.
16. GU 194.
17. DD 173f.
18. DD 177.
19. One is reminded of R. G. Collingwood's rather strident remark that 'what is thought to be a permanent problem P is really a number of transitory problems $P_1P_2P_3$...whose individual peculiarities are blurred by the historical myopia of the person who lumps them together under the one name P' (*An Autobiography* (Oxford, 1939) 69; on the historical nature of philosophical problems, see W. B. Gallie, *Philosophy and Historical Understanding* (London, 1964) 140–226). Jüngel attempts a brief historical sketch, DD 160–7 – though he tends to see the material in strongly linear terms and does not always appreciate the tasks of those he criticises. For historical material here, C. C. J. Webb's *Studies in the History of Natural Theology* (Oxford, 1915) is still valuable. See also the comments in A. R. Peacocke, *Creation and the World of Science* (Oxford, 1979) 7–22.
20. Cf. DD 175.
21. Ibid. 159.
22. GU 195.
23. DD 172.
24. Philadelphia 1980.
25. Hendry, *Theology of Nature* 14.

26. EC 190.
27. GEM 292.
28. ZF 26.
29. GEM 291.
30. EC 190; cf. ZF 26; GEM 292.
31. EC 190.
32. EV 8.
33. For the phrase see P. L. Berger, *A Rumour of Angels* (Harmondsworth, 1971).
34. GU 196.
35. E.g. DD 175, EC 189; WW 72.
36. EC 188.
37. Ibid. 187f.
38. For the phrase, see G. Ebeling, 'Die Klage über das Erfahrungsdefizit in der Theologie als Frage nach ihrer Sache' in *Wort und Glaube III* (Tübingen, 1975) 3–28, with GG 40 n. 49 (ET 32 n. 49). Further use of the concept is made by I. U. Dalferth in 'Christian Discourse and the Paradigmatic Christian Experience' (*NST* 1 (1980) 47–73) and *Religiöse Rede von Gott* (Munich, 1981) 471f. For surveys of current use of 'experience' as a theological category, see W. H. Ritter. 'Theologie und Erfahrung' (*Luther* 53 (1982) 23–37); R. Schaeffler, *Fähigkeit zur Erfahrung* (Freiburg, 1982); D. Lange, *Erfahrung und die Glaubwürdigkeit des Glaubens* (Tübingen, 1984).
39. GU 196.
40. G. Green, 'The Mystery of Eberhard Jüngel' (*RSR* 5 (1979) 34–40) 38.
41. GG 225 (ET 168).
42. Cf. DD 176.
43. Ibid.
44. Ibid.
45. MW 103.
46. EV 7.
47. MW 145.
48. WS 53.
49. MW 103.
50. GG 398 (ET 291); cf. MW 156 thesis 23.
51. MW 147.
52. EV 8.
53. GG 398 (ET 291).
54. Ibid.
55. Ibid. 390 (ET 285).
56. MW 154 thesis 4.
57. This is not to follow J. Martin in denying that parable and metaphor contain resources for discussing matters beyond the linguistic: 'Metaphor amongst Tropes' (*RelSt* 17 (1981) 55–66).
58. C. F. Evans, 'Parable and Dogma' in *Explorations in Theology* 2 (London, 1977) 133.

59. Ibid.
60. Ibid. 137.
61. EV 8.
62. Ibid. 9. Cf. D. Mieth, '"Natürliche" Theologie und "autonome" Ethik' in H. Weber and D. Mieth (ed.), *Anspruch der Wirklichkeit und christlicher Glaube* (Düsseldorf, 1980) 58–74.
63. GU 197.
64. Ibid.
65. In *The Transfiguration of the Commonplace* (Cambridge, 1981), A. C. Danto offers an aesthetic theory whose basic motif – as the title suggests – is structurally similar to Jüngel's natural theology.

Conclusion

1. For some of the uses of 'Christocentric', see C. F. Evans, 'Christology and Theology' in *Explorations in Theology* 2 (London, 1977) 101–120; L. Houlden, 'The Place of Jesus' in *Explorations in Theology* 3 (London, 1978) 40–52; D. M. MacKinnon, 'Christology and Philosophy' in *Borderlands of Theology* (London, 1968) 55–81; J. Milet, *God or Christ?* (ET London, 1981); W. Pannenberg, 'Christologie und Theologie' in *Grundfragen systematischer Theologie II. Gesammelte Aufsätze* (Göttingen, 1980) 129–45; J. Riches, 'What is a "christocentric" theology?' in S. W. Sykes and J. P. Clayton (ed.), *Christ, Faith and History* (Cambridge, 1972) 223–238; R. Williams, 'Christocentrism' in A. Richardson and J. Bowden (ed.), *A New Dictionary of Christian Theology* (London, 1983) 99f.
2. KMG 336.
3. KB 17.
4. Ibid. 18.
5. Ibid.
6. KBE 50.
7. On the multi-level nature of theological argument, see D. H. Kelsey, *The Uses of Scripture in Recent Theology* (London, 1975) 122–38, with S. Toulmin, *The Uses of Argument* (Cambridge, 1964) and *idem, Knowing and Acting* (London 1976) on the 'functional significance' of arguments: see esp. 221.
8. Cf. P. Wignall, 'Patterns in Theology' in S. W. Sykes, *The Integrity of Anglicanism* (London, 1978) 101–9.
9. AG 11f; GW 263.
10. ABC *passim*.
11. TWG 26–30.
12. EGE 239f.
13. GT 4.5; TL 231.
14. ZF 18f.
15. Ibid. 44–9; MW 110–51.
16. MacIntyre, *The Shape of Christology* 10. Cf. H. E. W. Turner, *Jesus the Christ* (London, 1976) 108–23.

17. KSV 301.
18. Ibid.
19. Ibid. 302.
20. EV 7.
21. Cf. Pannenberg's remark that in Barth's view of analogy 'the motive power is always transmitted from above to below' so that Barth 'grounds analogy both ontologically and noetically from God's side': 'Analogy and Doxology' in *Basic Questions in Theology I* 214 and n. 3.
22. KSV 302.
23. Ibid.
24. E. Käsemann, *Das Neue Testament als Kanon* (Göttingen, 1970) 376.
25. PJ 263.
26. See here C. F. D. Moule, *The Birth of the New Testament* (London, 1966); *The Phenomenon of the New Testament* (London, 1967); *The Origin of Christology* (Cambridge, 1977).
27. R. Williams, *The Wound of Knowledge* (London, 1979) 13.
28. J. D. G. Dunn, *Christology in the Making* (London, 1980) 266f. See also C. Tuckett, 'Christology and the New Testament' (*SJT* 33 (1980) 401–16) 402–6.
29. Kelsey, *The Uses of Scripture* 134.
30. T 137 (ET 108).
31. GG 207 (ET 155).
32. Ibid.
33. I. U. Dalferth, 'Christian Discourse and the Paradigmatic Christian Experience' (*NST* 1 (1980) 47–73) 63. The same point is well put by J. Rohls, 'Ist Gott notwendig?' (*NZSTh* 22 (1980) 282–96) 295: 'Dispensing on principle with proofs of God is certainly not required on theological grounds. Even though I contend that I have knowledge that God exists solely on the grounds of God's self-revelation in the person of Jesus, this does not release me from the task of establishing that it is *God* who reveals himself in Jesus, i.e. that something does in fact reveal itself in him.' See further H. Fries, 'Gott als Geheimnis der Welt' (*HKorr* 31 (1977) 523–9) 528f; Pannenberg, 'Analogy and Doxology' 211.
34. Wingren, *Theology in Conflict* 80; see further G. F. Woods, *Theological Explanation* (London, 1958) 3.
35. W. Pannenberg, *Grundfragen systematischer Theologie II*, 10.
36. Lash, *Theology on Dover Beach* 132f.
37. TC A.1.1.
38. See, e.g., GG 270f. (ET 199f.).
39. GB 468.
40. GG 428 (ET 313).
41. E. Gellner, *Legitimation of Belief* (Cambridge, 1974) 1–23; cf. *idem*, 'Explanation in History' in *Cause and Meaning in the Social Sciences* (London, 1973) 1–17.
42. Gellner, *Legitimation*, 10–13.
43. T. W. Adorno, 'Der Essay als Form' in *Gesammelte Schriften* 11.

Noten zur Literatur (Frankfurt/M, 1974) 9–33, 25. On Adorno and Christian theology, see now W. Brändle, *Rettung des Hoffnungslosen* (Göttingen, 1984).

44. T. W. Adorno, *Minima Moralia* (ET London, 1974) 18.
45. Cf. DA 178f., GST 16.
46. Barth, *The Christian Life* 3.
47. For what follows, see E. McDonagh, *Gift and Call* (Dublin, 1977).
48. WF 48.
49. Ibid., 59.
50. G. Outka, *Agape. An Ethical Analysis* (London, 1972) 151.
51. On Barth, see R. E. Willis, 'Some Difficulties in Barth's Development of Special Ethics' (*RelSt* 6 (1970) 147–55, esp. 152–5). On both Barth and Bultmann, see S. Hauerwas, *Character and the Christian Life* (San Antonio, 1975).
52. See KS 451–5.

Abbreviations

1. To Jüngel's works (dates refer to chronological bibliography)

ABC	1972a2	GDU	1980g	KSV	1971e	TA	1982b3
ACS	1970a	GEM	1975d	LG	1973c	TB	1970b
AG	1976c1	GES	1977d	LGT	1980e	TC	1972a3
AGH	1982c	GG	1977a	MA	1978f	TGA	1978g
AM	1976k	GGM	1976e	MTA	1962b	TGL	1960o
ANR	1980c	GI	1976b	MW	1974a	TL	1976a
B	1982d	GL	1973a	O	1976d3	Trin	1975a
BB	1968g	GM	1971d	P	1968a	TS	1973b
BK	1980b	GP	1979b	PC	1963b	TT	1978b
BP	1976c2	GS	1964b	PD	1984f	TV	1972e
BSV	1982b1	GST	1983f	PF	1976d6	TWG	1964c
D	1972f	GT	1977b	PG	1981a	UA	1964a
DA	1982b4	GU	1975e	PJ	1962a	VT	1968e
DAW	1979f	GUG	1968d	PN	1980d	VTD	1968c
DD	1975c	GW	1980a2	QSN	1972b	W	1976d2
DF	1976j	GWS	1969a	Reden	1979a	WDK	1976h
DSZ	1961	GZAC	1963a	RF	1976d7	WE	1978d
DUC	1972a4	H	1976d5	RL	1980a3	WF	1983b
DVB	1972a1	HG	1983e	RVG	1974c	WG	1976g
EC	1975b	LM	1971a	S	1966a	WMW	1969b
EG	1982b5	JW	1966b	Sak	1972c	WS	1971g
EGE	1966c	KB	1969d	SAT	1982e	WSF	1972d
EKB	1982b2	KBCL	1976m	SGW	1969c	WTG	1976d3
EV	1980a1	KBE	1968h	SJ	1978c	WW	1979d
FF	1980f	KBT	1968b	SS	1984b	ZF	1978a
FG	1968f	KBTT	1971f	SSP	1983c	ZH	1976f
FT	1967	KM	1966d	STS	1978h	ZL	1978c
G	1974b	KMG	1971c	T	1971b	ZZ	1976a1
GB	1968i	KS	1983g				

2. Other abbreviations

AnPhil	Année Philosophique	NST	New Studies in Theology
Att	Attempto	NZSTh	Neue Zeitschrift für
BTZ	Berliner Theologischer		systematische Theologie
	Zeitschrift	NZZ	Neue Zürcher Zeitung
BW	Bibel in der Welt	Prud	Prudentia
Cath	Catholica	PR	Philosophische Rundschau
CD	K. Barth, Church	PS	Process Studies
	Dogmatics (ET Edinburgh	Ref	Reformatio
	1956–75)	RelSt	Religious Studies
ChQ	Church Quarterly	RSPT	Revue des sciences
Coll	Colloquium		philosophiques et
ConDes	Congrès Descartes		théologiques
Cont	Continuum	RSR	Religious Studies Review
CTM	Currents in Theology and	Sem	Semeia
	Mission	SJT	Scottish Journal of
EK	Evangelische Kommentare		Theology
Ev	Evangel	StTh	Studia Theologica
EvTh	Evangelische Theologie	ThD	Theology Digest
ExpT	Expository Times	Them	Themelios
HKorr	Herder Korrespondenz	Theol	Theology
HeyJ	Heythrop Journal	ThPh	Theologie und Philosophie
Hok	Hokhma	ThQ	Theologische Quartalschrift
IJPR	International Journal for	ThSt	Theological Studies
	Philosophy and Religion	ThTo	Theology Today
Int	Interpretation	ThZ	Theologische Zeitschrift
JR	Journal of Religion	VF	Verkündigung und
JThCh	Journal for Theology and		Forschung
	Church	ZdZ	Zeichen der Zeit
KatBl	Katechetische Blätter	ZEE	Zeitschrift für evangelische
KS	Kant-Studien		Ethik
KTR	King's Theological Review	ZKTh	Zeitschrift für katholische
KuD	Kerygma und Dogma		Theologie
ModCh	Modern Churchman	ZNW	Zeitschrift für die
MT	Modern Theology		neutestamentliche
NB	New Blackfriars		Wissenschaft
NHP	Neue Hefte für Philosophie	ZThK	Zeitschrift für Theologie und
NS	Nietzsche-Studien		Kirche

Bibliography

1. Works by Jüngel

1961 'Der Schritt zurück: Eine Auseinandersetzung mit der Heidegger-Deutung Heinrich Otts' (*ZThK* 58 (1961) 104–22)

1962a *Paulus und Jesus. Eine Untersuchung zur Präzisierung der Frage nach dem Ursprung der Christologie* (J. C. B. Mohr (Paul Siebeck) Tübingen)

1962b 'Die Möglichkeit theologischer Anthropologie auf dem Grunde der Analogie: Eine Untersuchung zum Analogieverständnis Karl Barths' (*EvTh* 22 (1962) 535–57)

1963a 'Das Gesetz zwischen Adam und Christus. Eine theologische Studie zu Röm 5, 12–21' (*ZThK* 60 (1963) 42–68)

1963b 'Ein paulinischer Chiasmus. Zum Verständnis der Vorstellung vom Gericht nach den Werken in Röm 2, 2–11' (*ZThK* 60 (1963) 69–74)

1963c = 1962a, 2nd edition

1963d Review of G. Noller, *Sein und Existenz. Die Überwindung des Subjekt-Objektschemas in der Philosophie Heideggers und in der Theologie der Entmythologisierung* (Kaiser, Munich, 1962) (*EvTh* 23 (1963) 218–23)

1964a *Zum Ursprung der Analogie bei Parmenides und Heraklit* (Walter de Gruyter, Berlin)

1964b *Gottes Sein ist im Werden. Verantwortliche Rede vom Sein Gottes bei Karl Barth. Eine Paraphrase* (J. C. B. Mohr (Paul Siebeck) Tübingen)

1964c '"Theologische Wissenschaft und Glaube" im Blick auf die Armut Jesu' (*EvTh* 24 (1964) 419–43)

1966a 'Das Sakrament – was ist das?' (*EvTh* 26 (1966) 320–36)

1966b 'Jesu Wort und Jesus als Wort Gottes. Ein hermeneutische Beitrag zum christologischen Problem' in E. Busch, J. Fangmeier and M. Geiger (ed.), *Parrhesia. Karl Barth zum 80. Geburtstag* (EVZ, Zürich) 82–100

1966c 'Erwägungen zur Grundlegung evangelischer Ethik im Anschluss an die Theologie des Paulus. Eine biblische Meditation' (*ZThK* 63 (1966) 379–90)

1966d 'Der königliche Mensch. Eine christologische Reflexion auf die Würde des Menschen in der Theologie Karl Barths' (*ZdZ* 20 (1966) 186–93)

1966e = 1964b, 2nd edition

1966f = 1962a, 3rd edition

1967 *Die Freiheit der Theologie* (EVZ, Zürich)

1968a *Predigten. Mit einem Anhang: Was hat die Predigt mit dem Text zu tun?* (Kaiser, Munich)

1968b *Karl Barths Lehre von der Taufe. Eine Hinweise auf ihre Probleme* (EVZ, Zürich)

1968c 'Das Verhältnis der theologischen Disziplinen untereinander' in E. Jüngel, K. Rahner and M. Seitz, *Die praktische Theologie zwischen Wissenschaft und Praxis* (Kaiser, Munich) 11–45

1968d 'Gottes umstrittenes Gerechtigkeit. Eine reformatorische Besinnung zum paulinischen Begriff δικαιοσύνη θεου' in E. Jüngel and M. Geiger, *Zwei Reden zum 450. Geburtstag der Reformation* (EVZ, Zürich)

1968e 'Vom Tod des lebendigen Gottes. Ein Plakat' (*ZThK* 65 (1968) 93–116)

1968f 'Freiheitsrechte und Gerechtigkeit' (*EvTh* 28 (1968) 486–95)

1968g 'Bekennen und Bekenntnis' in S. Herrmann and O. Söhngen (ed.), *Theologie in Geschichte und Kunst. Walter Elliger zum 65. Geburtstag* (Luther-Verlag, Witten) 94–105

1968h 'Ansprache von Eberhard Jüngel, Karl Barth zu ehren' in *Karl Barth 1886–1968. Gedenkfeier im Basler Münster* (EVZ, Zürich), 47–50

1968i Review of E. Fuchs, *Marburger Hermeneutik* (J. C. B. Mohr (Paul Siebeck) Tübingen) under title 'Nicht nur eine geographische Bestimmung' (*EK* 1 (1968) 468f.)

1968j Review of H. M. Kuitert, *Gott in Menschengestalt. Eine dogmatisch-hermeneutische Studie über die Anthropomorphismen der Bibel* (Kaiser, Munich, 1967) (*EvTh* 28 (1968) 612)

1969a 'Gott – als Wort unserer Sprache' (*EvTh* 29 (1969) 93–116)

1969b 'Die Welt als Möglichkeit und Wirklichkeit. Zum ontologischen Ansatz der Rechtfertigungslehre' (*EvTh* 29 (1969) 417–42)

1969c 'Der Schritt des Glaubens im Rhythmus der Welt' in R. W. Meyer, ed., *Das Problem des Fortschrittes – heute* (Wissenschaftliches Buchgesellschaft, Darmstadt) 143–63

1969d 'Karl Barth' (*EvTh* 29 (1969) 621–6)

1969e 'Das dunkle Wort vom "Tode Gottes"' (*EK* 2 (1969) 133–8)

1969f 'Offener Brief an Herrn Pfarrer Johannes Weygand' (*EvTh* 29 (1969) 334f.)

1970a 'L'autorité du Christ suppliant' in E. Castelli (ed.), *L'infallibilité, son aspect philosophique et théologique* (Aubier, Paris), 201–8

1970b 'Die tödliche Blamage. Lukas 24, 1–6' in H. Nitzschke (ed.), *Auferstehung heute gesagt. Osterpredigten der Gegenwart* (Mohn, Gütersloh) 69–74

1970c Review of E. Güttgemanns, *Offene Fragen zur Formgeschichte des*

*Evangeliums. Eine methodische Skizze der Problematik der Form-
und Redaktionsgeschichte* (Kaiser, Munich, 1970) (*EvTh* 30 (1970)
447f.)

1970d Review of P. Knauer, *Verantwortung des Glaubens. Ein Gespräch
mit Gerhard Ebeling aus katholischer Sicht* (Knecht, Frankfurt/M,
1969) (*EvTh* 30 (1970) 510–12)

1970e Review of K. Bockmühl, *Atheismus in der Christenheit. Anfechtung
und Überwindung. Die Unwirklichkeit Gottes in Theologie und Kirche*
(Aussaat, Wuppertal, 1969) (*EvTh* 30 (1970) 570)

1971a 'Irren ist menschlich. Zur Kontroverse um Hans Küngs Buch
"Unfehlbar? Eine Anfrage"' (*EK* 4 (1971) 75–80)

1971b *Tod* (Kreuz-Verlag, Stuttgart)

1971c '"...keine Menschenlosigkeit Gottes..." Zur Theologie Karl
Barths zwischen Theismus und Atheismus' (*EvTh* 31 (1971)
376–90)

1971d 'Grenzen des Menschseins' in H. W. Wolff, ed., *Probleme bibli-
scher Theologie. G. von Rad zum 80. Geburtstag* (Kaiser, Munich)
199–205

1971e 'Zur Kritik des sakramentalen Verständnisses der Taufe' in
F. Viering (ed.), *Zu Karl Barths Lehre von der Taufe* (Mohn,
Gütersloh) 25–44

1971f 'Thesen zu Karl Barths Lehre von der Taufe' in ibid. 161–4

1971g (with K. Rahner) *Was ist ein Sakrament? Verstösse zur Verständi-
gung* (Herder, Freiburg). Pp. 11–40 = 1966b

1971h Review of P. Eicher, *Die anthropologische Wende. Karl Rahners
philosophischer Weg vom Wesen des Menschen zur personalen Existenz*
(Universitätsverlag, Freiburg, 1970) (*EvTh* (1971) 390–2)

1972a *Unterwegs zur Sache. Theologische Bemerkungen* (Kaiser, Munich)
In addition to items 1963a, 1963b, 1964b, 1966c, 1966d, 1968c,
1968d, 1968e, 1968f, 1969a, 1969b, 1969c, 1971a, this collection
contains:

1972a1 'Drei Vorbemerkungen'

1972a2 An expanded German version of 1970a, 'Die Autorität des
bittenden Christus. Eine These zur materialen Begründung der
Eigenart des Wortes Gottes. Erwägungen zum Problem der
Infallibilität in der Theologie'

1972a3 'Thesen zur Grundlegung der Christologie'

1972a4 'Was ist "das unterschiedend Christliche"?'

1972b 'Quae supra nos, nihil ad nos. Eine Kurzformel der Lehre vom
verborgene Gott – im Anschluss an Luther interpretiert' (*EvTh*
32 (1972) 197–240)

1972c 'Säkularisierung – Theologische Anmerkungen zum Begriff einer
weltlichen Welt' in K. Herbert (ed.), *Christliche Freiheit im Dienst
am Menschen: Deutungen der kirklichen Aufgabe heute. Zum 80.
Geburtstag von M. Niemöller* (Otto Lembeck, Frankfurt/M)
163–8

1972d 'Womit steht und fällt heute der christliche Glaube? Elementare
Verantwortung gegenwärtigen Glaubens' in *Spricht Gott in der*

Geschichte? Mit Beiträgen von F. H. Tenbruck, G. Klein, E. Jüngel, A. Sand (Herder, Freiburg) 154–77

1972e 'Der Tod als Verewigung gelebten Lebens – Tod und Zeit – die Hoffnung des Glaubens' (*Ref* 21 (1972) 219–23) = 1971b, 148–54

1972f '"Deus qualem Paulus creavit, Dei negatio". Zur Denkbarkeit Gottes bei Ludwig Feuerbach und Friedrich Nietzsche. Eine Beobachtung' (*NS* 1 (1972) 286–96)

1972g = 1962a, 3rd edition

1972h = 1971b, 2nd edition

1973a 'Gott ist Liebe: Zur Unterscheidung von Glaube und Liebe' in G. Ebeling, E. Jüngel and G. Schunack (ed.), *Festschrift für Ernst Fuchs* (J. C. B. Mohr (Paul Siebeck) Tübingen), 193–202

1973b *Theologie in der Spannung zwischen Wissenschaft und Bekenntnis* (Evangelische Zentralstelle für Weltanschauungsfragen, Stuttgart)

1973c 'Lob der Grenze' (*Att* 47/8 (1973), 12–15)

1973d = 1971b, 3rd edition

1974a 'Metaphorische Wahrheit. Erwägungen zur theologischen Relevanz der Metapher als Beitrag zur Hermeneutik einer narrativen Theologie' in P. Ricoeur and E. Jüngel, *Metapher. Zur Hermeneutik religiöser Sprache* (*EvTh* Sonderheft (1974) 70–122)

1974b *Geistesgegenwart. Predigten* (Kaiser, Munich)

1974c 'Redlich von Gott reden. Bemerkungen zur Klarheit der Theologie Rudolf Bultmanns' (*EK* 7 (1974) 475–7)

1975a 'Das Verhältnis vom "ökonomischer" und "immanenter" Trinität. Erwägungen über eine biblische Begründung der Trinitätslehre – im Anschluss an und in Auseinandersetzung mit Karl Rahners Lehre vom dreifaltigen Gott als transzendentem Urgrund der Heilsgeschichte' (*ZThK* 72 (1975) 353–64)

1975b 'Extra Christum nulla salus – als Grundsatz natürlicher Theologie? Evangelische Erwägungen zur "Anonymität" des Christenmenschen' (*ZThK* 72 (1975) 337–52)

1975c 'Das Dilemma der natürlichen Theologie und die Wahrheit ihres Problems. Überlegungen für ein Gespräch mit Wolfhart Pannenberg' in A. Schwann (ed.), *Denken im Schatten des Nihilismus. Festschrift für Wilhelm Weischedel zum 70. Geburtstag* (Wissenschaftliches Buchgesellschaft, Darmstadt) 419–40

1975d 'Der Gott entsprechende Mensch. Bemerkungen zur Gottebenbildlichkeit des Menschen als Grundfigur theologischer Anthropologie' in H.-G. Gadamer and P. Vogler (ed.), *Neue Anthropologie 6: Philosophischer Anthropologie I* (Thiema, Stuttgart) 342–72

1975e 'Gott – um seiner selbst willen interessant. Plädoyer für eine natürlichere Theologie' (*NZZ* (1975, Nr 218) 57f.)

1975f = 1964b, 3rd edition, with 'Epilegomena 1975'

1976a 'The Truth of Life. Observations on Truth as the Interruption of the Continuity of Life' in R. W. A. Mackinney (ed.), *Creation, Christ and Culture. Studies in Honour of T. F. Torrance* (Clark, Edinburgh) 231–6

1976b (with D. Rössler) *Gefangenes Ich – befreiender Geist. Zwei Tübinger Römerbrief-Auslegungen* (Kaiser, Munich) 7–18

1976c *Anfechtung und Gewissheit des Glaubens oder wie die Kirche wieder zu ihrer Sache kommt. Zwei Vorträge* (Kaiser, Munich)
This collection contains:

1976c1 'Anfechtung und Gewissheit des Glaubens. Wie bleibt die Kirche bei ihrer Sache?' = 1976i, 1976j (expanded)

1976c2 'Die Bedeutung der Predigt angesichts unserer volkskirklichen Existenz'

1976d *Von Zeit zu Zeit. Betrachtungen zu den Festzeiten im Kirchenjahr* (Kaiser, Munich)
This collection contains:

1976d1 'Von Zeit zu Zeit'

1976d2 'Weinachten – Freude am menschlichen Gott'

1976d3 = 1969e

1976d4 'Ostern – das Geheimnis des Gekreuzigten'

1976d5 'Himmelfahrt – Gottes offener Himmel über uns'

1976d6 'Pfingsten – Aufruhr zur Treue'

1976d7 'Reformationsfest – Freiheit unter Gottes Schutz'

1976e *Gott – für den ganzen Menschen* (Benziger, Einsiedeln)

1976f 'Zukunft und Hoffnung. Zur politischen Funktion christlicher Theologie' in W. Teichert (ed.), *Müssen Christen Sozialisten sein? Zwischen Glaube und Politik* (Lutherisches Verlaghaus, Hamburg) 11–30

1976g 'Warum gleich mit dem Fass geworfen? Über die Kunst, mit roter Tinte umzugehen. Offenes Brief von Eberhard Jüngel an Helmut Gollwitzer' in ibid. 41–9

1976h 'Wer denkt konkret?' in ibid. 111–17

1976i 'Anfechtung und Gewissheit des Glaubens. Auf der Suche nach der Sache der Kirche' (*EK* 9 (1976) 454–8)

1976j 'Die Freude am Erzählen wiedergewonnen, Geistliche Konzentration des kirklichen Lebens' (*EK* 9 (1976) 531–4)

1976k 'Der alte Mensch – als Kriterium der Lebensqualität. Bemerkungen zur Menschenwürde der Leistungsunfähigen Person' in D. Henke, G. Kehrer and G. Schneider-Flume (ed.), *Der Wirklichkeitsanspruch von Theologie und Religion. Die sozialethische Herausforderung. E. Steinbach zum 70. Geburtstag* (J. C. B. Mohr (Paul Siebeck) Tübingen), 129–32

1976m (with H.-A. Drewes) (ed.), Karl Barth, *Das christliche Leben. Die Kirkliche Dogmatik IV/4. Fragmente aus dem Nachlass. Vorlesungen 1959–61* (Theologisches Verlag, Zürich)

1976n = 1975b, in E. Klinger (ed.), *Christentum innerhalb und ausserhalb der Kirche* (Herder, Freiburg) 122–38

1976o 'Der Tod als Geheimnis des Lebens' in A. Paus (ed.), *Grenzerfahrung Tod* (Graz, Vienna) 9–39

1976p = 1976o, in J. Schwartländer, *Der Mensch und sein Tod* (Vandenhoeck und Ruprecht, Göttingen) 108–25

1977a *Gott als Geheimnis der Welt. Zur Begründung der Theologie des Gekreuzigten im Streit zwischen Theismus und Atheismus* (J. C. B. Mohr (Paul Siebeck) Tübingen)

1977b 'Gelegentliche Thesen zum Problem der natürlichen Theologie' (*EvTh* 37 (1977) 485–8)

1977c = 1977a, 2nd edition

1977d 'Gott entsprechendes Schweigen? Theologie in der Nachbarschaft des Denkens von Martin Heidegger' in *Martin Heidegger. Fragen an sein Werk. Ein Symposion* (Reclam, Stuttgart) 37–45

1977e = 1971b, 4th edition

1978a *Zur Freiheit eines Christenmenschen. Eine Erinnerung an Luthers Schrift* (Kaiser, Munich)

1978b (ed.) *Tübinger Theologie im 20. Jahrhundert* (*ZThK* Beiheft)

1978c 'Das Sein Jesu Christi als Ereignis der Versöhnung Gottes mit einer gottlosen Welt. Die Hingabe des Gekreuzigten' (*EvTh* 38 (1978) 510–17)

1978d 'Die Wirksamkeit des Entzogenen. Zum Vorgang geschichtlichen Verstehens als Einführung in die Christologie' in B. Aland (ed.), *Gnosis. Festschrift für Hans Jonas* (Vandenhoeck und Ruprecht, Göttingen) 15–32

1978e 'Zur Lehre von den Zeichen der Kirche' in G. Metzger (ed.), *Zukunft aus dem Wort. Helmut Class zum 65. Geburtstag* (Calwer-Verlag, Stuttgart) 113–17

1978f 'Mut zur Angst. Dreizehn Aphorismen zum Jahreswechsel' (*EK* 11 (1978) 12–15)

1978g (with E. Topitsch) 'Der Tod Gottes und der Atheismus. Anmerkungen zu einem Buch und eine Replik' (*EK* 11 (1978) 772–7)

1978h (with I. U. Dalferth) 'Sprache als Träger der Sittlichkeit' in A. Hertz *et al.* (ed.), *Handbuch der christlichen Ethik II* (Herder, Freiburg) 454–73

1978i = 1977a, 3rd edition

1979a *Reden für die Stadt. Zum Verhältnis von Christengemeinde und Bürgergemeinde* (Kaiser, Munich)

1979b *Geistesgegenwart. Predigten I und II* (Kaiser, Munich). This contains 1968a and 1974b, omitting the 'Anhang' to 1968a

1979c 'Am Anfang: Er. Hinweis auf eine geglückte Übersetzung' (*EK* 12 (1979) 284f)

1979d 'Wertlose Wahrheit. Christliche Wahrheitserfahrung im Streit gegen die "Tyrannei der Werte"' in S. Schelz (ed.), *Die Tyrannei der Werte* (Lutherisches Verlaghaus, Hamburg) 45–75

1979e 'Vom Kirchentag' (*EK* 12 (1979) 416f)

1979f 'Die andere Weinachtsgeschichte' in *Jesus: für heute geboren.*

Politiker, Autoren, Wissenschaftler antworten auf die Frage: Was bedeutet nun die Geburt Jesu? (Katzmann, Tübingen) 99–106

1979g = 1962a, 5th edition

1980a *Entsprechungen: Gott – Wahrheit – Mensch. Theologische Erörterungen* (Kaiser, Munich)
  In addition to items 1964a, 1967, 1971d, 1972b, 1972c, 1973b, 1973c, 1974a, 1975a, 1975b, 1975c, 1975d, 1975e, 1976k, 1976o, 1977b, 1978c, 1978f, this collection contains:

1980a1 'Vorwort'

1980a2 'Gottesgewissheit'

1980a3 'Recht auf Leben – Recht auf Sterben. Theologische Bemerkungen'

1980b 'Barth, Karl' in *Theologische Realenzyklopädie* 5 (Walter de Gruyter, Berlin) 251–68

1980c 'Anrufung Gottes als Grundethos christlichen Handelns. Einführende Bemerkungen zu den nachgelässenen Fragmenten der Ethik der Versöhnungslehre Karl Barths' in H. Weber and D. Mieth (ed.), *Anspruch der Wirklichkeit und christlicher Glaube. Probleme und Wege theologischer Ethik heute* (Patmos, Düsseldorf) 208–24

1980d 'Predigt über Num 13,2 – 14,5' in J. Brantschen and P. Selvatio (ed.), *Unterwegs zur Einheit. Festschrift für H. Stirniman* (Herder, Freiburg) 923–9

1980e 'Zur Bedeutung Luthers für die gegenwärtige Theologie' in L. Grane and B. Lohse (ed.), *Luther und die Theologie der Gegenwart. Referate und Berichte des 5. Internationalen Kongresses für Lutherforschung. Lund, Schweden, 14.–20. August 1977* (Vandenhoeck und Ruprecht, Göttingen) 17–79 (= 1978a)

1980f 'Freude über Freude' (*EK* 13 (1980) 728f)

1980g 'Glaube, der Unfreiheit überwindet. Auszüge aus einem Vortrag auf dem evangelischen Kirchentag 1979' (*KatBl* 105 (1980) 10–13

1980h 'Wege zum Frieden. Frieden als Kategorie theologischer Anthropologie' in H. Kunst (ed.), *Dem Staate verpflichtet. Festgabe für Gerhard Schröder* (Kreuz, Stuttgart) 21–35

1981a (with I. U. Dalferth) 'Person und Gottebenbildlichkeit' in F. Bockle, F.-X. Kaufmann, K. Rahner and B. Welte (ed.), *Christlicher Glaube in moderner Gesellschaft* (Herder, Freiburg) vol. 24, 57–99

1981b (with I. U. Dalferth) (ed.), Karl Barth, *Fides Quaerens Intellectum. Anselms Beweis des Existenz Gottes im Zusammenhang seines theologischen Programmes* (Theologisches Verlag, Zürich)

1982a = 1972c, 2nd edition

1982b *Barth-Studien* (Mohn, Gütersloh)
  In addition to items 1962b, 1966d, 1968b, 1968h = 1969d, 1971c, 1971e, 1971f, 1980c, this collection contains:

1982b1 'Vorwort'
1982b2 'Einführung in Leben und Werk Karl Barths' (= 1980b, expanded)
1982b3 'Die theologische Anfänge. Beobachtungen'
1982b4 'Von der Dialektik zur Analogie. Die Schule Kierkegaards und der Einspruch Petersons'
1982b5 'Evangelium und Gesetz. Zugleich zum Verhältnis von Dogmatik und Ethik'
1982c 'Anthropomorphismus als Grundproblem neuzeitlicher Hermeneutik' in E. Jüngel, J. Wallmann and W. Werbeck (ed.), *Verifikationen. Festschrift für Gerhard Ebeling zum 70. Geburtstag* (J. C. B. Mohr (Paul Siebeck) Tübingen) 499–521
1982d 'Bibelarbeit über 2 Timotheus 3, 14–17' (*BW* 19 (1982) 93–106)
1982e 'La signification de l'analogie pour la théologie' in P. Gisel and Ph. Secretan (ed.), *Analogie et Dialectique. Essais de théologie fondamentale* (Labor et Fides, Geneva) 247–58
1983a = 1978a, 2nd edition
1983b *Zum Wesen des Friedens. Frieden als Kategorie theologischer Anthropologie* (Kaiser, Munich)
1983c *Schmecken und Sehen. Predigten III* (Kaiser, Munich)
1983d 'Im Angesichts des Todes' in H. J. Schultz (ed.), *Luther kontrovers* (Kreuz, Stuttgart) 162–72
1983e 'Zur Lehre vom Heiligen Geist. Thesen' in U. Luz and H. Weder (ed.), *Die Mitte des neuen Testaments. Einheit und Vielfalt neutestamentlicher Theologie. Festschrift für Eduard Schweitzer zum 70. Geburtstag* (Vandenhoeck und Ruprecht, Göttingen) 97–188
1983f 'Das Geheimnis der Stellvertretung. Ein dogmatisches Gespräch mit Heinrich Vogel' (*ZdZ* 37 (1983) 16–22)
1983g 'Die Kirche als Sakrament?' (*ZThK* 80 (1983) 432–57)
1984a *Mit Frieden Staat zu machen. Politische Existenz nach Barmen V* (Kaiser, Munich)
1984b '"Auch das Schöne muss sterben" – Schönheit im Lichte der Wahrheit. Theologische Bemerkungen zum ästhetischen Verhältnis' (*ZThK* 81 (1984) 106–26)
1984c 'Pater im Glauben' (*EK* 17 (1984) 237f)
1984d (with K. W. Müller) (ed.), Rudolf Bultmann, *Theologische Enzyklopädie* (J. C. B. Mohr (Paul Siebeck) Tübingen)
1984e 'Das Geheimnis der Stellvertretung' (*BTZ* 1 (1984) 65–80) (= 1983f)
1984f (with M. Trowitzsch) 'Provozierendes Denken. Bermerkungen zur theologischen Anstössigkeit der Denkwege Martin Heideggers' (*NHP* 23 (1984) 59–74)
1984g 'Menschwerdung des Menschen' (*EK* 17 (1984) 446–8)
1984h 'Einleitung: Die Barmer Theologische Erklärung als Bekenntnis der Kirche' in M. Rohkrämer (ed.), Karl Barth, *Texte zur Barmer Theologischen Erklärung* (Theologischer Verlag, Zürich) IX–XXII

2. English translations

1971 'God – as a Word of Our Language' in F. Herzog (ed.), *Theology of the Liberating Word* (Abingdon, Nashville) 24–45 (= 1969a)

1975 *Death. The Riddle and the Mystery* (St Andrew Press, Edinburgh) (= 1971b)

1976 *The Doctrine of the Trinity. God's Being is in Becoming* (Scottish Academic Press, Edinburgh) (= 1966e)

1976 'The Relationship between "Economic" and "Immanent" Trinity' (*ThD* 24 (1976) 179–84) (= 1975a, summarised)

1983 *God as the Mystery of the World. On the Foundation of the Theology of the Crucified One in the Dispute between Theism and Atheism* (Clark, Edinburgh) (= 1978i)

3. Works about Jüngel

Barth, U., 'Zur Barth-Deutung Eberhard Jüngels' (*ThZ* 40 (1984) 296–320, 394–415)

Breuning, W., 'Überlegungen zu Jüngels interessantem Versuch der Weiterführung des Analogieverständnisses' in J. Brantschen and P. Selvatio (ed.), *Unterwegs zur Einheit. Festschrift für H. Stirniman* (Herder, Freiburg, 1980) 380–98

Duquoc, C., 'Les conditions d'une pensée de Dieu selon E. Jüngel' (*RSPT* 65 (1981) 417–32)

Fries, H., 'Gott als Geheimnis der Welt. Zum neuesten Werk von Eberhard Jüngel' (*HKorr* 31 (1977) 269–79)

Geyer, H.-G., 'Gottes Sein als Thema der Theologie' (*VF* 11 (1966) 3–37)

Green, G., 'The Mystery of Eberhard Jüngel. A Review of his Theological Programme' (*RSR* 5 (1979) 34–40)

Härle, W. and Herms, E., 'Deutschsprächige protestantische Dogmatik nach 1945. II. Teil' (*VF* 28 (1983) 1–87) 21–9

Kern, W., 'Theologie des Glaubens, vorgestellt anhand von Eberhard Jüngel' (*ZKTh* 104 (1982) 129–46)

König, A., 'Le Dieu crucifié. Peut-on parler du Dieu crucifié? (Moltmann et Jüngel)' (*Hok* 17 (1981) 73–95)

Lønning, P., 'Zur Denkbarkeit Gottes. Ein Gespräch mit Wolfart Pannenberg und Eberhard Jüngel' (*StTh* 34 (1980) 37–71)

O'Donovan, L. J., 'The Mystery of God as a History of Love. Eberhard Jüngel's Doctrine of God' (*ThSt* 42 (1981) 251–710

Peters, A., 'Gedanken zu Eberhard Jüngel's These: Gott als Geheimnis der Welt' in H. Burkhardt (ed)., *Wer ist das – Gott? Christliche Gotteserkenntnis in der Herausforderungen der Gegenwart* (Giessen, 1982) 178–89

Robinson, J. M., 'The New Hermeneutic at Work' (*Int* 18 (1964) 346–59)

Rohls, J., 'Ist Gott notwendig? Zu einer These von E. Jüngels' (*NZSTh*

22 (1980) 282–96)

Seim, J., 'Wovon sprechen wir eigentlich, wenn wir "Gott" sagen?' (*EvTh* 38 (1978) 269–79)

Wainwright, G., 'Today's Word for Today III: Eberhard Jüngel' (*ExpT* 92 (1981) 131–5)

Zimany, R., 'Perspectives from Jüngel's Theology' (*CTM* 11 (1984) 154–67)

Index